SPORTS DEVELOPMENT

Sports development is an important emerging field of academic study with a distinct contribution to make to wider social, cultural, economic and education policies and practices.

Sports Development: Policy, Process and Practice provides a detailed, authoritative and dependable guide to all aspects of the subject.

This popular course text examines the roles of those working in and around sports development and explores how professionals can devise better and more effective ways of promoting interest, participation or performance in sport.

Now in its second edition, *Sports Development* has been updated to include discussion of contemporary debates about mass participation, social inclusion, talent development, the Olympic Games, elite performance and policy evaluation.

It includes chapters covering:

- Sports policy
- Developing 'Sport for All?': inequality and inclusion
- Community sports development
- PE and school sport
- Sports development and health
- Resourcing sports development
- Sports development and sports coaching
- Researching and evaluating sports development

Sports Development: Policy, Process and Practice represents an invaluable resource for university and further education students, researchers and those working in sports development and should be essential reading for all those wanting to prove themselves effective in this area.

Kevin Hylton is Senior Lecturer in Sport and Recreation Development in the Carnegie Faculty of Sport and Education, Leeds Metropolitan University.

Peter Bramham is Reader in Sport and Leisure Policy at the Carnegie Research Institute, Leeds Metropolitan University.

SPORTS DEVELOPMENT

Policy, process and practice

Second edition

EDITED BY KEVIN HYLTON AND PETER BRAMHAM

Routledge
Taylor & Francis Group

LONDON AND NEW YORK

First published 2001
This second edition published 2008
by Routledge
2 Park Square, Milton Park, Abingdon, Oxon, OX14 4RN

Simultaneously published in the USA and Canada
by Routledge
270 Madison Avenue, New York, NY 10016

Routledge is an imprint of the Taylor & Francis Group, an informa business

© 2008 selection and editorial matter Kevin Hylton and Peter Bramham;
individual chapters © the contributors

Typeset in Zaph Humanist and Eras by
Keystroke, 28 High Street, Tettenhall, Wolverhampton
Printed and bound in Great Britain by
TJ International Ltd, Padstow, Cornwall

British Library Cataloguing in Publication Data
A catalogue record for this book is available from the British Library

Library of Congress Cataloging in Publication Data
  Sports development: policy, process and practice / edited by Kevin Hylton and
  Peter Bramham.
     p. cm.
  Includes index.
  ISBN 978–0–415–42182–9 (hardcover) — ISBN 978–0–415–42183–6 (softcover)
  1. Sports—Great Britain. 2. Sports administration—Great Britain.
  3. Sports—Social aspects—Great Britain. 4. Sports and state—Great Britain.
  I. Hylton, Kevin, 1964– II. Bramham, Peter.
  GV605.S76 2007
  796.0941—dc22

ISBN13: 978–0–415–42182–9 (hbk)
ISBN13: 978–0–415–42183–6 (pbk)
ISBN13: 978–0–203–93947–5 (ebk)

ISBN10: 0–415–42182–9 (hbk)
ISBN10: 0–415–42183–7 (pbk)
ISBN10: 0–203–93947–6 (ebk)

CONTENTS

1 INTRODUCTION   1

Peter Bramham and Kevin Hylton

2 SPORTS POLICY   10

Peter Bramham

3 DEVELOPING SPORTS PRACTICE   25

David Jackson

4 DEVELOPING 'SPORT FOR ALL?': ADDRESSING INEQUALITY IN SPORT

Kevin Hylton and Mick Totten

5 COMMUNITY SPORTS DEVELOPMENT

Kevin Hylton and Mick Totten

6 PARTNERSHIPS IN SPORT

Stephen Robson

ILLUSTRATIONS

TABLES

CONTRIBUTORS

Peter Bramham is an experienced lecturer and researcher who has spent over thirty years in academic life in several higher education institutions in the UK. He has published work in conjunction with colleagues in the UK and across Europe and regularly makes conference contributions in the broad leisure and sport policy area. He has served on the Leisure Studies Association (LSA) National Executive Committee and he acted as Chair of the LSA. He was appointed Reader in 2004. Peter's research interests include research into leisure and sport policy, history and social theory; globalisation, leisure, sport and the city; and gender relations and physical activity. Recent publications include 'Habits of a lifetime?: Youth, generation and lifestyles' in P. Bramham and J. Caudwell (eds) *Sport, Active Leisure and Youth Cultures* (2005), and, with C. Critcher, 'Devil still makes work' in J. Haworth and A.T. Veal (eds) *Work and Leisure Thirty Years On* (2005).

Anne Flintoff is Reader in Physical Education in the Carnegie Research Institute, Leeds Metropolitan University. She has been involved in school PE as a teacher, teacher trainer and researcher for over twenty years. Her higher education teaching, research and consultancy have centred on issues of equity and social inclusion, and she publishes regularly in academic and professional journals. She is a member of the advisory board of the *PE and Sport Pedagogy* journal. Recent publications include, with S. Scraton (eds) *Gender and Sport: A Reader* (2002) and 'Gender and PE' in K. Green and Hardman (eds) *Physical Education: Essential Issues* (2005), and, with K. Hylton and J. Long (eds) *Young People and Active Leisure: Theory, Policy and Participation* (2005).

Kevin Hylton is Senior Lecturer in Sport and Recreation Development and Course Leader for the MA Sport, Leisure and Equity in the Carnegie Faculty of Sport and Education at Leeds Metropolitan University. Kevin's research interests include 'race', racism and anti-racism in sport, community sports development and inclusion. Kevin's PhD focused on 'race', sport and equality in local government. A founder member of the black sports forum (BEMSport) in Yorkshire, Kevin has worked with a number of governing bodies on issues of equity, such as the Badminton Association of England, ILAM, Sport England and UK Sport. Kevin works as an advocate of 'race' and ethnicity issues with Sport Leeds, the strategic policy body for Leeds. Recent publications include *An Evaluation of Sportsweb: Reaching the Parts Other Coaches Can't Reach* (2003) and, with J. Long and A. Flintoff (eds)

Evaluating Sport and Active Leisure for Young People (2005). Kevin is writing *'Race' and Sport: Critical Race Theory* for Routledge (forthcoming).

David Jackson is Principal Lecturer and International Development Co-ordinator in the Carnegie Faculty of Sport and Education, Leeds Metropolitan University. David spent five years as Principal Sports Officer, where he played a leading policy-making role in Leeds Leisure Services with responsibility for sports development. He has also been an active member at regional and national level of the National Association of Sports Development (NASD) with a particular interest in sports policy, education and professional development issues. David was a member of the editorial team for the first edition of *Sports Development: Policy, Process and Practice.*

Jonathan Long is Director of the Carnegie Research Institute, Leeds Metropolitan University. He has directed some fifty research projects for external clients. His experience embraces all stages of the research process from design to dissemination and his research uses both quantitative and qualitative techniques. Jonathan's major research interests centre around leisure policies and practices related to social change and issues of social justice. Recent research in sport and leisure has been involved with racial equality, social capital and social inclusion. He is the author of *Researching Leisure, Sport and Tourism: the Essential Guide* (2007), was a founding member of the editorial board of *Leisure Studies* and is now on the board of other journals. He is an Academician of the Academy of Social Sciences.

John Lyle is Professor of Sports Coaching at Leeds Metropolitan University and an Adjunct Professor at the University of Queensland. He established the first professional diploma in Sports Coaching and the first Master's degree in Coaching Studies in the UK, and has played a significant role in the development of sports coaching as an academic field of study. He is the author of the influential textbook *Sports Coaching Concepts* (2002). John has contributed widely through publications, presentations, master classes, working groups and other media to academic and professional developments in sports coaching. John's academic experience is complemented by a considerable personal experience as a volleyball coach, and engagement in consultancy, policy and the delivery of coach education.

Jim McKenna is Professor of Physical Activity and Health and leads the Active Lifestyles research theme at Leeds Metropolitan University. He joined Leeds Met in 2005 after eighteen years at the University of Bristol. Jim's research portfolio is diverse, ranging from health-related behaviour change to the relevance and application of positive psychology to sport and physical activity. He is working on a number of projects relating to the promotion of physical activity with young people (Derby City), ageing adults (Project OPAL), psychological resilience (Everest West Ridge expedition, 2006) and the role of exercising in workplace performance (International Walking Project).

Stephen Robson is Senior Lecturer in Sport and Recreation Development and Management in the School of Leisure and Sport Management at Leeds Metropolitan University. Stephen worked in sports development in Middlesbrough Council before coming to the university. Stephen's work with local health authorities and sports development has generated an interest in partnership working. Stephen represents the university on the national Higher Education Institutions' Curriculum Group for sports development, which is working towards an industry endorsement scheme for Sports Development degrees.

Mick Totten is Senior Lecturer in Community Leisure and Recreation, Leeds Metropolitan University. He started working life in community theatre, before moving back to sport to become a Community Sports Leader with the initial Action Sport project in Leeds in the mid-1980s. He combined his interest in sport and drama with inner-city youth work and with young people with physical disability in social work. He then worked for five years in further education teaching on sport, leisure and drama courses before joining the staff at Leeds Met in 1995. At Leeds Met Mick teaches Community Sport, Sociology and Sport Development. He completed postgraduate work in community sport and community arts, and consultancy work in community leisure and sport.

FOREWORD

Derrick Anderson, CBE
Chief Executive, Lambeth Borough Council

Since the publication of the first edition (2001) there has been a massive increase in the field among practitioners, policy makers, academics and students. Being the first substantive text in the field the first edition went some way to establish sports development as an important topic. The book reflects the engagement of the authors with this burgeoning field as it has been welcomed in the international community and been reproduced in Chinese and e-book format. The London Olympic Games 2012 and Beijing 2008 are conspicuous examples of this need for sound education in sports development, policy and practice. The work of this group of Carnegie staff is to be applauded for its timing and contribution.

The second edition of *Sports Development: Policy, Process and Practice* develops key issues in relation to community sport, health, equalities, partnership working, policy and practice. It also introduces the new chapters of sports coaching, PE and school sport, and researching and evaluating sports development that have emerged as distinct and important policy areas since 2001. Consequently, the second edition continues to argue that traditional views of the sports development profession must be disrupted in order to include those from other fields and disciplines. The span of the subjects covered makes it invaluable to both those involved in academic work and those engaged in front-line activities in either a paid or voluntary capacity.

In the tradition of the first edition the book presents its arguments using a combination of case studies and optional exercises. The subject matter has been carefully thought through so as to present what are complex issues in an accessible manner. The authors of *Sports Development* have certainly risen to the challenge of bringing out the essence of sports development. They have produced a second edition that holds as much interest for the academic as for the practitioner as they focus our gaze on the philosophies and processes which are fundamental to the practice.

Once again I commend this book to you as a good read and great value in its contents, analysis and observations.

Derrick Anderson D.A. has an academic background in psychology, PE and social work. His professional life has spanned the fields of the arts, sports and local government at practitioner, strategic and policy-making levels. He was Deputy Director of the original Action Sports Programme in the West Midlands between 1982 and 1985. He is a member of the Arts Council of England. He was a member of the Ministry of Sport – Sports Implementation Strategy Group until 2003, an independent member of the West Midlands Cultural Consortium until 2004 and Chair of Sport England West Midlands Board until his departure for London in 2006. He holds positions on a variety of bodies ranging from non-executive director on the Home Office General Executive Board, to member of the Board of Sport England London and was, until joining Lambeth, a member of the Nations and Regions Committee for the London 2012 Olympics. His interests include working with aid and development agencies in Southern Africa and the Caribbean, and in recent years he has volunteered regularly in Mozambique.

ACKNOWLEDGEMENTS

The editorial team would like to thank colleagues in the Carnegie Faculty of Sport and Education at Leeds Metropolitan University for their support in the writing of this book. We would also like to thank Rachel Thornton for her administrative efforts.

Thanks also go to our colleagues in local authority sport Paul Senior and Peter Smith at the Learning and Leisure Department in Leeds, and Zuby Hamard and Ikram Butt, Taj Butt and Steve Warner at Bradford Sport and Leisure Services for their collaboration on the community sports development case studies.

The authors and publishers are grateful to the copyright owners for permission to reproduce material acknowledged in the captions to figures and at the foot of tables. Whilst every effort was made to ensure the accuracy and acknowledgement of the information contained within Figures 1.3, 3.1 and 9.2–3 and in Tables 4.1, 4.3 and 9.1, Sport England cannot be held responsible for any errors, omissions and/or the completeness of such information. Sport England accepts no liability for the consequences of error and/or omissions or for any loss or damage suffered as a result. Where the information contains third-party intellectual property Leeds Metropolitan University and/or the publishers have sought all necessary consent, permission and/or clearance in such third-party intellectual property.

Every effort has been made to contact copyright holders for their permission to reprint material in this book. The publishers would be grateful to hear from any copyright holder who is not acknowledged here and will undertake to rectify any errors or omissions in future editions.

K.H.
P.B.

CHAPTER ONE

INTRODUCTION

Peter Bramham and Kevin Hylton

This chapter sets out the distinctive philosophy and structure of the second edition of the book. The four editors of the first edition argued that sports development must be 'used to describe processes, policies and practices that form an integral feature of the work involved in providing sporting opportunities' (Hylton, Bramham *et al.*, 2001: 1). This book again advocates that sports development should be thought of as comprehensive inclusive processes which engage the broadest spectrum of policy makers, agencies, organisations, practitioners and participants. Gone are the days of traditional departmentalism as PE staff, teachers, coaches, facility managers, youth and community workers and last but not least Sports Development Officers have to take cognisance of new policy frameworks that demand strategic partnerships and inter-professional co-operation, all within a performance-driven culture. The chapters in the second edition of the book are testimony to how sports development has been drawn into new debates about mass participation, social inclusion, talent development and elite performance as well as into justifying its distinctive contribution to wider educational, social and economic policies and practices.

The structure of the new book reflects this broader engagement with this developing field and expanding remit for sports development. All the original chapters have been updated. The chapter on law has been withdrawn, as it will feature in a forthcoming Routledge book on *Sport and the Law*, with Hazel Hartley as the sole author. In addition there are three newly commissioned chapters on youth sports policy, researching and evaluating sports development and finally coaching. All chapters in the second edition have been written by staff working in the Carnegie Faculty of Sport and Education at Leeds Metropolitan University. Consequently the book as a whole offers a distinctive account of sports development which has been enriched by researching and teaching undergraduate and postgraduate courses at Leeds. It also reflects the breadth of staff experience, commitment and professional engagement in the field of sports development as staff supervise both dissertations and student work experience/placements, attend and contribute to academic and practitioners' conferences and are actively involved in research, curriculum development and training, at both a national and local level.

Given the strengthening lobby and funding for elite sport development, it is quite common to hear the argument that sport and recreation development is the traditional responsibility of Sports Development Officers (SDOs). This residual view is not the approach taken here. Sports development is more accurately a term used to describe policies, processes and practices that form an integral feature of work involved in providing sporting opportunities and positive sporting experiences. Such a process-oriented perspective leads to the challenging (and uncomfortable for some) radical conclusion that PE staff, teachers, coaches, facility managers, community outreach workers, youth workers, health specialists, policy makers and many others, including SDOs, are all engaged in sports development work. However, within this occupational matrix, a mixed economy exists of volunteers, paid professionals, policy makers, academics and practitioners. These sectional interests have created a policy space, a perplexingly dynamic environment, within which this work takes place. There are good times when sports policy and funding have been robustly promoted and in bad times collectively defended against retrenchment. However, considerable tensions exist between different actors and institutions. Such conflict and dissonance arise from competing discourses, policies and practices. Indeed, substantial academic research has highlighted a history of political tension between advocates of elite sports development and wider mass participation (see Houlihan and White, 2002). These tensions are clearly present in the history of sport in the UK as well as in other nation states, such as Australia and Canada (see Green and Houlihan, 2005).

Dissonance further emerges in developments to establish a coherent organisation to articulate the views of those involved in sports development in the UK. The paradox occurs as the new Institute for Sport Parks and Leisure (ISPAL) has the job of defining policy and standards for its members in sports development whilst there are many more professionals in other sectors who could legitimately lay claim to sports development activity. A task such as this is not without risk, for, although time can be spent fine-tuning the semantics of what is and who is involved in sports development, to define it is to exclude something. However, there are practical implications for this necessary exercise because to professionalise a sector a professional association must know who its members are, especially if it intends to advocate for *them* and to meet the *needs of the members and the sector.*

For an industry that has been increasingly accused of being piecemeal and *ad hoc* as well as unco-ordinated and fragmented, sport has an opportunity to secure a co-ordinated shift in its governance and overall funding. At this time it is apparent that sport is high on the agenda for government for a whole host of reasons that range from the frantic focus on healthy lifestyles and obesity issues to the increasing focus on world class sports events such as the 2012 Olympics in London. There is a lot at stake. Sports development workers are famed for being flexible, dynamic and opportunistic . . . Cometh the hour, cometh the profession? The Sports Minister, Richard Caborn, announced that:

> If we are to prove that the sector can address the government's agendas across the UK, and on what it can do for others, be it tackling the obesity crisis in health, greater social inclusion in our communities and of course producing world-class

2

talent for our 2012 athletes and beyond – then it needs to be fit for purpose and ready to deliver.

(ISPAL, 2006)

Sports development then is an ambiguous and contested term. The use and some would argue misuse of the term can be appreciated by a closer examination of what each word is describing. *Sports* have at times been narrowly defined in terms of competitive, rule-governed games, involving some degree of physical activity and exercise. *Development* conjures up ideas of maturation, of education: the gradual consolidation of knowledge; the teaching of competences and practical skills. Consequently, to develop someone or something suggests a transition through progressive stages where new and improved outcomes are both possible and desirable. But put two strange words together, each drawing on different vocabularies, like *sports* and *development*, and what do you get? A new hierarchy or range of meanings emerges. What if there is an unequal intonation on each half, as in '*sports* development' or conversely 'sports *development*'? Does a change in emphasis signify different fields of policy and practice, where professional actors have different scripts or roles to interpret? But what if we are dealing with a new hybrid word, a compound noun, made up of equal halves, as in 'sports development'?

Philosophers, linguists and others have warned against the mistaken belief that we can define a word so precisely and accurately as to distil the essence of the meaning of the word itself. The definition acts as a sieve to include or catch all essential characteristics, whilst excluding all non-essential elements or meanings. So we have a word that catches sport or 'sportiness' and beyond lies 'non-sportiness'. This is an example of just one language game where words act as direct mirrors of reality. There are other language games which focus on how people use words: meaning is use. The meaning of a particular word becomes a 'form of life'; it depends on how people use the word in their everyday lives.

But naming is everything as it expresses one element of a distinctive discourse which links knowledge, power and practice. For example, health studies have documented a 'medical model' for health – the medical model gives doctors power to manage the illness of others who are cast in the dependent role of patients. Doctors can lay claim to superior scientific knowledge about how the body functions, how medicines work in clinical trials, and so on, leaving the patient to take on trust the knowledge and professional expertise of the medical practitioner. It is primarily a 'curative model' of health, with the doctor intervening when the patient is sick or suffering some form of illness. By way of contrast there is a 'preventative model' of health, often favoured by alternative medicine, which seeks to encourage healthy lifestyles. Consequently the correct diet, exercise regime and lifestyle choices (i.e. avoiding smoking, unsafe sex, drug and alcohol abuse) will prevent morbidity and avoid invasive medical intervention. In this version of health, often drawing on Oriental philosophy rather than Western science (see, for example, the 'mindful exercise' of Tai Chi or Yoga exercises), the individual becomes an active agent seeking or choosing a healthy lifestyle rather than a patient waiting for hospitalisation and surgery.

So academic discourses, the naming of key concepts, policy prescriptions recommending intrinsic and extrinsic benefits of sport, changing organisation structures and leadership styles, new coaching regimes and so on, must all not be taken lightly. So sport or sport development cannot be taken for granted. Indeed, the word 'sports' itself has been remarkably broad and flexible; walking briskly, camping and step aerobics have all been included as sports activities, and have received support from a range of organisations involved in *sports development*. Ultimately it may be easier (and more helpful) to hold fluid and non-dogmatic views on what do or do not constitute sports, given the ever-changing landscape within the world of sport, recreation and leisure. Sporting landscapes and discourses have become more permeable if one factors in the growing moral panic about obesity and health (see Gard, 2004) as sports projects are often anxious to claim health benefits for participants (see Long, Welch *et al.*, 2002).

Those engaging in sports development must be in the business of devising better and more effective ways of promoting interest, participation or performance in sport. This apparently neat account of sports development nevertheless obscures the arguably more important issues of who has the responsibility for this activity, and questions around where, how, why and ultimately what should be done.

These issues became apparent when studying the introduction of Sport England's Active Sports Programme in 1999. Whilst Active Sports Co-ordinators and their colleagues championed the programme as a tool for sports development to play a more complete role in government policies of social inclusion, some sports development officers and others were critical of what they defined as further policy overload or what Michael Collins later termed 'Initiative-itis' (Collins, 2003: 218). Although heated debates and disagreements between policy makers and those on the 'front line' responsible for service delivery afflict all sectors, sports development is particularly vulnerable because of the characteristics of sport. In simple terms, there are some who believe that sports development should be used to meet broader social, political, economic and cultural aims; the contemporary cross-cutting, joint working agendas which stress sport's externalities. Meanwhile, others contend that 'sport for sport's sake' is the only legitimate battlecry therein emphasising the intrinsic benefits of sport participation. Whilst naturally another group would argue that sport was equally capable of defending itself on both fronts. There are clearly different intrinsic and extrinsic rationales for sports policies and provision. Sports development is an area where passions can run high and, as one should expect with enthusiasts, parochial and self-interested views are frequently found. Again, contrary to the general view, politics at both macro (central government) and more micro (local authorities, governing bodies) levels have played a major part in policy formulation in sports development. High-profile examples have been the establishment of the Community Sports coach scheme, the introduction of the Olympic themed National Lottery games and the construction of the new Wembley stadium. At a more local level, there have been the Community Sports Networks and the emergence of specialist sports colleges and PESSCL developments. The years leading up to the London Olympics 2012 will provide a wealth of examples of central and local government involvement in sport, with support and resistance from local communities.

4

The important and contentious area facing sports development has been the need to work at both grass-roots levels and elite sport. Disagreements as to where the focus should be and disputes about the importance of each, have bedevilled the policy area. The Sports Council, and more recently Sport England and others, have attempted to provide a means of identifying the different roles and responsibilities for those involved in sports development from the lowest to the highest levels of achievement. The first and some would say clearest sports development continuum locates development on a hierarchical basis from foundation, participation, performance and excellence (see Figure 1.1). The sports development continuum model has been used by diverse organisations to provide a logical coherence to their plans, policies and strategies for sport. As with all models it offers an idea of how things 'ought to be' in a perfect world rather than how things necessarily operate in each situation. (See also Figures 1.2 and 1.3.)

This simple and powerful model of sports development has been further modified and refined by sports agencies to articulate new policy agendas and initiatives. These issues

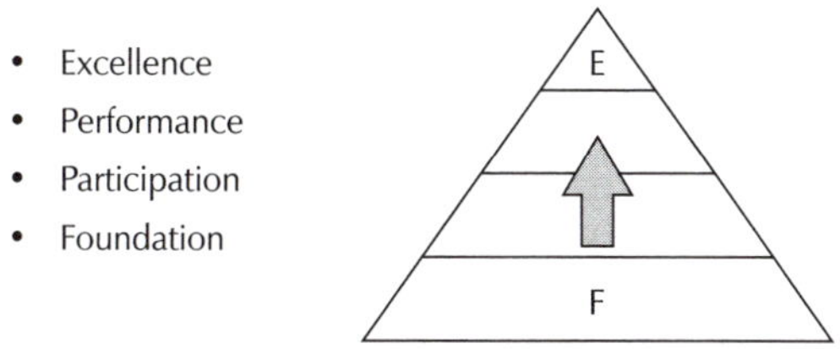

- Excellence
- Performance
- Participation
- Foundation

Figure 1.1 The traditional sports development continuum

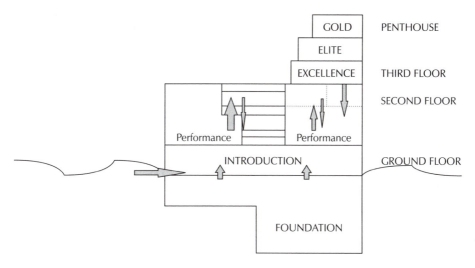

Figure 1.2 The house of sport

Source Cooke (1996).

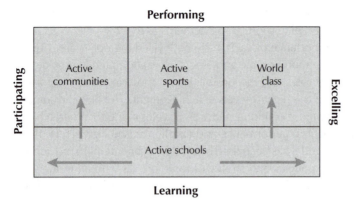

Figure 1.3 Sport England: the active framework

Source Sport England.

and themes are explored throughout the chapters that follow. Chapter 2 defines the key stages in public policy analysis and the politics of decision making: policy formulation, implementation and policy evaluation. Here the major political traditions of conservatism, liberalism and social reformism are introduced and the implications of hybrid ideologies from the New Right and New Labour are explored for sports policy and state provision. The second half of this chapter provides an overview of current policy debates, highlighting ambiguities and ambivalences in sport policy which provide for continuity and change.

Chapter 3 considers how the introduction of Best Value represents the most recent manifestation of central government's interest in resourcing public sector sports development provision. This chapter examines the roles of the public, voluntary and commercial sectors in a context of greater financial accountability, customer service and performance awareness. Economic, political and social dimensions and their impact on the world of sports development are considered here. A particular focus falls on the changing face of local government provision with its increasing emphasis on partnerships across sectors.

Chapter 4 focuses on Sport for All and in particular equality in sport, as, just like in wider society, it is not yet a reality. This chapter outlines some of the key discussions in relation to equality terminology before focusing upon recent case studies in governing bodies and local government. This work investigates policy and practice in sport and offers 'active sociology' as a tool for the critical, inquisitive sports professional.

Chapter 5 illustrates the wider current and historical context that makes up the work of community sports development. Community sports developments as the development of communities through sport and as the development of sport through communities are key dimensions of a continuum which are clarified here. The diversity of rationales and working practices of this community sports continuum are explored, drawing upon case study material and good practice in the UK. The second half of this chapter explores different theoretical perspectives which will help sports professionals clarify community sports policy and practice.

Chapter 6 builds upon the work of the first edition by exploring the benefits and problems experienced by organisations working together. It reflects upon the growth of strategic partnerships encouraged today where more flexible state and government agencies are encouraged. The chapter provides an overview of the benefits such alliances have realised, with particular reference to a successful multi-agency initiative, Sport Leeds. The range of benefits accruing from working together is documented just as limitations are considered as a by-product of less rigorously structured alliances. The final section introduces organisational theory as one lens through which to view partnerships. The chapter concludes with a detailed case study of a county sport partnership (West Yorkshire Sport).

Chapter 7 examines the changing policy universe of youth sport and physical education (PE). The nature and scope of physical education and physical culture among young people is explored in what is described as a 'crowded policy space'. Central government has intervened with a national strategy in PE – the PE and School Sport Club Links (PESSCL) (DfES/DCMS, 2003) and recognises the importance of building links between opportunities in curriculum PE and those physical activity contexts outside school. In particular, the chapter explores ways in which particular conceptions of PE and school sport benefit some groups and marginalise others. It examines the challenges facing different agencies working in partnership to implement change.

Chapter 8 considers how health promotion specialists throughout the UK are becoming increasingly sympathetic towards the notion of sport and physical activity as positive health interventions. It is now generally accepted that physical inactivity is an independent risk factor for coronary heart disease. This represents a major challenge for health care providers and promoters of healthy living. The chapter focuses upon how sports managers can use the provision of fun and informal physical activity opportunities as a means of introducing people to the world of sport. Practical examples of successful collaboration between sport and health care are presented.

Chapter 9 discusses economic resources for sport and the different rationales which drive commercial, public and voluntary sector provision. Individual and collective sporting experiences are shaped by both material and human resources, and the focus of this chapter settles on public policy and funding. The chapter assesses the emergence and impact of National Lottery funds, Sport England policies and New Labour's Game Plan (2002) on elite performance and sports participation. This chapter also considers how providers of sporting opportunities have sought to maximise the potential of past and current funding environments.

Chapter 10 goes beyond the initial question of a particular interrelationship between coaching and development to ask (1) Does the social agenda of much of grass-roots sports development require a particular form of coaching? (2) Is sports development adequately served by the 'quality' of coaching provided? (3) Does coach education provide sufficient preparation for achieving social and other objectives? (4) Is there a 'threshold' level of coaching activity, beyond which the term is most aptly applied, and does sport development activity generally reach this threshold, with implications for professionalisation?

Chapter 11 examines research and evaluation in sports development which have become areas of increasing concern for sport policy makers and practitioners seeking to develop an increasing evidence base to support the resourcing of policy initiatives. Practitioners and students in sport studies are encouraged to familiarise themselves with techniques to gather data and related information about what they do and how they do it to ensure the efficacy of practice. Reference is made to sports development policy and practice with a further development of the research rationale and techniques used in the Sportsweb case study introduced in Chapter 5 by Hylton and Totten.

This book covers a wide range of material and although the authors agree that a systematic reading of the content is advisable it could be just as fruitful to enjoy each chapter in its own right. The case studies are set at the end of most chapters as an opportunity to showcase some of the main ideas and in some cases they are an opportunity for further discussion in professional and academic terms. The situation in sport in 2001 when the first edition was written was different from the world today, whilst experience would suggest that many core issues remain. Equality is still a key concern for sports providers and potential participants; partnerships and joint working are prominent in policy discourses; sport must justify itself even more forcefully to funding agents; policy on elite and community sport are regular discussion issues at all levels of policy; and as always events continue to remind us that sport and politics are inextricably linked. Due to these and related issues this second edition provides interesting and compelling perspectives and debates on sports development policy and practice.

REFERENCES

Cabinet Office (2002) *Game Plan: a Strategy for Delivering Government's Sport and Physical Activity Objective*, London: Cabinet Office.

Collins, M. with Kay, T. (2003) *Sport and Social Exclusion*, London and New York: Routledge.

Department for Education and Skills and Department for Culture Media and Sport (2003) Physical Education and School Sports Club Links, http://www.dfes.gov.uk/pesscl.

Gard, M. (2004) An elephant in the room and a bridge too far, or, Physical education and the 'obesity epidemic', body knowledge and control, in J. Evans, B. Davies and J. Wright (eds) *Body Knowledge and Control*, London: Routledge.

Green, M. and Houlihan, B. (2005) *Elite Sport Development, Policy Learning and Political Priorities*, London and New York: Routledge.

Houlihan, B. and White, A. (2002) *The Politics of Sport Development: Development of Sport or through Sport?* London and New York: Routledge.

Hylton, K., Bramham, P., Jackson, D. and Nesti, M. (eds) (2001) *Sports Development: Policy, Process and Practice*, London and New York: Routledge.

ISPAL (2006) http://www.myispal.org.uk.

Long, J., Welch, M., Branham, P., Butterfield, J., Hylton, K. and Lloyd, E. (2002) Count me in. The Dimensions of Social Inclusion through Culture and Sport. Report to the Department for Culture Media and Sport, http://www.leedsmet.ac.uk/ces/lss/research/countmein.pdf.

CHAPTER TWO

SPORTS POLICY

Peter Bramham

This chapter provides a general introduction to understanding the policy process and then focuses on sports policy in the UK. It outlines key stages in public policy and then explains the nature of three political ideological traditions that have shaped both government policy and policy institutions in post-war years. Ideology is crucial to understanding these generic processes, since sports policy occupies a contested space on the margins of mainstream government policies on education, health and social services. The final section concludes with a brief discussion of sports policy and policy networks to illustrate how political traditions place different values on sport's intrinsic and extrinsic costs and benefits. Sport may be valued intrinsically for its own sake because it develops personal skills, competition, individual self-esteem and fun for participants. Sport can also produce wider externalities, by making a valuable contribution to other government policy with respect to national prestige, to foreign policy and international diplomacy, to tourism and city regeneration, to local community development, to health, as well as helping to redress social divisions around class, 'race', gender and disability. This fault line in sports policies and practices[1] helps to account for both continuity and change in the UK.

UNDERSTANDING THE POLICY PROCESS

One starting point for most policy analysts is a descriptive model of discrete stages in the overall policy process. Jones, Gray *et al.* (1994) traced three main stages in the policy journey: *initiation, formulation* and *implementation*. Others further subdivide this threefold division to provide a more precise account.[2] One detailed model which has dominated policy literature has been provided by Hogwood and Gunn:

Stages in the policy process

- Deciding to decide (issue search or agenda-setting).
- Deciding how to decide (or issue filtration).
- Issue definition.
- Forecasting.
- Setting objectives and priorities.

- Options analysis.
- Policy implementation, monitoring and control.
- Evaluation and review.
- Policy maintenance, succession or termination.

But even this more sophisticated model of stages in the policy process has problems. The authors openly acknowledge some themselves:

> Viewing the policy process in terms of stages may seem to suggest that any policy episode is more or less self-contained and comprises a neat cycle of initial, inter-mediate and culminating events. In practice, of course policy is often a seamless web involving a bewildering mesh of interactions and ramifications.
>
> (Hogwood and Gunn, 1984: 24)

The above model therefore provides an explanatory heuristic device or ideal type for rational decision making: policy makers define policy problems, plan policy strategies, implement best policies and evaluate policy outcomes. The cycle then starts up again in the light of outcomes from original policy intentions. Policy makers often appeal to this systemic model in order to justify choices among alternatives and to legitimate outcomes. Policy development can then be presented as a rational process, and articulated simply as a neutral and technical discourse. All policy 'tick boxes' are systematically covered and audited. There are clear stages in decision making, objective professional advice taken, plans are agreed and policy outcomes evaluated. Policy is defensively grounded in good practice and 'common sense'.

In practice, policy can be irrational, pragmatic and incremental, driven forward or sub-verted by powerful vested interests. Policies slip the grasp of policy makers; create unintended consequences, stubbornly 'working behind the backs' of people and their good intentions. For example, when cities compete to host international sporting mega-events, conventional rationality, realistic time scales, forecasting, accurate budgets and data analyses may disappear. Decisions to locate summer or winter Olympic Games have been clearly shaped by global politics of international sports federations, internal tensions within transnational agencies, media sponsorship, scheduling and advertising, as well as by legitimate lobbying, and by serendipity (see Horne, 2006); in the post-mortem after the Olympic Committee's decision to award the 2012 Games to London in 2005 there were media stories about one delegate voting for London by mistake.[3]

Maurice Roche's (1994) detailed case study of Sheffield City Council's decision to host the World Student Games in the 1990s has documented that policy decisions were taken with limited economic forecasting, crucial financial information suppressed from public debate and democratic processes bypassed. Short- and long-term costs and benefits, as well as the legacy or heritage of sporting venues, have been the focus of much debate and research. The 2002 Commonwealth Games in Manchester told a similar story, with short-falls in funding alongside fierce political and economic controversy over the decision to pass the City of Manchester Stadium over to Manchester City FC. Indeed, many community groups in Barcelona, Athens and London have run anti-Olympic bid protests on account of each bid's social, cultural, economic and environmental impact on disadvantaged neighbourhoods but they have tended to gain little media coverage or political influence.

Such marked deviations from the rational model of decision making have led writers such as Simon (1960) and Lindblom (1959) to describe policy makers as exhibiting 'bounded rationality', informed by partial knowledge, hamstrung, with limited room for manoeuvre by powerful structural forces, as satisfactory rather than perfect solutions are sought to expedite pressing policy issues. Politicians rarely solve long-term policy problems but quickly move on to other problems as they appear on the political and media agenda. They seldom wait to judge and evaluate earlier decisions. Success and failure in policy terms may have little to do with rational decision making to solve long-term problems but rather more to do with short-term gain to appease interested parties, to secure re-election and to maintain control over the policy process. Indeed, it is sometimes argued that sports policy has gained in political significance due to its general public appeal and as other major intractable socio-economic problems have become less susceptible to local, regional or even national initiatives.

A distinction can be drawn between 'insiders' and 'outsiders' in the policy arena. 'Insiders' usually carry discrete professional, commercial or departmental interests and are committed advocates of policy, and 'outsiders' are those experts who lay claim to offer a more detached, analytical and holistic approach. The 'outsiders', often social science academics interested in politics, society and organisational behaviour, gather contextual knowledge of policies and processes at work, whereas 'insiders' have careers in consultancy, PR and marketing, in partnerships, projects and research networks. The sports policy universe becomes an increasingly crowded place, with politicians, political advisers, civil servants, local government officers, non-departmental public bodies, think tanks, consultancy firms, journalists and academics all seeking to make an impact (see Figure 2.1).

Figure 2.1 Types of study of public policy making

Source Hogwood and Gunn (1984), cited in Ham and Hill (1993: 8).

IDEOLOGIES

If one wants to understand how public policy works, it is helpful to start at the policy studies end of the continuum by examining broad ideological assumptions that not only direct policy but also underpin the very institutions that shape and deliver policy. Consequently, before spelling out three ideologies or major traditions of *conservatism*, *liberalism* and *social reformism*, it is worthwhile to clarify how ideologies work in general.

Political ideologies are best described as reflections *of* the world and reflections *on* the world. They prescribe how the world ought to be and offer a guide or mandate for policies and action. One function of political ideology is to provide a particular perspective on the world and to highlight key issues, debates and problems that need to be tackled. Ideologies not only provide an understanding of how the world works but also map out mission statements as to how the world needs to change and to be managed.

In the 'restricted' view, ideology refers to different political ideas debated and contested between and within political leaders, parties and party activists. It is the narrow politics of Westminster, of national and local news broadcasts, of local government debates and plans. In the more 'relaxed' or broader view, ideologies permeate and mediate economic, social and cultural life. Coherent frameworks of attitudes and interpretation shape practices in families, at work, in mass media, in education and in local communities. Commonsense ideas or discourses about what is 'natural', about men, about women, social class, sexuality, 'race', age, ethnicity and so on are all powerfully embedded in institutions, in relationships and in language. One useful concept here is *interpellation*, as ideologies literally speak to concerns of people by addressing them as individual subjects and articulating *their* unique problems and their personal resolution. To take the case of racism against minority ethnic groups and asylum seekers, when tight immigration rules and repatriation offer instant 'solutions' to problems of unemployment, poor housing, poor education and so on. Racist political parties can target white working-class communities as those most neglected by existing political parties and policies. In various distorted ways racist messages tackle silences in mainstream policy discourses as demands for equity and justice in policy outcomes are dismissed as excessive 'political correctness'.

In conventional accounts of policy analysis and rational decision making, political ideologies provide values, ideals and mandates for action, whereas policy sciences provide technical knowledge and advice to administer policies effectively and efficiently. Politics provides the chosen value-laden ends, with policy and administration securing appropriate means to achieve political ends. This separation between political values and facts of policy administration is one cornerstone in Weber's view of social science. Politics and political debates are inevitably grounded in different values and beliefs about how the world ought to be – differences of opinion are inevitable and irreconcilable. Politics is a battlefield, fought by warring tribes with different values. By way of sharp contrast, Weber argues that social science must be value-free. It must produce knowledge about the world as it is. Social research must be objective, neutral and unbiased and not subjective, partisan or committed to some form of politics. As individual citizens we can voice and act upon personal beliefs and idiosyncratic prejudices, but as social scientists and researchers we must exercise value freedom and remain neutral.

This boundary between facts and values, between science and ideology has been fiercely contested throughout the history of social sciences. More recent developments in post-modern analysis argue that many claims of scientific method to secure objective detached knowledge are bogus. Like any other stock of knowledge, science does have its own coherent ontology, epistemology, and its own distinctive logical techniques for generating and testing data. Scientific method celebrates technique by collecting reliable data via experimentation, causal analysis and accurate measurement. But it can no longer claim to provide a single universal objective truth about the world, as there are other discourses to listen to . . . non-Western, non-scientific and so on. Science does have its own coherent discourse but this is just one approach among many. Other voices can provide distinctive and different narratives about the world, how it works and who and what is important. One needs only to think of the criticisms of mainstream science and technology from the radical politics of Marxism and feminism, black critical studies and 'green' politics of environmentalism. Within these counter traditions there are many internal debates. Processes of globalisation, the Information Age (Castells, 1996) and scientific knowledge itself are all directly challenged by religion, most powerfully from fundamentalists who reassert Christian, Islamic or Buddhist traditions and teachings.

Postmodern times offer a variety of such discourses. In the past, in modernity, it was felt that science alone could provide universal laws to explain natural and social worlds. Politics and policy makers would be knowledgeable and could legislate to impose order. It was as if natural and social worlds were gardens that could be carefully cultivated and improved by knowledgeable policy makers. With postmodern thinking, the ideal of an orderly garden gives way to diversity and disorder. Neat horticulture is no longer an option as relativism thrives, like weeds and wilderness. We all live in what Giddens (2001) calls a 'runaway world', where all nation states are permeated by transnational processes of migration, global communications, environmental pollution and global warming. Moreover, life is a babble of competing voices of different sorts of gardeners, different experts each providing conflicting advice. It is hard to choose or know who to trust. In postmodern times, risk and uncertainty seem inherent features of decision making.[4] Public policies lag behind new science and technologies, as people now must face what Giddens (1991) terms manufactured risk in ordinary everyday life. Public policies may even seem to make things worse with nuclear power, global warming and genome research.

POLITICAL IDEOLOGIES

Conservatism

One strategy of dealing with uncertainty and accelerated change is to turn to the past and rely upon tradition. Conservatism has deep historical roots and emerged as a coherent political ideology of the aristocracy to resist the 1789 political revolution in France that demanded democracy, political representation and citizenship. Conservative ideas sought to legitimate the *status quo* and protect it from democratic demands for equality. For conservatism, existing inequalities were natural, pre-ordained and inevitable, even God-given; people should accept their position in the world and perform their defined roles within tried and tested institutions. The *status quo* was a moral order, ordained by religion, by monarchy, and ingrained in custom and practice.

The three core values of the French revolution, *liberté*, *egalité* and *fraternité*, still divide modern political ideologies. For conservative thinkers, fraternity is not possible under the conditions of equality and liberty – they simply produce chaos and anarchy. Conservatism as a political tradition is clearly anti-individualistic, as individuals are not citizens with political rights but are subjects who must be loyal and obedient to the state or monarchy. In conservative ideology, the state is seen as a powerful organism that has the will to strongly destroy external and internal enemies that threaten its lifeblood. All people therefore intuitively, intimately and instinctively belong to the nation state – they are born into it, they constitute its tribe – with a common language, with communal institutions, shared heritage, history and landscape. For an updated exposition of conservative ideas Scruton (2001) maps out the key values of tradition, allegiance and authority. Linked with its fear of democracy, such values carry shades of totalitarianism. However, these tendencies are tempered by the conservative affinity with pragmatism and intuition that permit conservative political ideologies to absorb incremental changes rather than to remain blindly committed to defending the past. In the words of Burke, in *Reflections on the Revolution in France* (1790), one must 'change in order to conserve'. Modern conservatism aims to be a living museum rather than a mausoleum.

Liberalism

If the origins of conservatism lay with the French aristocracy straining to protect privilege in turbulent revolutionary times, liberalism was the political creed of the emerging commercial middle classes, the bourgeoisie, made up of industrialists, financiers and intellectuals. Liberalism throughout the Age of Enlightenment demanded individual freedom in thought and deed from control by tradition and privilege, embedded in the institutions of church and monarchy. Liberalism as a political ideology stresses both individualism and democracy: individuals should be free from governance, free to exercise rights to property, free speech and political suffrage. A contract is struck between the individual and the state: the individual is free to maximise his/her self-interest but s/he must abide by legislation to guarantee order. Individual citizen rights can be written down as constitutional guarantees protected by the courts against state encroachment and any misuse of authority and power. Some liberal writers fear democratic utilitarian institutions pursuing 'the greatest happiness of the greatest number' as the tyranny of the majority may generate legislation that impinges on individual self-interest.

The main function of the liberal or minimalist state is to provide law and order, a secure context within which individuals are free to maximise their own self-interests, in an open market environment. It is a nightwatchman state. Unlike conservative ideology, liberalism demands a clear divide between private and public spheres, as the state has no justification for penetrating the boundary between its own public domain and civil society. Institutions of family, education, work and mass media are private concerns; they must be free from state intervention. Market forces, equations of supply and demand through delicate price mechanisms, are the lifeblood of liberalism and of consumer choice. Adam Smith's 'invisible hand of the market' is seen as the most efficient and, more important, most just means to maximise individual self-interest and to distribute scarce resources. Governmental bureaucracy and state regulation serve only to distort market forces, to weaken work discipline and to discourage profit maximisation and capital accumulation. These liberal themes and others have recently been developed and promoted by Hayek and Friedman. Both have been strong advocates of monetarism that demands a minimal state whose major function is to control the money supply and check destabilising inflation.

In the world of politics, democracy enables individuals to choose their own rulers through representation and even more direct forms of democracy may be possible at a local or community level. In a similar democratic vein, individuals are free to organise themselves into pressure groups to protect their collective interests and to influence political parties in both shaping and implementing policies. Such pluralism denies the concentration of power into a strong state and encourages governments to seek public consent to legitimate and secure their policies among citizens.

Social reformism

If the political ideology of conservatism developed in the pre-industrial eighteenth century, and liberalism blossomed in the industrial capitalism of the nineteenth century, social reformism is very much the product of the twentieth century. It grew out of a range of working-class movements that sought government intervention to mitigate the intended and unintended consequences of market forces. Confronted with capitalist economics that spawned gross inequalities of income, capital and property, social reformists stressed the need for equality, for the state to redistribute resources in order to protect wage labourers and the poor, particularly those groups who were unable to sell their labour power through force of circumstance – the sick, mentally ill, children, the unemployed, the elderly.

In the early part of the twentieth century, radical sections of the working class looked to Marxist ideologies and revolutionary struggle to destroy class inequalities as well as political dominance of the state by the ruling class. In sharp contrast, social reformists were disenchanted with socialism and Marxism, feeling that gradual change or reform was both possible and desirable. Rather than overthrowing capitalism by civil war and establishing a communist state, social reformism argued, equality in capitalism could be achieved by political intervention in the form of a welfare state. Governments had a major role to play: they should own and plan sectors of the economy, guarantee minimum wages and income support for all by redistributing wealth from the rich to the poor through direct taxation. The welfare state should abolish poverty and deprivation by providing health care, social services, education and adequate housing. It would be funded out of taxation, social insurance paid by the working population and by a growing economy. It would also witness the growth of a powerful public sector bureaucracy, staffed by professionals and semi-professionals who would set standards of care and define appropriate levels of social need and provision.

For social reformism, individual freedom could not be realised under the conditions and constraints of inequality, so substantial central and local government intervention would have to be targeted at disadvantaged groups. For example, children could not be expected to develop their full potential if they were trapped in poverty, living in inadequate, overcrowded housing, learning at under-achieving schools and playing outside in damaged communities. Consumer choice was no real option for the working classes unless the state intervened to manage capitalism and its social consequences. In social reformist ideology, government had to deal with market failure, with negative consequences or externalities in markets, and had to control monopolistic and oligopolistic practices that generated surplus super-profits for business and commerce. Many of the key ideas of social reformism have been articulated by Titmuss (1958). He argued that one of the key values that should inform welfare is altruism, which is closely linked to fraternity. Citizens should seek to generate collective welfare for the greater good rather than pursing their own self-interest, often at the expense of others. To illustrate his position he contrasts the gift relationship of blood donorship in the UK with the market relationship of blood sales in the United States. In the UK healthy donors provide good blood for nothing whereas in the United States many disadvantaged groups sell their own blood, possibly contaminated by drugs and problems of ill health, to supplement their meagre income.

After considering the three traditional ideologies that have dominated UK political institutions in the post-war period, namely *conservatism, liberalism and social reformism*, we are now better placed to make sense of two ideological hybrids which have shaped governance during the past thirty years. Stated boldly, 1980s New Right ideas *mix conservatism and liberalism* whereas commentators see New Labour, from the late 1990s and on into the millennium, as a mix of *liberalism* and *social reformism*.

The New Right

New Right ideas were developed in the UK from the 1970s on through a variety of think tanks and pressure groups, including notably the Institute of Economic Affairs, the Adam Smith Institute and many others. They were dissatisfied with the institutional legacy of the post-war welfare state, underpinned by social reformism, arguing that state intervention was inefficient, ineffective and led to dependence on the state rather than encouraging responsibility and self-reliance. No part of the institutional structure of welfarism was exempt from criticism – politicians promised to increase public expenditure and services to secure re-election; bureaucrats maximised their own budgets and departmental power, whilst professionals denied choice to the individual. These criticisms in academic circles led to the elucidation of *public choice* theory that demanded restructuring the state and introducing market forces. Voters must be made to pay more directly for public services received, which must be shaped by the tested disciplines of the private sector – profitability, entrepreneurship, income generation, customer care, quality audits and performance-related pay.

Although New Right ideas were a clear restatement of liberalism in the face of an established social reformist welfare state, it was more than that. The startling contradiction or paradox in the heart of New Right thinking was its fusion of market liberalism with elements of its arch ideological enemy, conservatism. The New Right was a mixture of the two – a strong nation state and a strong deregulated market. In the persona of Margaret Thatcher the Conservative Party in the 1980s was driven forward to restructure the welfare state and change its relationship with local government. Throughout two decades, central government introduced a series of fiscal and legislative measures to control local government expenditure as well as open up local professionals to New Right thinking, enshrined in such initiatives as the Community Charge, Standardised Spending Assessments, rate capping, Local Management of Schools and Compulsory Competitive Tendering (see Henry, 2001). Quangos and agencies were created to implement policy and the Audit Commission could assess the performance of central and local government departments against market ideals measured in performance indicators of cost, efficiency and customer care.

New Labour

It has been suggested that British elections are lost by governments rather than won by the opposition. Indeed, it was the failure of Conservative supporters to turn out on election day, tactical voting in marginal seats and general disenchantment with Tory sleaze that resulted in a landslide majority for the Labour Party in 1997. Having modernised the party by distancing itself from its trade union and socialist roots, the Blair government accepted continuing New Right economic policies as parameters to guide the first two years of new government. There were substantial continuities in policies such as Best Value, Public–Private Business Partnerships (PPBPs) and Private Finance Initiatives (PFIs) as well as privatisation. Indeed, some writers felt that New Labour was nothing but Blair's presidential style and his pragmatism to choose 'whatever works' in policies. Others saw New Labour as a progressive discourse in postmodern politics because traditional ideologies had lost popular support and their traditional class alignment. Governments could no longer deal with growing individual aspirations, globalisation, new technologies and transnational migration (Kelly, 2003). If New Right ideology drew on liberalism and conservatism, New Labour was another hybrid, finding its direction from mixing neo-liberalism and social reformism. Guided by think tanks such as Demos and the Institute for Public Policy Research (IPPR) as well as by the prolific writings of Anthony Giddens (see 1998, 2000, 2002), Labour presented itself as offering a 'Third Way' to deal with these 'New Times' of globalisation. New Labour argued that neither the 'first way' of liberal capitalism nor the 'second way' of state socialism was viable. A free unregulated market and the planned collective socialist state were anachronisms. Indeed, Blair targeted the 'forces of con-servatism' (of both left and right) in his millennium speech as major opponents to progressive politics. Since re-election in 2001 and 2005 the language of New Labour has stressed monotonously and remorselessly modernisation and reform of public services. Marxist academics[5] and Old Labour see current reforms and finance strategies in health, education and workfare as covert privatisation and marketisation. There is a 'hollowing out' of governance. Nation states must open themselves up to competition from global market forces, to new technologies and to flexible patterns of work whilst trying to fill a growing democratic deficit of declining voter interest by devolving power to the local state and community organisations.

POLITICAL TRADITIONS, QUANGOS AND SPORTS POLICY

Major political ideologies of conservatism, liberalism and social reformism clearly offer different prescriptions for public policy; they define the preferred relationship between nation state, civil society and markets. Several writers have spelt out what sports policies would look like if driven directly by political ideology (see Whannel, 1983; Bramham and Henry, 1985; Wilson, 1988; Bramham and Henry, 1991; Henry, 2001).[6] There is also a wealth of cross-national literature on how socialist ideas have shaped sports policies in communist nation states (see Riordan, 1978).

Political traditions direct public policy as well as mapping out contours of key institutions which define and empower stakeholders in the policy process. In the post-war UK, policy has been shaped by social reformism in the domain of culture, leisure and sport. Conservative and Labour governments gradually set up quangos such as the Arts Council, the Sports Council and the Countryside Commission to plan and develop facilities and opportunities. In 1994 the Department of National Heritage empowered agencies to distribute National Lottery funds. Despite changes in governments, this 'arm's length' approach to policy has been both politically and ideologically expedient by providing institutional continuity. Governments provide subsidy and appoint quango personnel but are not directly accountable in Parliament for policy decisions and outcomes. This is in no way to suggest that sports policy is an ideologically battle-free zone. Sports policy cannot avoid moral panics in the media about national elite sports performance, alcohol and drug abuse, football hooliganism, racism and sexism, childhood obesity and so on. The sports policy universe is inevitably drawn into each government's political ideology and policy agenda.

Detailed histories of the development of UK sports policy are already well established. Accounts have been provided by Sports Council personnel (Coughlan, 1990; Pickup,

1996), by academics writing policy textbooks (Houlihan, 1991; Henry, 1993; Haywood, Kew et al., 1995; Houlihan and White, 2002), as well as a range of detailed studies evaluating various policy initiatives; e.g. for the unemployed (Glyptis, 1989), for community sport (Lentell, 1994; Haywood, 1994; McDonald, 1995), and for women (Talbot, 1979; Hargreaves, 1994).

Establishment of the Sports Council in 1972 was a response to successful lobbying by voluntary governing bodies organising sport (NGBs), orchestrated by the Central Council for Physical Recreation (CCPR), but was also a clear expression of conservative beliefs in the intrinsic value of sport. Sport and recreation were also seen as means to deal with disaffected youth. National culture had to be preserved within the next generation as the 1960s witnessed growing moral panic about the corrosive impact of American media and consumer culture. The 'expressive' revolution of sex, drugs and rock-'n'-roll diluted the traditional authority of the family, school and community. Equally, black youth were scapegoated as the cause of inner-city problems rather than victims, as news media amplified 'mugging' into a symptom of a violent, racially divided society (Hall, Critcher et al., 1978). Youth work and sport were therefore seen as crucial ingredients to divert youth, particularly those unemployed and living in inner-city working-class neighbour-hoods away from crime and delinquency and into sport and active lifestyles.

Youth sport, whether organised by PE teachers, youth development workers, coaches and sports animateurs or the police, was and still is defined as a crucial site to re-establish moral values, healthy lifestyles and so rebuild fragmenting communities and avoid social exclusion. These themes have been popularised by Robert Putnam's (2000) idea of 'social capital': US bowling leagues had acted as social glue, binding together healthy community networks. High-achieving schools, excellent health and care services, high rates of employment and sporting opportunities all served to build local relations of trust; good neighbouring to suppress high rates of family breakdown, of crime, delinquency and social disorder. Conservatism defined the performance of national teams in international sport as an important indicator of successful sports policy. Conservatism valued the volun-tary sector in sports organisations (see Roberts, 2004), particularly traditional male 'English' team games, such as cricket, rugby and football. Failures in World and Olympic Games were read as significant historical indicators of decline in UK culture and competitiveness. Consequently, tension between national elite performance and local community par-ticipation, albeit often focused in targeted populations, has been the hallmark of post-war UK sports policy. Shifting priorities in sports policies have been conflated in the Sports Council's sporting pyramid, a continuum from foundation, to participation, performance and on to elite excellence. A broad base of mass participation and talent identification of young athletes was perceived as essential for excellence in elite performance. Sports development should increase sports participation, whilst simultaneously providing sporting and coaching pathways to elite performance.

If the Conservative government was attracted to sport mainly because of its intrinsic ben-efits, during the 1970s a social reformist Labour government was keen to promote sporting opportunities as an integrated part of a comprehensive welfare state. Such an inclusive approach was heralded in the 'Sport for All?' campaign. One important physical expression of this policy appeared in the planning, management and development of sports facilities. Local authorities, encouraged by Regional Sports Councils, invested heavily in both large-scale and community-based facilities. As with other aspects of state welfare provision, there developed a growing professionalism within the public sector around the marketing and delivery of leisure services. At the same time, there was growing dissatisfaction with social reformism, mounted by New Right ideas around public choice. Sports policy was now felt to be dominated by local government. The nature of sports provision was seen to be inefficient, ineffective and unnecessary.

New Right ideology argued that government subsidy in sport was inappropriate. Individuals should be free to meet their sporting wants through the commercial or voluntary sectors rather than having their sporting needs defined by distant quangos or central or local government. Olympic elites and national governing bodies should look to business sponsorship for support rather than rely on welfare subsidies from a 'nanny state'. However, faced by inner-city riots, the New Right Thatcherite government was not completely deaf to the extrinsic benefits of sports provision for troublesome youth. During the 1980s, unemployed and black minorities were drawn into a variety of community-based sports leadership schemes, financed by urban aid programmes. This was the emergence of what came to be seen as the new profession of sports development through the 'Action Sport' programme (see Hylton and Totten, Chapter 5).

Another paradox of New Right policies at this time was the growth of diverse government quangos to bypass the power of local authorities and to weaken the collective professional base and trade union rights of public sector producers. The Thatcher hegemonic New Right project vaunted a minimalist state yet simultaneously presided over the expansion of a wide range of government agencies and quangos. Traditional government bureaucracies and civil servants were viewed by the New Right as self-serving inefficient bureaucrats and the Sports Council itself was subjected to numerous reviews which raised severe doubts about its future policy direction and possible continuation.

During the mid-1990s the Major government pragmatically breathed new life into the Sports Council through National Lottery funding and with its commitment to the UK Sports Institute to secure excellence. The government reasserted the intrinsic benefits of team sports and introduced a raft of policy initiatives in *Sport: Raising the Game* (1995) to strengthen sporting opportunities within the PE curriculum and within extra-curricular activities. Emergence of the Youth Sports Trust provided new pathways for youth sport through TOP initiatives in combination with the National Coaching Foundation's 'Champion Coaching' scheme. Some commentators argued that media panic about the loss of school playing fields and sports opportunities has overstated the crisis in youth sport (Roberts, 1996).

Since the 1990s New Labour has pursued similar sports objectives as New Right administrations.[7] But it is a complicated narrative. During the first years of this century, government departments such as the DCMS and the Social Exclusion Unit in the Cabinet Office have put increasing pressure on Sport England, NGBs and local authorities to demonstrate how sporting outcomes contribute to its broader policy agenda related to social exclusion (Collins and Kay, 2003). With its PESSCL initiatives, the Labour government has also funded education and sporting partnerships between Specialist Sports Colleges and NGBs both to increase mass participation and to identify talent and gifted young athletes. Deep-seated contradictions between intrinsic and extrinsic rationales for sport abound and are glossed over in sports policy discourse. For example, the presentation bid, strongly supported by New Labour, to host the 2012 Olympics in London illustrated sport's complex position in relation to broader government agendas of social, economic and cultural policies. A multi-racial group of inner-city school children were taken along to help Lord Coe justify the British bid, as if they were to be the main beneficiaries of the Olympic sporting facilities. It is this capacity of sport to offer governments help in achieving wider policy goals which explains continuity in support for sports policies, albeit from governments working from different ideological scripts.

In a globalised world in which transnational economic, environmental, security and cultural forces reign supreme, even transcending nation state boundaries, sports policies continue to offer national governments the illusory temptation that ideologically based interventions can make a difference. Whether in bidding for mega-events, changing mass participation rates in sport, or using activities to regulate disorderly youth, sports policy remains, and has even grown in political salience in the twenty-first century.

NOTES

1   The subtitle of Houlihan and White's book (2002), *Development of Sport or Development through Sport*, captures this tension. However, it is not simply a case of *either* one *or* the other, but rather *both* one *and* the other, as is implied by their final chapter, 'Development of sport and/or development through sport?' (pp. 206–31).
2   See, for example, a fivefold division by F. Forman, *Mastering British Politics* (1991): policy germination, policy formulation, decision making, policy execution and policy fulfilment.
3   This alleged mistake occurred in one of the early elimination rounds which would have meant that Paris or Madrid would have been awarded the 2012 Olympic Games.
4   See Beck (1992) for a full discussion of how the development of scientific knowledge and technological intervention seems to mean that no one knows and, worse still, no one is in control.
5   See S. Hall, 'New Labour has picked up where Thatcherism has left off', *Guardian*, 6 August 2003.
6   See Yule (1990) for a discussion on how a political counter-ideology such as feminism would shape sport and leisure policy.
7   Towards the end of its first term of office New Labour produced a prescriptive national sports strategy (see DCMS, 2001) *A Sporting Future for All: The Government's Plan for*

Sport, and DCMS/Strategy Unit, *Game Plan: A Strategy for Delivering the Government's Sport and Physical Activity Objectives*).

REFERENCES

Beck, U. (1992) *The Risk Society: Towards a New Modernity*, London: Sage.

Bramham, P. and Henry, I. (1985) Political ideology and leisure policy, *Leisure Studies*, 4(1): 1–19.

Bramham, P. and Henry, I. (1991) Explanations of the organisation of sport in British society, *International Review for the Sociology of Sport*, 26: 139–50.

Castells, M. (1996) *The Rise of The Network Society*, Oxford: Blackwell.

Collins, M. and Kay, T. (2003) *Sport and Social Exclusion*, London and New York: Routledge.

Coughlan, J. (1990) *Sport and British Politics since 1960*, London: Falmer Press.

Department for Culture Media and Sport (2001) *The Government's Plan for Sport: A Sporting Future for All*, London: DCMS.

Department for Culture Media and Sport and Cabinet Office Strategy Unit (2002) *Game Plan: A Strategy for Delivering Government's Sport and Physical Activity Objectives*, London: HMSO.

Department of National Heritage (1995) *Sport: Raising the Game*, London: HMSO.

Forman, F. (1991) *Mastering British Politics*, London: Macmillan.

Giddens, A. (1991) *Modernity and Self-identity*, Cambridge: Polity Press.

Giddens, A. (1998) *The Third Way: The Renewal of Democracy*, Cambridge: Polity Press.

Giddens, A. (2000) *The Third Way and its Critics*, Cambridge: Polity Press.

Giddens, A. (2001) *The Global Third Way Debate*, Cambridge: Polity Press.

Giddens, A. (2002) *Where Now for New Labour?*, Cambridge: Polity Press.

Glyptis, S. (1989) *Leisure and Unemployment*, Milton Keynes: Open University Press.

Hall, S., Critcher, C. *et al.* (1978) *Policing the Crisis: Mugging, the State and Law and Order*, London: Macmillan.

Ham, C. and Hill, M. (1993) *The Policy Process in the Modern Capitalist State*, London: Harvester Wheatsheaf.

Hargreaves, J. (1994) *Sporting Females: Critical Issues in the History and Sociology of Women's Sports*, London: Routledge.

Haywood, L. (ed.) (1994) *Community Leisure and Recreation: Theory and Practice*, Oxford: Butterworth Heinemann.

Haywood, L., Kew, F. *et al.* (1995) *Understanding Leisure*, Cheltenham: Stanley Thornes.

Henry, L.P. (1993) *The Politics of Leisure Policy*, Basingstoke: Macmillan.

Henry, I. (2001) *The Politics of Leisure Policy*, Basingstoke: Palgrave.

Heritage, Department of National (1995) *Sport: Raising the Game*, London: Stationery Office.

Horne, J. (2006) *Sport in Consumer Culture*, Basingstoke: Palgrave Macmillan.

Houlihan, B. (1991) *Government and the Politics of Sport*, London: Routledge.

Houlihan, B. and White, A. (2002) *The Politics of Sport Development*, London: Routledge.

Jones, B., Gray, A. *et al*. (1994) *Politics UK*, London: Harvester Press.

Kelly, P. (2003) Ideas and agendas in contemporary politics, in P. Dunleavy, A. Gamble, R. Hefferman and G. Peele (eds) *Developments in British Politics*, Basingstoke: Palgrave Macmillan.

Lentell, B. (1994) Sports development: goodbye to community recreation? in C. Brackenridge (ed.) *Body Matters: Leisure Images and Lifestyles*, Brighton: LSA Publications.

Lindblom, C. (1959) The science of muddling through, *Public Administration Review*, 19: 79–88.

McDonald, I. (1995) Sport for All: RIP? A political critique of the relationship between national sport policy and local authority sports development in London, in S. Fleming, M. Talbot and A. Tomlinson (eds) *Policy and Politics in Sport, Physical Education and Leisure*, Eastbourne: Leisure Studies Association.

Pickup, D. (1996) *Not another Messiah: An Account of the Sports Council, 1988–1993*, Edinburgh: Pentland Press.

Putnam, R. (2000) *Bowling Alone: The Collapse and Revival of American Community*, New York: Simon & Schuster.

Riordan, J. (ed.) (1978) *Sport under Communism*, London: Hurst.

Roberts, K. (1996) Young people, schools, sport and government policies, *Sport, Education and Society*, 1(1): 47–58.

Roberts, K. (2004) *The Leisure Industries*, London: Palgrave Macmillan.

Roche, M. (1994) Mega-events and urban policy, *Annals of Tourism Research*, 21(1): 1–19.

Scruton, R. (2001) *The Meaning of Conservatism*, Basingstoke: Macmillan.

Simon, H. (1960) *Administrative Behaviour*. London: Macmillan.

Talbot, M. (1979) *Women and Leisure*, London: SSRC/SC.

Titmuss, R. (1958) *Essays on the Welfare State*, London: Allen & Unwin.

Whannel, G. (1983) *Blowing the Whistle*, London: Comedia.

Wilson, J. (1988) *Politics and Leisure*, London: Allen & Unwin.

Yule, J. (1990) Gender and leisure policy, *Leisure Studies*, 11(2): 157–73.

CHAPTER THREE

DEVELOPING SPORTS PRACTICE

David Jackson

This chapter sets out to provide a brief resumé of developments in sports provision from an historical perspective, linking key moments to changes in different sectors. Debates around policy issues are related to the contemporary political, social and economic contexts. A number of important themes emerge, in particular the changing role of local government as both direct provider of services and facilitator for partnerships, working with and through the voluntary and commercial sectors. The historical perspective taken here examines and reflects upon policy and practice experienced in the public sector and how these relate to other players in the sporting arena. Over recent years financial and market-led pressures have become more prevalent alongside changing economic and cultural values. At the highest levels of central government, political enthusiasm for sport has fluctuated but a significant level of interest in sport and recreation has always been evident. However, since 1997 the policies of the New Labour government have driven a sporting agenda based around the search for improved international performance and the need for sport to fulfil wider social objectives relating to health, inclusion, employment, crime reduction and urban regeneration.

A close examination of the history of sports development in the UK reveals a reality of irregular evolution. New Labour's commitment to sport and physical activity as detailed in *Game Plan* (DCMS/Cabinet Office, 2002) will be examined later in the chapter. This iconic statement of government intent provides the current framework to which sporting organisations must now relate. In the vacuum left by previous Conservative administrations, specifically in relation to strategic planning and policy direction in sport, local authorities were often left to take the lead in both direct and indirect provision. A historical perspective highlights the important links between central and local government policy development and implementation and the experience of individuals' sporting lives at all levels across the nation.

Best Value in public service provision was conceived by New Labour in an attempt to improve service delivery across local government. Improving the quality of delivery of public service sports services was as much a part of this new vision as were other traditional local government services. The clear intention was to shift the philosophy to 'joined-up thinking' across public, voluntary and commercial sectors, with local government acting as catalyst and facilitator. There is a long history of fragmented approaches by different agencies and services in sports development, although there has been greater success in partnership working in recent years. The changing policy environment impacts on the voluntary sector, and to a lesser extent on the commercial sector, as the powerful arguments in favour of an integrated approach are fully felt.

Best Value has itself evolved from the drive towards improved value for money and the demand for greater accountability in public services which gathered momentum during the 1980s and 1990s. This was led by a New Right philosophy which gave dominance to market forces and growing 'marketisation' of the public sector was experienced throughout many nation states of the developed world. During the 1980s the major policy manifestation of the Conservative administration that impacted on sport was the introduction of Compulsory Competitive Tendering (CCT), established by the Local Government Act 1988. This legislation targeted a wide range of local government services, including management of sports and leisure facilities, with the aim of introducing greater financial awareness and accountability in local authority provision. This legislation sought to encourage commercial sector involvement in the running of public sector sports and leisure facilities. That only a very small number of contracts were won by commercial operators in the initial rounds of contract bidding revealed that this latter aim was largely unfulfilled. Although perceived in some quarters as such, this was not an attempt at full-scale 'privatisation'. It clearly was, however, an attempt at instilling a more businesslike and entrepreneurial focus into the provision of local sporting services.

The implementation of CCT highlighted a major tension between financially driven contracted services and broader cultural and social aims associated with traditional sports development, both within leisure departments and schools. This pressure is still in evidence today but with perhaps differing emphases. It is questionable that the progression to Best Value would have ever been achieved without this policy initiative and the requirement for reflection that the impetus of impending marketisation instilled. This all seems some distance when viewed from the earliest stages of government involvement in sport and recreation. Analysis of the history of the development of sport clearly reveals halting progress in public, voluntary and commercial activity. These changes were frequently accompanied by partisan legislation or were shaped by various cultural influences as well as by demographic or socio-economic changes. The balance between these has changed over history.

THE EARLY DAYS

At the end of the decade in which England won the World Cup, the 'swinging sixties' took off and the Beatles were the most famous pop group on earth, there were only a handful of sports centres across the UK. Terms and concepts such as sports development, performance indicators, customer care and quality management were more than a decade away. According to Torkildsen (2005) the sport and recreation sector was overwhelmingly

26

david jackson

about voluntary sport, with clubs, governing bodies and local sporting and community associations delivering activity on the ground. The 1970s and mid-1980s experienced rapid and massive public investment in specially designed sport and leisure facilities as well as the recruitment of a professional and skilled work force. Driven by local authorities, the emphasis was on increasing opportunities to participate in sport by providing state-of-the-art indoor swimming pools and sports halls, often located on the same site. The public were generally very enthusiastic recipients of these facilities and at this juncture few dissenting voices were to be heard across the political spectrum. There was clear latent demand for improved sports development and facility expansion. However, this was not the first time that local government had played a key role in the expansion of sport and recreation facilities with a primary focus of sports participation.

Concerns over public health, disease and hygiene, especially in the overcrowded and cramped conditions of the large Victorian industrial cities, impacted on both local and national government. The late Victorian and Edwardian era, up until the period before the First World War (1914–18) witnessed increases in legislation and provision in relation to education, health and safety at work and representation of workers. For the most part, however, little was made of sport and recreation. Nevertheless, as McIntosh (1984) has pointed out, public authorities were increasingly aware of the need to ensure that the working classes had access to health and physical recreation opportunities. Public baths, for both swimming and personal hygiene, became a feature of many cities and larger towns. Parks and open spaces were increasingly planned. The focus clearly was on 'recreation' sustaining the physical fitness and mental health of huge numbers of people, working in often dangerous, dirty and morale-sapping conditions. This provision of physical recreation facilities tended to be in working-class areas usually located on the edge of inner cities. This traditional, utilitarian and functional view of sport and recreation is still recognisable in late 1990s policy developments by the New Labour government and was updated in its first term in Sport England's policy document, *The Value of Sport* (Sport England and Local Government Association, 1999a). Sports development expenditure is justified in terms of unequivocal externalities: sport is good for health, experienced both at an individual and community level, and essential in terms of securing social order. These approaches echo much earlier times when games, chariot races and 'bread and circuses' were provided by the Roman emperors to keep the populace in its place (see McIntosh, 1984).

During the inter-war years the UK was preoccupied with managing the decline of a fragmenting empire, surviving world economic recession in the 1930s and worrying about the rise of Nazi Germany. In part to prepare the population for the eventuality of war, the government enacted the Physical Training and Recreation Act 1937. However, beyond the development of new 'flagship' bespoke facilities such as Wembley Stadium for football, White City for athletics, and in physical education the establishment of Carnegie College and Loughborough, little real change was evident. Again, sport and recreation development post-1945 was largely non-existent, as the country faced more fundamental problems of rebuilding shattered infrastructure and sustaining without American aid a badly damaged economy. As competitive sport at international levels began to be re-established in the following decade it became clear that British sportsmen and sportswomen could no longer be relied upon to achieve easy victories. Indeed, in some sports notable high-profile failures shook national self-confidence and searching questions were asked in political circles and in sports governing bodies. These chastening experiences contributed to increases in coach education and to the appointment of national coaches in sports such as football and athletics. During the next forty years this cycle of media- and politician-led inquests into the perceived demise of British sport in international competition would repeat itself many times. Again, the usual answer would involve much hand wringing and *ad hoc*, inadequate and ill conceived responses.

THE POST-WAR PERIOD

It can be argued that the 1960s did witness major events which had a significant and long-lasting impact on sports development in the UK. The formation in 1965 of the Central Council for Sport and Recreation (CCPR) represented a key moment in the decade as far as governing bodies of sport were concerned. The CCPR provided a unified voice for a disparate group of sports and so encouraged a more planned and strategic approach in the provision of sporting opportunities. Through its ever-growing band of technical officers and development staff the CCPR was successful in helping to improve the quality of facilities, coaches and coach educators. In addition, and arguably of greater importance, this organisation was highly effective in attracting media interest and political support for its various campaigns and policies via an Advisory Sports Council between 1965 and 1972. So effective was the CCPR in this respect that when the Sports Council was established in 1972 by royal charter, ostensibly to replace the CCPR and develop its work, high-level political support resulted in the continuation of this body, albeit in emaciated form. The CCPR transferred most of its resources and staff over to the newly created Sports Councils. However, its new incarnation continued to represent the governing bodies of sport and maintained a high profile in British sport.

Much of the tension and outright animosity that appeared subsequently between the CCPR and the Sports Council reflected wider developments taking place. Within many areas of the economy, and the service sector in particular, differences in terms of funding, operational climate and political influence were increasingly evident between voluntary organisations and other providers such as local government. The residual resentment that accompanied this tension would make an already complex and unsystematic sports development industry even more difficult to guide strategically. This would seriously undermine the effectiveness of those organisations such as the Sports Council, charged with bringing efficiency and order into recalcitrant and at times chaotic areas of operation. This greater desire to bring direction and control through planning and strategic approaches increased during the decade. This 'corporate' strategy was associated elsewhere with strident efforts to challenge the prevailing establishment with its traditional, amateurish and conservative mores. The 1960s were a time of new freedoms, of emerging youth cultures and sustained economic prosperity, all of which were uncomfortable with following an establishment line as readily as previous, more deferential generations.

One further crucial landmark during the 1960s was the findings reported by the Wolfenden Committee (1960) in terms of sport development for children and young people. The so-called 'Wolfenden gap' identified that one major reason for declining sport participation levels among young people was the result of weak and often non-existent links between school sport and local clubs. In simple terms, huge numbers of committed young sports participants were failed by the system upon leaving school at either fourteen or fifteen years of age. The sporting life of those going on to university generally continued whilst, for the rest, the ages (fourteen to eighteen years) at which they joined the work force often coincided with the end of their careers in sport. Wolfenden raised the political temperature and had a major impact on the formation of a sports policy lobby, and contributed to an increased role for local authorities in the provision of sporting opportunities. Local authorities began a massive programme of facility provision during the 1970s. Torkildsen (1999) has pointed out that sport and leisure centres were provided by local authorities in both rural and urban areas and across the political divide, as a mood of optimism and expansion spread to all areas of public services. A powerful agenda of social welfare and quality of life, coupled with an increasingly hedonistic and leisure-orientated environment, offered the optimal conditions for investment in sport. Local authority provision of sport and leisure centres had escalated from four in 1970 to over a thousand by the end of the decade.

By directing funding to encourage local authorities to invest in increased provision, Sports Council grant-aid policies fuelled this development apace. The CCPR, as representatives of a large voluntary sector in sport and individual sports governing bodies (NGBs), did manage to highlight other concerns, particularly after failures in the international sport arena. However, the general pattern was set. Local authorities' 'flagship' facility provision was the most important and visible expression of the collective drive to achieve Sport for All. In this climate, little time was allocated to identifying how successful this mass-facility approach was in terms of increasing sports participation. Focus was on supply-side provision and, consistent with approaches across other business and commercial environments, it was felt that if products were good, success and demand would follow. Marketing, targeting and sophisticated differential pricing policies were generally overlooked.

As this huge capital programme of facility development expanded, greater pressure built up, especially in the larger urban areas, for local authorities to compete with their neighbouring authorities, by providing the best, 'state of the art' facilities for their residents. Internally, local politicians representing housing, leisure (sport and arts) and education put intense pressure on authorities' budgets to gain more funds for major building and construction works. Finally, given that these sport and other facilities in education and housing represented an important source of civic pride, local political groupings vied with each other and promised increased provision should the voters bring them to power. However, the Sports Councils were at last starting to raise serious questions about just how effective this 'build, build and build' policy had been. Some realistic evaluation of what had and would be achieved was not only inevitable but also highly desirable.

The major policy shift came in 1979 when the new Conservative government swept into power on the back of a radical New Right agenda to combine market economics with traditional one-nation Conservatism. The marriage of this 'odd couple' would seem ill conceived at times during the next decade and eventually would result in the emergence of New Labour in the 1990s. Indeed, New Labour, in common with what some cast as more self-centred and individualistic times, does not so much represent a marriage but rather the cohabitation of two irreconcilable positions, market economic liberalism on the one hand and the collectivism of social reformism on the other. In terms of sport development little substantial change occurred during the 1980s as the Conservative government devoted its energies to more pressing economic and macro-structural concerns beyond sport. However, the functionality that sport appears to offer to successive governments assumed greater significance in the new, evolving environment.

In the inner-city riots of 1981 doubts were raised about how successful local authorities had been in attracting traditionally low participant groups to use sport and leisure facilities and about the effectiveness of investment in sporting infrastructure in maintaining social control. There was little subtlety in connecting sport with alleviating social unrest. Collins and Kennett (1999) have revealed that in many cases those people closest to facilities, perhaps surprisingly, used them least and that this situation was most pronounced within the inner-city areas of large urban conurbations. Partly to address this issue the Sports Council set up the Action Sport initiative to bring sporting opportunities closer to local communities. However, whilst McIntosh and Charlton (1985) had many positive things to say about both the theory and the practice of Action Sport programmes, others such as Haywood (1992, 1994) criticised agencies for paying lip service to genuine community development and for continuing to use top-down approaches to managing sports development.

Towards the end of the1980s attention was refocused on considering sporting success at the highest level. The National Coaching Foundation (now Sportscoach UK) took on a major role in enhancing coach education and the Sports Council began to divert a more significant proportion of resources to performance and excellence levels of the sports development continuum. At the end of the decade a change in funding and managing sport would return facility-based sport development to the top of the agenda.

THE MARKETISATION OF SPORT

Following the massive developments which resulted from local government reorganisation in 1974 after the Bains Report, there was a period of relative prosperity in national and local government finances. This allowed councils to carry on the building bonanza sparked by many outgoing authorities and was a clear example of the power of both local politician and officer alliances in newly professionalised departments. It was also an affirmation of the arrival of leisure and sport as significant and legitimate areas for policy intervention.

30
david jackson

While central government was delivering a consultation paper on the future of sport and recreation and establishing through the Sports Council an agency for developing and disseminating policy, finance was released to a local government system with relative autonomy to spend as it pleased. The recognition of sport as a major factor in the lives of both individuals and communities and people's increasing awareness of the benefits of well-being put pressure on local authorities to make more provision. They were more than happy to oblige, as this was a political 'win–win' situation.

> The publication, in 1975, of the White Paper, *Sport and Recreation*, confirmed the place of sport and recreation services as a legitimate element of the welfare state and also reiterated a conventional rationale for intervention, namely a concern with social order, international prestige, and individual well-being.
>
> (Department of the Environment, 1975)

By 1979 things were about to change. The government led by Margaret Thatcher began a journey of policy intervention at national and local levels that was not directly aimed at sport but which had a major impact on the delivery of sporting opportunities. At national level there was indifference to sporting issues. Sports policy was reactive and uncoordinated and there did not appear to be any substantial thought applied to policy area. However, the government's agenda for local authorities was to have a significant effect on sport and recreation.

The major themes of New Right philosophy associated with the Thatcher years revolved around freedom of the individual and the primacy of free markets. Resultant policy developments were aimed at a reduction in the role of the state at both national and local levels and the introduction of market forces to shape provision of public services. As applied to local government, these policies were introduced in a limited way in the Planning and Land Act 1980, where an enforced tendering regime was imposed for contracts in relation to building and highway construction and maintenance. However, in the Local Government Act 1988, under the banner of Compulsory Competitive Tendering (CCT), a range of services previously provided by local government work forces were exposed to free competition in the market place. This was an enforced system of marketisation that initially covered refuse collection, catering and school meals, street cleaning and lighting, vehicle maintenance and grounds maintenance. After a consultation exercise, the management of sports and leisure facilities was added to the list. This had a major impact on the way that local authorities defined their role both as a direct provider of sporting opportunities and as a facilitator for other deliverers in the sporting matrix.

Much of the government's policy deliberations which resulted in the CCT legislation revolved around notions of 'value for money' in public services and around the premise that, no matter how good services appeared to be, local government could not prove that it was providing value for money unless it was tested against private sector entrepreneurs in fair and open competition. Indeed, according to the New Right doctrine, exposure to competition was deemed to be the only way that such proof could be secured. To support this forceful argument in relation to the specific management function of sport and leisure management, the Audit Commission produced two documents that set out the case for changing the *status quo* and adopting a more positive stance in favour of the marketisation of services. The first of these, *Sport for Whom? Clarifying the Local Authority Role in Sport and Recreation* (1988), sought to establish some general issues about provision that needed more serious consideration than had been previously given. These rested on a view that there was a lack of strategic planning, policy direction and financial accountability in provision. In other words, a great deal of public money was spent and possibly wasted without sufficient application to the philosophy and practical implications of what was done.

> But whatever their social aims, local authorities also need financial objectives if they are to manage their facilities properly. Local authorities have found it hard to strike the right balance between social and financial objectives.
>
> (Audit Commission, 1988: 27)

In summary there were a number of issues.

- Investment decisions to provide facilities were often poorly thought through in relation to other organisations that might make provision if assisted.
- The ongoing revenue costs of facilities were not considered over a sufficient life span and therefore left a burden on future budgets for upgrading and renovation to meet future customer expectations.
- Blanket pricing subsidies that were perceived as achieving social objectives of opening opportunities to the disadvantaged often only supported the new leisure lifestyles of mainly males from professional and managerial backgrounds.
- The lack of any demonstrable monitoring of the true costs and effectiveness of services provided meant that these burgeoning activities that were constantly added were insufficiently accountable.

In effect there was a damning indictment that local government was unclear about what it was doing or why it was doing it, and that there was a lack of accountability right across the country.

In order that authorities were better able to prepare for the rigorous regime of CCT they were advised to:

- Make strategic plans that encompassed the whole of their geographical areas (whilst also bearing in mind issues of local competition with neighbouring authorities).
- Consider the widest range of options for the providers of services, especially the voluntary sector.
- Take a long, hard look at pricing, admissions and programming policies so that they might improve their record on targeting special and disadvantaged groups.
- Start to set some performance measurement parameters.

To help them through this process the Audit Commission produced the second of its documents, *Local Authority Support for Sport: A Management Handbook* (1989). Whereas *Sport for Whom?* (1988) had been aimed at policy and strategic management tiers of senior politicians and chief officers, this new advice was about 'hands-on' process issues and became a working bible for many officers charged with setting up their organisation to comply with legislation.

It was at this point that many but not all authorities became embroiled in strategies for resisting CCT that involved embracing the letter of the law, if not necessarily the spirit. They failed to come to terms with planning Best Value services for the widest community but rather became engaged in trench warfare that revolved around internal reorganisation and the erection of artificial barriers that gave the appearance of evenhanded compliance with new legislation.

The vast majority of contracts were won by in-house work forces (Direct Service Organisations, DSOs) that were reconstituted operational arms of the local authority departments, but despite their often long-standing commitment to sport, previously valued services that were not as commercially viable in this new culture were often put to the sword in the name of financial efficiency or indeed survival. There was some anecdotal evidence to suggest that this situation often occurred where ailing in-house contracting arms were given more leeway to vary the detail of specifications in order to enhance their income potential than might have been afforded to any external private sector contractor.

The bias against quality in community-based social and welfare services was more manifest in the management of sport and leisure facilities as the sole management function to be subjected to the tendering regime, quite different in character from refuse collection or street lighting. These latter services are to a greater extent finite and measurable; it is possible to quantify how many dustbins need emptying each week and where they all are. Moreover, customers have their dustbins emptied every week or their street lights maintained whether they like it or not. They have little choice in the matter and are charged for the service whether used or not. It became very clear to many operators of sports facilities that customers had to be attracted, retained and nurtured with innovation and quality services or serious consequences would follow.

The economic recession in the early 1990s, alongside a range of other factors, including changes in competing sport and leisure activities, in demographic profiles, education policy and increasing pressure on local government budgets, forced financial imperatives increasingly to the fore. The political, welfare and social aspirations of a wide range of sporting communities came under pressure. Many did not survive and attempts to implement strategies of equity and equality received lip service at a time when there was increasing awareness of the importance that sport had for the nation, for local communities, especially ethnic minorities, and for individuals. The emerging sports development arena whose main function was to reach these previously neglected sporting communities was a clear casualty of this focus on bottom-line financial calculations:

there is also evidence that the policy (CCT) has resulted in a reduction in sports development activity and a preference for activities that generate a more rapid return on investment.

(Sports Council, 1993: 5)

Having acknowledged that the rigidity of the CCT regime across many services resulted in over-emphasis on quantity in financial terms at the expense of quality as seen as welfare or social services, the Labour government set out after 1997 to redress this imbalance by setting out the principles of Best Value.

BEST VALUE

In short CCT has provided a poor deal for employees, employers and local people. CCT will therefore be abolished.

(DETR, 1998: 6)

The duty of Best Value has been an integral part of New Labour's ambitious modernising agenda for local government which includes democratic renewal, community leadership, a new ethical framework, reformed local government finance and Best Value in service delivery. The duty of Best Value as laid down for local authorities is 'to secure continuous improvement in the way in which functions are exercised, having regard to a combination of economy, efficiency and effectiveness' (Local Government Bill, 1998 in Sanderson, 1999). Professor Ian Sanderson has described the overall philosophy of Best Value as having its foundations in the principles of:

- Systematic review of all services as the basis for identifying and addressing weaknesses in performance.
- Setting clear standards and improvement targets for both cost and quality of all services.
- Putting the interests of local people first and giving them a greater say in setting service standards and assessing performance.
- Responsibility to central government for meeting national standards for designated services.
- Enhanced community leadership and partnership working to address cross-cutting issues facing local citizens and communities.
- Commitment to ensuring the most effective, efficient and economic means of service delivery, using competitive processes where appropriate.
- Improved reporting and accountability for performance to local people as taxpayers, customers and citizens.
- Rigorous audit and inspection processes to provide an external check on information, processes and performance.
- Intervention by central government where authorities 'fail to remedy clear performance failure'.

In the application of this new policy process to sport there are a number of issues that require examination. In the context of local authority sports provision this required councils to be 'continually improving the quality and cost of local services delivered to local people' (Sport England, 1999b: 2).

Since the introduction of this new approach to service delivery there has been a continual evolution of both policy ideas and responses by local authorities. The most significant developments have been participation in Best Value pilots and development of some credible Performance Indicators (PIs), all of which has been underpinned by incorporating sport and recreation in a new 'cultural block' for Comprehensive Performance Assessment (CPA). This shift in thinking by the Audit Commission (and by definition government) has recognised, after a great deal of time, the value that culture adds to national and local life. The long history of sport's fragile position as a discretionary service may not have ended but the fact that it was now defined as an integral part of service provision perhaps makes it less likely to suffer the neglect which has been visited upon it on occasion in the past.

The system under the CPA is based on self-assessment with key performance indicators in the area of sport and recreation consisting of quantifiable measurement of value and customer satisfaction. What is perhaps surprising is the lack of any PI connected with physical activity. Throughout the government's development of policy relating to sport and recreation through a succession of documents and interventions culminating in *Game Plan* (2002), the emphasis has clearly been around increasing participation rates to significantly higher levels than are currently (or have ever been) achieved. The target of having 70 per cent of the population being physically active for thirty minutes three times per week has been viewed with some scepticism in many quarters but it has nevertheless provided a target at which to aim. That this major declaration of intent has no identifiable measure within the framework which reviews the investment made by local government in sport and recreation does seem anomalous. Whilst there are clearly difficulties in attributing value to qualitative issues with respect to the population's perceptions of experiences in sport and recreation, not making use of the CPA to track this key indicator is an omission waiting to be rectified.

The shifting nature of public policy and investment in sport and recreation at the beginning of the twenty-first century has placed local government in a key position as facilitator and co-ordinator of service provision. There has been a shift in how councils have reflected on their own direct provision and how they match and enhance what is done through other sectors. Services are often viewed in the round across traditional departmental divides to accommodate the essentials of strategically planned, 'joined-up' provision. Thus, for example, whilst Leisure Services Departments still exist for operational functionality, their strategic thinking embraces services for young people across boundaries of education and social services and vice versa.

From a sporting perspective one of the major challenges is the nurturing of partner-ships with the voluntary sector and connections with national policy development and investment in school sport. Underneath a layer of strategic thinking in Regional Sports

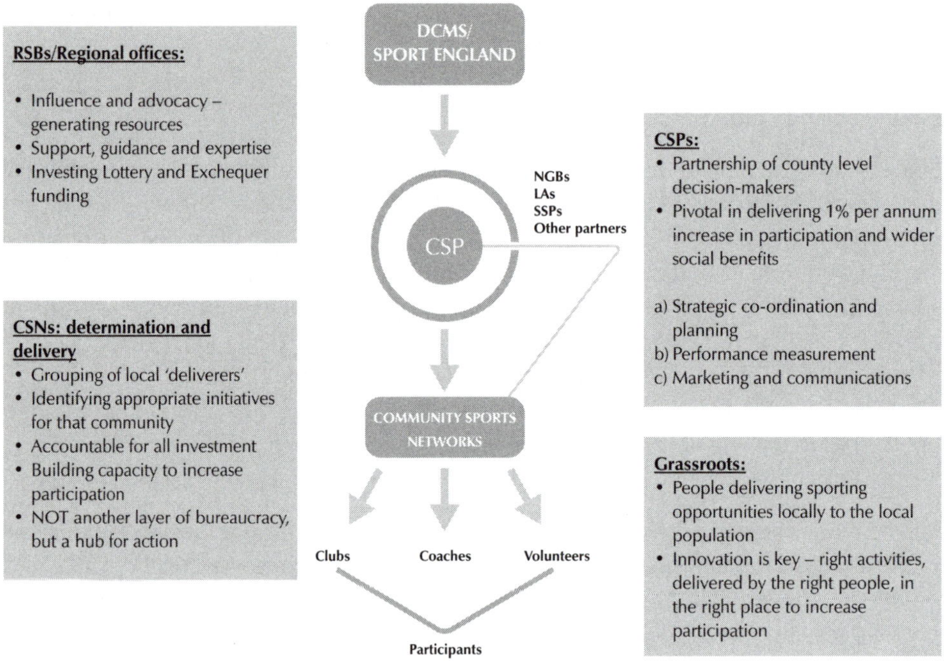

Figure 3.1 The single system for delivering sport in the community

Source Sport England (2007b), www.sportengland.org/singlesystem.ppt#272,3,slide 3, reproduced by courtesy of Sport England.

Boards (RSBs), the County Sports Partnerships (CSPs) (Sport England, 2007a) programme is Sport England's framework for connecting all the pieces of the sporting puzzle in geographical areas. It consists of a network of forty-five partnerships across England, bringing together national governing bodies of sport, the myriad clubs and volunteers they embrace, plus local authority provision, coaching networks and School Sport Partnerships (SSPs).

Massive support for physical education and school sport has been made in recent years through the Department for Education and Skills and this is to be welcomed after some years of neglect. The PESSCL (Physical Education and School Sport Club Links) strategy and the development of Sports Colleges and SSPs through an investment package of over £1.5 billion between 2003 and 2008 (DfES, 2007a, b) represents a massive shift in thinking and funding action. There is concern, however, that community endeavours may not be able to match high expectations of delivery of such an ambitious strategy without parallel resources to support local authority departments and the necessary infrastructure of vol- untary sporting clubs, which have been such a significant feature of the sporting life of the nation in the past.

All these complex interactions are ultimately aimed at achieving very disparate goals outlined in the central strategic document to which all agendas relate. *Game Plan: a Strategy for delivering Government's Sport and Physical Activity Objectives* (DCMS/Cabinet Office, 2002) was the culmination of government thinking aimed at providing strategic guidance to policy objectives discussed in *A Sporting Future for All* (DCMS, 2000). *Game Plan* sets out broad areas for action in relation to:

- Increasing participation.
- Improving international performance.
- Support for major events.
- Better delivery.

Whilst aimed at developing and improving sporting performance at all levels the clear message from government is that sport and physical activity matters because of the social objectives to which it can contribute. Often termed the 'cross-cutting agenda', these objectives are about key issues that the government clearly sees as priorities:

- Promoting health to combat economic incapacity. The Prime Minister, Tony Blair, asserts in his foreword to *Game Plan* that 'physical inactivity currently [2002] costs the nation at least £2 billion a year (or 54,000 lives lost prematurely').
- Using the education system to deliver improvement in participation and educational attainment.
- Tackling crime and drug problems.
- Tackling social inclusion issues.
- Generating a 'feel-good factor' at all levels but particularly through international success.

Whilst in the past all those involved in the provision of sporting opportunities were working to different agendas that did not necessarily fit together in any strategic way, there does now seem to be more coherence of approach. The governmental lead in policy and strategy across different departments, supported by real investment, has potential to provide coherence and success in achieving the range of identified objectives.

- UK Sport has the lead in improving international performance and raising the UK's profile on the world stage. The impetus of the 2012 London Olympics will be widespread not only in terms of lead-up and delivery of the event itself but also from its legacy, an essential ingredient in London (and the UK) being awarded the Games.
- The education system has clear frameworks in place and funding from both government and the National Lottery to support programmes and, in collaboration with partners in the Youth Sport Trust, for example, has templates for positive change.
- Sport England has strategic plans to co-ordinate activity at national, regional and local level that involve all necessary agencies, including local authorities and national governing bodies who can act together more effectively than in the past.
- Local authorities have the role of both primary provider and local and regional facilitator and, through the Best Value processes, have mechanisms for planning and delivering services and co-ordinating effort with relevant agencies.

Within agencies at all levels there is recognition of the multi-faceted roles that sport plays in the life of the nation, local communities and individuals. There is growing acknowledgement of the intrinsic value of sport and that the impetus needs to be maintained. But, whilst there is general optimism about the general thrust of policy delivery opportunities, there are ongoing concerns about the level of resources that needs to be sustained, particularly in local government departments and in grass-roots sports clubs. For all the pieces of the jigsaw to fit properly there is still a great deal of attention needed to consider resource issues.

SUMMARY

When the New Labour regime came into power in 1997 and began to formulate policy and strategies for delivery, much was made of the concept of 'joined-up thinking' to ensure strategic fit and the optimal use of resources. Though not approaching a state of grace there are clear indications that that is taking place at both central and local government levels. An example from the DCMS web site (Table 3.1) shows that the Public Service Agreement (PSA) targets that have been prioritised are in fact clearly linked to those of other departments.

Table 3.1 Public Service Agreements in sport

DCMS Sports Division plays a key role in the delivery of a range of government Public Service Agreement (PSA) targets:

PSA Target 1.

Enhance the take-up of sporting opportunities by five- to sixteen-year-olds so that the percentage of schoolchildren in England who spend a minimum of two hours each week on high-quality PE and school sport within and beyond the curriculum increases from 25 per cent in 2002 to 75 per cent by 2006 and to 85 per cent by 2008, and to at least 75 per cent in each School Sport Partnership by 2008. (Joint target with Department for Education and Skills.)

PSA Target 2.

Halt the year-on-year increase in obesity among children under eleven by 2010, in the context of a broader strategy to tackle obesity in the population as a whole. (Joint target with Department for Education and Skills and Department of Health.)

PSA Target 3.

By 2008 increasing the number who participate in active sports at least twelve times a year by 3 per cent, and increasing the number who engage in at least thirty minutes of moderate intensity level sport at least three times a week by 3 per cent.

Source Sport England, www.culture.gov.uk/what_we_do/sport/ (2007).

The broad brush of moving policy into practice is for the most part well established and those involved at a strategic level now perhaps have a clearer view of their organisational roles than has been the case in the past. The reality, however, is that the practical implications of succeeding in achieving current objectives are complex and rely heavily on promoting vigorous partnerships supported by the appropriate resources.

FAIRFAX METROPOLITAN DISTRICT COUNCIL

In the changing environment of local government, the new Active Sport and Recreation Department at Fairfax MDC has been grappling with the rigours of Best Value for over five years, following the demise of the CCT regime. Although the process of CCT was resource- and energy-sapping, with seemingly little pay-off for the council-taxpayers of the District, there was a growing understanding of the need to undergo some rigorous evaluation of the rationale for deciding what services were delivered, at what cost and for whom. Best Value has become a tool that is honed to improve the quality of services that the department delivers directly but which can also be used to examine and influence the whole sporting picture for the District. To this end the lead officers and politicians in the Department (which has now itself come under the banner of 'Young People's Services', which also includes Education and parts of Social Services) are the driving force behind the Active Fairfax Board. This is the strategic body which oversees and co-ordinates all the leading stakeholders in sports provision in the District. This forum, which includes representatives of NGBs, grass-roots clubs, professional teams and education institutions, has an eye on the government's agenda and also the Regional Sports Board for their area.

Whilst this wider partnership is making progress, there are tensions between all the players, as they all have their own agendas and priorities. Balancing everyone's needs and commitments is at times difficult. The economic climate within the Department is quite taxing as stringent financial controls require difficult decisions to be made about service delivery. Capital expenditure for new developments outside education is often not seen as high-priority and revenue budgets are squeezed year on year, leading to difficulties in maintaining buildings and staffing levels at desired levels. The fact that there are Best Value reviews to be undertaken every three years and that the service is now part of the Culture Block in the Comprehensive Performance Assessment process does have some influence in how budgets are allocated but it is clear the whole service is under pressure. In order to examine ways in which some of this pressure might be eased, moving the whole service to trust status is being seriously considered. Although this will mean some loss of political control, it might well provide opportunities for tax relief and a more flexible operational methodology that could release finance and benefit the service as a whole. Politicians, officers and the work force are all approaching the prospect cautiously but it may well be a solution for the future. There are a number of well-established trusts elsewhere that have managed to make the switch and improve the quality of sports provision for local people.

REFERENCES

Audit Commission (1988) *Sport for Whom? Clarifying the Local Authority Role in Sport and Recreation*, London: HMSO.

Audit Commission (1989) *Local Authority Support for Sport: A Management Handbook*, London: HMSO.

Collins, M. and Kennett, C. (1999) Leisure, poverty and social inclusion: the growing role of passports to leisure in Great Britain, *European Journal of Sports Management*, 6(1): 19–30.

Department for Culture Media and Sport (2000) *A Sporting Future for All*, London: DCMS.

Department for Culture Media and Sport and Cabinet Office (2002) *Game Plan: A Strategy for Delivering Government's Sport and Physical Activity Objectives*, London: DCMS/ Cabinet Office.

Department for Culture Media and Sport (2007) *What We Do*. Available: http://www.culture.gov.uk/what_we_do/Sport/.

Department for Education and Skills (2007a). Available: http://www.teachernet.gov.uk/teachingandlearning/subjects/pe/.

Department for Education and Skills (2007b). Available: http://www.teachernet.gov.uk/teachingandlearning/subjects/pe/nationalstrategy/.

Department of Environment Transport and the Regions (1998) *Modernising Local Government: Improving Local Services through Best Value*, London: HMSO.

Department of the Environment (1975) *Sport and Recreation*, Cmnd 6200, London: HMSO.

Fromm, E. (1994) *The Art of Listening*, London: Constable.

Haywood, L. (1992) *Leisure in the 1990s: Rolling back the Welfare State*, Brighton: Leisure Studies Association.

Haywood, L. (ed.) (1994) *Community Leisure and Recreation*, London: Heinemann.

Houlihan, B. and White, A. (2002) *The Politics of Sports Development*, London: Routledge.

McIntosh, P. (1984) *Sport in Society*, London: Macmillan.

McIntosh, P. and Charlton, V. (1985) *Action Sport: An Evaluation of Phase One*, London: Sports Council.

Sanderson, I. (1999) Unpublished presentation forming part of the National Evaluation of Best Value Pilot Programme.

Sports Council (1993) *Compulsory Competitive Tendering Sport and Leisure Management: National Information Survey Report*, London: Sports Council.

Sport England (1999) *Investing in our Sporting Future*, London: Sport England. Available: http://www.english.sports.gov.uk.

Sport England (2007a). Available: http://www.sportengland.org/national_csptoollkit.pdf.

Sport England (2007b). Available: http://www.sportengland.org/singlesystem.ppt.

Sport England and Local Government Association (1999a) *The Value of Sport: Best Value through Sport*, London: Sport England. Available: http://www.english.sports.gov.uk.

Sport England and Local Government Association (1999b) *Delivering Best Value Through Sport*. London: Sport England. Available: http://www.english.sports.gov.uk.

Torkildsen, G. (1999) *Leisure and Recreation Management*, London: E. & F.N. Spon.

Torkildsen, G. (2005) *Leisure and Recreation Management*, London: Routledge.

Wolfenden Committee on Sport (1960) *Sport and the Community*, London: Central Council for Physical Recreation.

CHAPTER 4

DEVELOPING 'SPORT FOR ALL?'

Addressing inequality in sport

Kevin Hylton and Mick Totten

Sport has been consistent in its claims to be an arena where we can play unfettered by the inequities of a wider society which could learn much from the way sport is played, organised and conducted. The power of sport to transform individuals and communities is a popular argument evident in sport policy and practice at all levels (Polley, 1998; Houlihan and White, 2002; Bramham in this edition). The original 'Sport for All?' campaign was a creation of the early 1970s and has long since been succeeded by a multitude of campaigns and causes. But the ideals of 'Sport for All?' still have resonance today as a clarion call for all involved in sports development. Former Prime Minister Tony Blair, outlined with the Central Council of Physical Recreation (CCPR, 2002: 2) how sport needs to be encouraged as a tool of social policy, but with the caveat that he was no longer satisfied with the anecdotal evidence that 'sport is good for you'. Despite its attractions, the reality of 'Sport for All?' has never been fully achieved, and successes remain incomplete and partial. Gains have been made, but massive inequalities still remain. However, tackling inequality must continue as a central premise and aim of sports development. In order to tackle inequality, inequality itself must be better understood. If the aim is to foster 'inclusion', then 'exclusion' and its social context must be better identified and understood.

CONTENT AND PROCESS

This chapter examines the nature and extent of inequality in sport, and outlines strategies to tackle inequality through sport and recreation development policy and practice. The first sections draw out some of the challenges and issues that sports development workers have been engaged in when trying to provide Sport for All. It commences with an analysis of how inequality is exhibited, and can be identified within sport. It then explains how that inequality is linked with broader social processes in society. Sport and society are in symbiosis. Sport is directly influenced by society, which in turn is influenced by sport, and as a consequence many of the wider processes of society express themselves in the realm of sport. Loosely translated, where there are prejudice, discrimination, power differentials and social exclusion in wider society they will also be manifest in sport.

The chapter considers how inequality can be understood in sport and society. The use of sociology is viewed as an essential and important weapon in the armoury of an effective sports professional. The authors draw on sociological theory and analysis to gain a deeper understanding of the issues. Four differing interpretations (or perspectives) offer the sports development worker and policy maker alternative views of issues surrounding equality and inequality in sport. These are applied to sport, sport development and Sport for All. These views enable the sports professional to understand that competing views or arguments are grounded in the way that other people see the world and sports development. Having established the social context of inequality in sport, the authors then analyse significant strategic policy responses and specific examples of practice in the light of previous theory and argument. Political and policy implications are explored in a case study of good practice, alongside other related examples, of the way in which different organisations have attempted to develop Sport for All.

INEQUALITY AND SPORT

Sports development has been at the cutting edge of what are seen as innovative and refreshing approaches to traditional sports provision. Despite constraints within their organisations, sports workers today are attempting to offer more opportunities to the public. The house of sports development was built on the foundations of Sport for All, which has always been an ideal rather than a coherent realisable object. This ideal can be viewed from differing perspectives which 'open up' interesting views on sport and recreation and their development. Sports development professionals are challenged to plan, implement and monitor equality work in sport (Sport England, 2001; Jowell, 2002). Furthermore, cultural shifts that have to take place in each organisation for long-term change need to go hand-in-hand with political and social change. Sustainable strategic planning becomes a realistic proposition only when both resources and commitment are in close attendance. Recent years have seen significant investment in sport as a legacy of the New Labour government.

Social exclusion and inclusion

Persistent barriers to participation can be understood as 'social exclusion'. Social exclusion is more than exclusion from sport. Social exclusion was one of the major foci of the United Nations World Summit on Social Development in 1995. Social exclusion is typified by social and economic boundaries and by continual aggravation of differences and divisions in the life chances of members of the same society. For example, divisions can be expressed *socially* in terms of gender differences in sport; economically in terms of differences in income; or *culturally* through ethnic differences. 'Exclusion' and 'inclusion' affect individuals in different ways, but ultimately have a decisive impact on overall quality of life. The establishment of a Social Exclusion Unit (SEU) by the government in 1997, and Minister Hilary Armstrong's announcement of a new task force in 2006 that would put it even closer to the heart of government, give a clear indication of the continued value of sport as a tool to combat social exclusion. The SEU states that social exclusion happens:

> When people or places suffer from a series of problems such as unemployment, discrimination, poor skills, low incomes, poor housing, high crime, ill health and family breakdown. When such problems combine they can create a vicious cycle.
> (Social Exclusion Unit, 2006)

Sports development workers need to be conscious of the evident common ground which sport shares with other 'social' services working towards social inclusion. Such recognition enabled New Labour to coin the phrase 'joined-up thinking and policy making'. This phrase emphasises the potential of working partnerships and the economies of scale that may be afforded. Shared professional knowledge and integrated resources across departmental areas can improve services. These mutual areas of interest become fields for integrated coherent policies and are often referred to as 'cross-cutters'. Cross-cutters enable professionals to work together to reduce social exclusion and include:

- Community development.
- Lifelong learning.
- Social cohesion.
- Community safety.
- Active healthy lifestyles.
- Social and economic regeneration.
- Job creation.
- Equal Opportunities.
- Crime prevention.
- Environmental protection.

All the above emphasise that sport must not be considered in isolation from other aspects of society.

Social exclusion and 'Sport for All'

The demand for 'joined-up thinking' in 1999 confirmed that sport should be used as one instrument within a broad diet of activity influenced by the government and related stakeholders. An agenda to combat social exclusion subsumes Sport for All and other institutionalised equality work. *Inclusion through sport* and *inclusion in sport* are positive steps on a much broader agenda for those defined as socially excluded (Room, 1995; Levitas, 1998; Collins and Kay, 2003). In effect, these considerations give some insight into the potential and limits of sport and sports development in the twenty-first century. Where inequality remains an issue for social groups and sports development even the often ambiguous benefits of sport will remain unachievable.

Activities relating to equality in sport have become more prominent since the Commission for Equality and Human Rights (formed in 2007) was established. This forced, at the very least, a minimal change in the way sport is managed and developed. The dissolution of the Commission for Racial Equality, the Equal Opportunities Commission and the Disability Rights Commission has forced public organisations to reconsider how they structure their policies and practices in relation to equality. For example, in England the launch of the Equality Standard (2004) drew together what had been previously a fragmented set of agendas and systems concerning ethnicity, gender and disability into a common system of management. The Equality Standard was a joint project of four home country Sports Councils and UK Sport, with the support of the Central Council of Physical Recreation, the English Federation of Disability Sport, Sporting Equals and the Women's Sport Foundation. The authors advocate a commitment towards more equality development work within sport as a primary responsibility for sports providers. So the proviso to implement the Equality Standard as a mandatory condition of the national funded agreements between Sports Councils, sports governing bodies, and regional sports organisations and their partners, is a small but significant and welcome step forward. Subsequent analysis will consider the nature of inequality and how it can be tackled.

Understanding equality and inequality

A number of authors (Rawls, 1971; Desai, 1995; Mithaug, 1996) have tried to articulate the elusive concept of equality, which consistently provides thinkers with a kaleidoscope of choices as to its constituency, and subsequent eventual achievement. Like academics, professionals in sport have competing views on equality, which is one reason why there are inconsistencies in approach. Bagilhole (1997: 7) prefers to deploy Equal Opportunities only in inverted commas, as she defines it as such a contested notion. Similarly, the rhetoric in sports development, concerning Sport for All, is another indicator of a philosophy of provision which has been interpreted inconsistently. The notion of equality itself is ambiguous as it implies that it constitutes an achievable end point. Clearly *true equality* is impossible, even in the most equitable of societies. Here the saying 'some are more equal than others' makes sense as it hints at the relative nature of equality and inequality. In a modern, globalised, capitalist society it is an inevitable part of the human condition to experience some level of inequality (Blakemore and Drake, 1996). Therefore, Blakemore and Drake's (1996) view that we cannot have equality but must always be 'working towards it' encapsulates the elusiveness of equality in sport. However, the necessity of underpinning sports development policies and practices with equality principles is crystal clear.

In everyday life there will be social groups who experience direct or indirect discrimination because of any combination of age, social class, gender, religion, sexuality, disability, 'race' and/or ethnicity. Both individuals and organisations in sport are affected by and are implicated in this discriminatory behaviour and therefore it is incumbent upon these entities within sport to make sport as equitable as possible. But whilst working towards equality might be a priority for some within sports provision, practice has shown it not to be as high on the agenda for others. There are some whose philosophy is such that they would argue for the state to leave providers to compete for custom. This would allow the open market to provide for a range of public needs, without subsidising public facilities and services, and take the burden away from the public sector (LeGrand, 1991; Coalter 1998). The irony of this position is that the profit-orientated, competitive nature of the unregulated market creates inequality, exclusion and community breakdown in the first place (Ledwith, 2005). So involvement of the public sector is imperative to provide a safety net for those most vulnerable and traditionally excluded (Clarke, 1994).

As a result of differing personal, political and institutional views on the nature of equality, different approaches are taken to sport policy and practice that range from radical to minimal. There is a growing body of research around inequality in sports development that highlights patterns and trends that act as drivers of counter-initiatives. There are different approaches to identifying inequality in sport. Inequality can be considered 'macroscopically' where it can be observed or tracked across sections of society or comparatively between different societies. It can also be analysed 'microscopically' in relation to more specific contexts. Inequality can be considered 'quantitatively' in terms of the numbers or percentages participating. But it can also be considered 'qualitatively' in terms of distinctive reasons behind the *how?* and *why?* people participate and their experiences of participation or spectating in sport (Veal, 1992; Gratton and Jones, 2004; Long, 2007).

Trends in participation patterns: the quantitative analysis of sport

Quantitative analysis of participation relies mostly on surveys of participation, in particular: who does or does not participate, frequency, costs and other measurable factors. Analysis can focus on sport as a whole, or on types of sports, or on specific activities. Participation rates are sometimes monitored in isolation, but more usefully when set against other 'variables'. Most commonly variables will include 'socio-economic' factors which characterise the 'demographic' composition of a population. These factors might include age of participants, gender, social class, occupation, level of educational attainment, wealth, ethnicity, access to car use, and others. These variables when set against levels of participation reveal 'patterns of participation'. Such patterns can be compared with average, or expected, levels of participation. When specific variables reveal levels of participation which are significantly above or below average, one can conclude that that variable has an influence in predicting likelihood of participation. For example: women, those with physical impairment, or the unwaged, are significantly less likely to participate in snowboarding than men, the able-bodied or the highly paid. Collectively, patterns of participation highlight trends which reveal disparities in participation. These can then be used to identify specific groups or populations in society less likely to participate, such as the elderly, the disabled, many women, certain ethnic groups, the unwaged and others. These can then be considered 'priority groups' in terms of focusing initiatives to promote and increase participation. This common strategy of 'targeting' can concentrate efforts to 'include' the previously 'excluded'. Initiatives might take the form of policies, specific projects or innovation around established or new structures. In so doing there is more likelihood for participation to increase in that group, so changing patterns of participation, and decreasing inequalities in sports participation (see Tables 4.1 and 4.2).

By analysing Table 4.1 one can deduce that participation in sport, games and physical activities varies by socio-economic group: the 'higher' the group the more likely participation becomes. Overall, an individual's socio-economic status appears to bear a direct relationship to ability to participate in physical activities, thus reflecting social inequalities.

By analysing Table 4.2 a few aspects can be surmised: overall, men participate more frequently than women; younger people participate more commonly than older people; again socio-economic status betrays a direct relationship to participation; finally, those who are married are less likely to participate than others. So sex, age, class and marital status all appear to have a strong influence on the likelihood of participation. Other socio-economic factors can be expected to exert similar variations in participation. This reveals that ability to participate manifests itself in many different ways. All these inequalities pose challenges to Sport for All and for sports development to resolve.

Table 4.3 shows not only that there are overall variations in sports participation, but also that there are differences in the 'types' of activities chosen by people. This table illustrates that different social groups participate more and less frequently in different types of sport, games, and physical activities. This would appear to reflect elements of diversity and inequality in both opportunities as well as tastes. Quantitative methods of analysis are useful in identifying such broad patterns in participation, but do not really uncover their full *meaning*.

Participatory experiences: the qualitative analysis of sport

Qualitative analysis of participation is much less common in sport than quantitative analysis, even though it is increasing in popularity in many sport disciplines (Gratton and Taylor, 2004; Long in this edition). As such it is a type of research which could, or should, be developed. It is more likely to be used by academics than by policy makers or practitioners. This is because it is not only costly in terms of both time and resources, but also because it reveals more complex information which is open to differing interpretation. Such complexity is often perceived as too resource-intensive to be worthwhile. Additionally, the findings are often perceived as too challenging to be implemented and translated into practice.

Qualitative research veers away from a preoccupation with numbers and concentrates on the *meaning* and *significance* of participation. It offers deeper insights into the motivations of participants and the social significance of their participation. It often employs methods like semi-structured interviews, focus group discussions or observations of practice to gain

Table 4.1 Participation in sport in England, 2002

Active sports, games and physical activities	National Statistics socio-economic classification							
	1.1	1.2	2	3	4	5	6	7	8	England
	Large employers & higher managerial	Higher professional	Lower managerial & professional	Intermediate	Small employers & own account workers	Lower supervisory & technical	Semi-routine	Routine	Never worked & long-term unemployed	
At least one activity (exc. walking)	82.5	80.6	75.5	63.1	65.1	62.6	53.4	48.8	45.3	65.6
At least one activity	89.1	88.9	84.2	72.7	74.0	72.0	64.6	59.9	53.5	74.9
Base (all adults)	858	1131	3068	1051	1266	1607	1646	1628	317	12841

Source Sport England (2002:16).

Notes Participation rates in the 12 months before interview by National Statistics Socio-economic Classification (% of respondents). Adults aged 16+.

Table 4.2 Sports-related activities, by gender, age, socio-economic group and marital status, September 2005 (%)

	Doing any sport or exercise		Going to live sporting event	
	Weekday	Weekend	Weekday	Weekend
All	32	29	11	15
Men	39	38	17	23
Women	26	21	5	8
18–24	47	41	14	20
25–34	42	36	11	18
35–44	34	32	12	17
45–54	29	30	9	15
55–64	30	28	13	13
65+	19	15	7	9
AB	45	42	13	19
C1	41	37	12	17
C2	34	29	14	18
D	17	16	6	8
E	12	10	6	8
Marital status				
Married	31	28	11	14
Not married	35	31	11	15

Source Leisure Time, February 2006, Leisure Intelligence, Mintel.

Note Base: 2,102 adults aged 18+.

insights. It concentrates on the 'social relations of participation', how people behave and what that behaviour means to them and to others. Understanding how and why people behave and relate to each other in particular ways, and what that signifies, is at the root of sports participation and choice. Behaviour can be seen to be structured in particular ways and linked to broader social influences.

The interrelation of sport and society is manifest as social influences are brought to sport, and as influences are exported from it to wider society. The analysis of sport must also encompass other more informal manifestations such as recreation and play. Sport is a social activity, partly composed of elements which might involve some form of competitive activity. Analysis must extend beyond the playing field, into the locker room, and for some even into the bar afterwards as well! These are all a part of sport and sports cultures.

If you were to observe behaviour in a multi-sport and social club bar you could focus on the influence of gender, class, ethnicity, disability or age. Sticking with gender, it is most likely, though not always the case, that women and men would behave differently and adopt different behavioural roles in the same setting. Different groups and individuals of

Table 4.3 Sports, games and physical activities

| Active sports, games and physical activities | National Statistics socio-economic classification | | | | | | | | | |
	1.1 Large employers & higher managerial	1.2 Higher professional	2 Lower managerial & professional	3 Intermediate	4 Small employers & own account workers	5 Lower supervisory & technical	6 Semi-routine	7 Routine	8 Never worked & long-term unemployed	England
Walking	47.1	46.2	41.7	32.7	30.0	29.4	28.5	23.5	19.5	34.1
Any swimming	24.0	19.9	17.7	13.7	11.9	11.2	8.8	7.8	7.4	13.9
Swimming: indoor	20.6	17.2	15.8	11.5	10.5	9.2	7.8	6.8	6.4	12.1
Swimming: outdoor	5.3	4.7	3.4	2.7	2.8	2.7	1.4	1.3	1.0	2.9
Keep fit/yoga	20.8	18.3	15.3	14.8	11.1	9.4	7.1	6.3	4.6	12.2
Cycling	13.0	12.0	11.5	6.5	8.1	7.2	6.3	6.8	7.5	9.0
Snooker/pool/ billiards	9.9	9.2	9.6	10.2	9.4	9.1	8.5	7.0	5.5	9.2
Weight training	11.4	8.5	7.3	6.9	5.1	4.0	4.0	2.5	2.0	5.9
Running (jogging, etc.)	10.3	8.1	6.6	5.2	3.3	3.4	2.2	2.3	3.2	5.0
Golf	9.5	8.4	6.1	4.2	4.9	3.6	1.8	1.7	0.0	4.5
Any soccer	6.1	5.4	5.5	4.2	4.8	4.7	3.3	3.8	4.2	4.8
Soccer: outdoor	5.0	4.2	4.4	3.1	4.3	4.0	2.7	3.1	4.2	3.9
Soccer: indoor	2.7	2.3	2.6	1.5	1.2	1.7	1.2	1.3	1.0	1.8
Tenpin bowling/ skittles	4.8	4.0	3.9	4.2	3.2	3.1	2.9	2.0	0.3	3.3
Tennis	3.1	4.0	2.7	1.8	1.7	0.5	0.8	0.5	1.0	1.9
Badminton	2.8	3.6	2.4	1.5	1.4	1.6	1.3	0.7	0.9	1.8
Fishing	1.1	1.1	1.2	1.5	2.5	2.3	1.6	1.5	0.8	1.6
Any bowls	1.8	1.0	1.1	1.1	1.3	1.6	1.1	1.4	0.0	1.2

Carpet bowls	1.1	0.6	1.0	1.0	1.3	0.5	0.9	0.0	0.8
Lawn bowls	0.9	0.5	0.2	0.4	0.5	0.7	0.6	0.0	0.5
Weight-lifting	2.0	1.9	1.7	1.2	1.0	1.1	1.1	0.5	1.3
Table tennis	1.8	2.0	1.2	1.1	0.9	1.5	0.2	1.1	1.2
Squash	2.1	1.5	1.1	0.8	1.0	0.2	0.4	0.3	1.2
Horse riding	1.7	1.2	1.0	1.8	0.8	0.7	0.5	0.9	1.1
Martial arts (inc. self-defence)	1.3	1.3	1.2	1.7	0.5	0.5	0.9	0.9	0.9
Shooting	0.9	0.9	0.9	0.9	1.1	0.7	0.6	0.0	0.8
Basketball	0.9	0.7	0.5	0.8	0.4	0.3	0.1	1.6	0.7
Sailing	1.2	0.7	0.2	0.8	0.3	0.1	0.3	0.4	0.5
Cricket	0.7	0.9	0.3	0.2	0.5	0.4	0.2	0.0	0.6
Climbing	0.6	0.6	0.7	0.4	0.3	0.3	0.1	0.0	0.5
Motor sports	1.0	0.7	0.3	0.7	0.5	0.4	0.3	0.2	0.6
Ice skating	0.9	0.4	0.5	0.7	0.5	0.6	0.3	0.6	0.5
Skiing	1.5	0.5	0.5	0.0	0.2	0.0	0.1	0.0	0.4
Rugby	0.8	0.5	0.2	0.1	0.3	0.2	0.3	0.3	0.4
Netball	0.4	0.4	0.2	0.5	0.4	0.1	0.2	0.0	0.3
Hockey	0.5	0.3	0.5	0.1	0.2	0.1	0.3	0.0	0.3
Canoeing	0.4	0.4	0.3	0.2	0.1	0.1	0.2	0.0	0.3
Volleyball	0.3	0.4	0.5	0.1	0.3	0.1	0.0	0.0	0.2
Athletics – track and field	0.2	0.1	0.2	0.3	0.0	0.1	0.1	0.0	0.2
Windsurfing, boardsailing	0.1	0.2	0.1	0.3	0.1	0.1	0.1	0.0	0.2
Gymnastics	0.4	0.2	0.5	0.2	0.4	0.0	0.2	0.0	0.3
At least one activity (exc. walking)	60.5	51.2	42.9	43.1	38.8	31.0	29.4	26.1	43.4
At least one activity	76.1	67.3	57.3	56.6	54.0	46.6	42.7	36.7	58.3
Base (all adults)	858	3068	1051	1266	1607	1646	1628	317	12841

Source Sport England (2002:16).

Notes Participation rates in the four weeks before interview by National Statistics socio-economic classification (% of respondents) Adults aged 16+.

the same sex could also be seen to behave differently towards each other. Such analysis would focus on the role of gender in influencing and determining behaviour. Different views of masculinity and femininity can be detected to result in different 'engendered' role behaviours. The setting or social space might be seen to be dominated by a specific gender, or a particular type of masculinity or femininity. This might differ in some way from another context, like a rugby club bar: however, the resulting atmosphere might still make some groups or individuals feel more or less welcome. That in turn might lead to partial exclusion of certain groups through perceptions of discomfort or simply feelings of alienation or disengagement. Those groups are unlikely to be attracted to that setting or organisation while those gender norms prevail despite best official efforts to countenance an open-door policy. Fully including those excluded groups is unlikely to occur without first challenging, then changing, that prevailing 'gender order' or culture. The same observation but focused on class, ethnicity or disability would be as likely to generate similar results and conclusions. A prevailing class or ethnicity, or a prevailing cultural perspective, or attitude towards disability could all be identified. As with other forms of hegemony dominant views and actions can be seen to include or exclude.

Dominant cultures are often revealed as similar in patterns across many sports settings. Consequently these specific cultures can become normalised to appear to shape and create expectations across sport as a whole. To be more inclusive those dominant cultures need to be challenged or resisted in some way. Evidence of such resistance could be exemplified by the likes of women's rugby teams, who could be seen to be invading and culturally challenging what was once exclusively male territory. This can be understood as individual social 'agents' acting against the prevailing norms of social 'structure'. The complexities of beginning to address cultural change in practice deter many attempts from the outset. So in relation to gender, class or ethnicity, the prevailing order or culture persists, and with them so too does exclusion. The inherent difficulty in addressing participation in a qualitative way signals why it is less common. But until participation is addressed in a qualitative way, exclusion will continue to manifest itself and therein lies a challenge for sports development!

Barriers to participation

Promoting inclusion and tackling exclusion involve identifying inequalities. Ultimately inequality is shaped by different social, cultural, political and economic processes. Using previously identified quantitative and qualitative methods of analysing participation, the same influences crop up regularly. Key influences include disposable income, levels of educational attainment, occupational status, social class, culture, ethnicity, gender, sexuality, age, ability and disability.

These social influences can either empower or discourage sports participation. In terms of exclusion, influences can also act as potential 'barriers to participation'. These can be further categorised as physical, economic, motivational, cultural and political. Physical barriers to participation include the location of facilities, activities and services, and physical access into and within those facilities, activities and services. Economic barriers relate to affordability, cost and perceived value at that cost. Motivational barriers to participation relate to the perceived absence of value in activity, or towards a conflict with self-image when viewed in the light of the perceived image of an activity. Cultural barriers to participation include direct conflicts with codes, customs and conventions or values inherent in an activity, or perhaps less directly, with a discomfort associated with the perceived cultural image of an activity. Political barriers to participation relate to feelings of alienation from or lack of ownership over the existing choice of provision. This may stem from a lack of representation, consultation or involvement in decision making about provision and design which may generate feelings of being disenfranchised from provision. These barriers are all issues which sports development must grapple with in order to promote inclusion. Cultural and political barriers provide particularly complex challenges for sports development.

Alienation can occur at a local level in relation to a particular facility. One anecdotal example would be an aerobics group within an area of multiple deprivation in Leeds who preferred to participate in the local community centre rather than in the local sports centre. (The community centre was a blighted Portakabin in the *car park* of the sports centre!) For these local participants there was an invisible cultural barrier preventing entrance to the sport and leisure centre. This perceptual barrier conveyed class values and tastes which were alien to the locals, whereas 'outsiders' were the mainstay of those participating. The community had little sense of 'ownership' of the local authority facility on their doorstep. A further example, but at a civic level, were the feelings of many of the people of Sheffield towards the provision for the World Student Games. Again perceptions of loss rather than gain clouded community views of this new sports provision. Concerns were raised about local access to international facilities. Why were local community centres not built? Why were local sports centres closed in the shadow of this massive spend on prestige capital investments? Similar risks attach themselves to the London 2012 Olympic and Paralympic preparations, where local businesses are already being driven out by compulsory purchase orders on the land. Those excluded in the East End of London may need many things but it is debatable that elite sports stadia are top priorities on their long list of needs. And promises of jobs and investment are beholden to the practices of large corporations who may be as likely to drain the money away to outside interests (Rigauer, 2000; Hargreaves, 2002; Schirato and Webb, 2003).

All the previously highlighted barriers can exclude and lead to feelings of 'this isn't for me'. Remedying inequalities and overcoming barriers involves development strategies. These must challenge the inequitable nature of existing provision. There are limitations as to what can be achieved solely within sport. Many barriers draw their foundations from broader processes and institutions in society. But if the barriers are physical, economic, motivational, cultural and political, then so too are the solutions. If sports development strategies can address structural issues, then they are on the way to establishing facilities and services valued and supported by the majority of the community rather than a privileged few.

INEQUALITY AND SOCIETY

The social context of inequality

Sport is more than just an activity. It has far more meaning for the individual, and significance to society. It does not exist in a vacuum and there is a plethora of evidence to demonstrate its place as a vital social tool and cultural product:

> Nelson Mandela understands the powerful role that sport can play in changing people's lives – both on and off the sporting field. The London 2012 Olympic Games shares the same vision. The Games in London will help to build new bridges of understanding between cultures and nations and leave a legacy of much needed new sporting venues and facilities that will continue to change people's lives for generations to come.
>
> (Coe, 2006)

Unequal processes and practices in society are contributory reasons for why sport and recreation development professionals have a difficult job in developing Sport for All. Inequality exists on the field of play and it exists also in the rest of society. Analysis must embrace a more comprehensive social enquiry beyond the unique institutional framework which constitutes 'sport' itself; it must also consider society!

Inequality and discrimination

Sport institutions are constituted by members of society whose actions influence inclusion and exclusion. To varying degrees they may work towards, or indeed against equality in society. Among groups who are traditionally excluded in society, some have regularly been the focus for sport development. Gender, disability, 'race' and ethnicity have preoccupied the attention of many policy makers, practitioners and social commentators who recognise inequalities in the location of women, disabled people and black people to positions of power and control in sport. Class, age and sexuality have been considered less systematically, but their influence on life-chances should not be underestimated. There are few people from these excluded groups in managerial and administrative positions in sport and this has a clear qualitative impact on the opportunities for individuals from these groups to access sport and recreation (Sport England, 2002).

Inequality in sport and society can be caused through discriminatory practices and processes which can occur intentionally or unintentionally at three different levels:

- Individual (micro).
- Institutional (meso).
- Societal (macro).

kevin hylton and mick totten

All levels are interrelated in that everyone is part of and contributes to society. The industry of sports development is a reflection of larger processes and practices which continue in wider society. The societal (macro) issues which impact on us all in our day-to-day lives are carried with us into sport. So where there are power and structural advantages which accrue for or against particular groups in society they are likely to be replicated in sports development in diverse ways. For example, discrimination against disability in sport can be:

Individual-level discrimination (micro)

Disabled people are regularly the focus of active direct prejudice and stereotyping by others through discrimination, and are therefore disadvantaged. Stereotypes in relation to physicality such as frailty and ability have often limited the participation of disabled individuals. These constraints may have the effect of filtering disabled athletes away from some sports and channelling them into others. It is very similar to the concept of 'stacking' in other areas of sport. Emphasis on the needs of the individual rather than on collective needs and rights means that isolated piecemeal change and good practice occur but remain elusive and unsustainable for all. This has the effect of stereotyping/stigmatising disabled people rather than challenging/deconstructing sport and society's response to disability.

For example: a manager treats local young people coming into a leisure centre unfavourably, which could be interpreted as a series of isolated incidents. However, where the manager or any other staff members frequently discriminate against people on the grounds of culture, class, age, sex, ethnicity or disability they would be discriminating at a personal level. This behaviour might also be a combination of overt and/or covert discrimination and a further complication could be that it might be conscious or unconscious. Overt behaviour is the easiest to identify, although responses to any type of discriminatory action are never simple, and often inadequate.

Institutional-level discrimination (meso)

Disabled people are underrepresented among major institutions and policy makers of sport and this again is a mirror image of society. DePauw and Gavron (2005: 13) summarised institutional barriers to disabled people in sport as:

- Lack of organised sport programmes.
- Lack of informative early experiences.
- Lack of access to coaches and training programmes.
- Lack of accessible sport facilities.
- Limiting psychological and sociological factors.

For example, where a manager encourages discrimination or where the centre or local authority does not have policies and systems (remedies and/or sanctions) to ensure staff awareness of these discriminatory actions (or non-actions!) it could be said to be per-petuating institutional discrimination. Again this activity (or inactivity) by an organisation might be overt or covert, intentional or unintentional.

Societal-level discrimination (macro)

On an even more fundamental level a responsible society would take away any obstruc-tions in public arenas, buildings and services such as transport, education, health and housing (Rheker, 2000). A disabling society favours a *medical* model of disability where the individual is seen as a patient, rather than a social model which accepts that economic, social and political processes militate against people with disabilities; these processes are reproduced in sport. Saraga (1998) outlines how 'able-bodiedness' is seen as the norm and that disability becomes a euphemism for people who are somehow defective or impaired. This process has been described as 'disablement' but has some utility in initiating a more constructive critical dialogue on the way disabled people are structurally oppressed. Writers in sport are beginning to focus on these under-theorised norms that are sometimes seen as 'invisible' due to the lack of analysis on them (Messner, 1992; Scraton and Flintoff, 2002; Long and Hylton, 2002; Collins and Kay, 2003; Fitzgerald, 2005; Gilborn, 2005; Hylton, 2005).

For example, society has practices and processes which are (to varying degrees) knowingly or unknowingly discriminatory. This leisure centre drew its staff from members of society who (to varying degrees) inherited and reflected these broader prejudices.

Equity and equality

The idea of equity or fairness is a term that is often used interchangeably with equality. However, equality is different and more complex, as it has both descriptive and specific components. Edwards (1990) suggests that Equal Opportunities are in effect equal oppor-tunities to compete for rewards, and hence to be unequal. He suggested that previous historical differences between groups must be taken into account in terms of who has, and who has not, got access to opportunities in sport. Sport England advocates sports 'equity' and has sports 'equity' trainers involved in working with national governing organisations and local authorities. Equity is a more arbitrary and vague concept than equality, as an individual or organisational view of 'fairness' can be dominant where a more purposive collective view of equality would be more specific. Clarity in this area must be reached if people in sport intend to work towards equality and inclusion as positive outcomes. In addition, it is important to note that equality does not necessarily imply equity as equality may be advocated for reasons other than equity, as we will see later in this chapter. Significantly, the Sport Equality Standard (2004) at the very least presents a shared equality discourse that makes institutional equity more transparent, accountable and relative to good practice across sports development. Regulated equality or Equal Opportunities (as it is otherwise known) attributes something more credible to the rhetoric of equity.

kevin hylton and mick totten

Equality in practice

Working towards equality in different contexts can take interesting turns depending on the strategy(ies) employed by practitioners and policy makers. As institutions operate in differing contexts it is clear that some will adopt policies to suit their own philosophies or politics (see Table 4.4). Equality of opportunity implies that all persons, regardless of their background, should be given equal access to the same facilities, services, employment and other conditions. Statutes such as the Sex Discrimination Act 1975, the Race Relations Act 1976, and Disability Discrimination Act 1995 and the more recent Equality Act 2006 make it unlawful to discriminate in the provision of goods, facilities and services. Equality of opportunity, equality of condition and equality of outcome are three significant policy foci for understanding equality processes in sports development.

Table 4.4 Views on equality in sport and society

B. Bagilhole (1997)

- *Equality of opportunity*. There is recognition here that all social groups need equal access to facilities and services.
- *Equality of condition*. Here it is acknowledged that even where access is open there may be material and cultural disparities that need to be considered. These may revolve around travel, cost, religion, physical access, timing and environment.
- *Equality of outcome*. Here the impact of historical disadvantages is considered. Action is taken to privilege marginalised groups; this is sometimes referred to as positive or affirmative action.

I. Forbes (1991)

- *Liberal*. Traditional liberals believe that the state should not interfere in the life-chances of individuals. It is the market that will provide where there are needs. Competition should be left unfettered.
- *Neo-liberal*. Traditional liberal values around the market are adapted with a social agenda. The market is central to a strong community, although inequality is recognised as needing to be checked by a social welfare, hence the New Right.
- *Radical*. A radical perspective criticises the conservative nature of traditional liberals and the liberal nature of advocates of New Right politics. Equal Opportunities will reconstitute inequality only if it does not take a radical 'alternative' approach.

S. Cunningham (1992)

- *Minimalist*. Holders of a minimalist ideology base equality on merit and the removal of barriers to achievement. Here the market offers individuals the chance to compete to be unequal, procedure-led policies are adopted which are 'race' and gender blind, and rewards are awarded on merit alone.
- *Maximalist*. This view refers to more radical activism. Practical outcomes that transform the *status quo* (social change) are the main focus of this activity in opposition to a minimalist incrementalism or procedural approach.

Table 4.4 continued

N. Jewson and D. Mason (1992)

- ▥ *Liberal*. The authors refer to this as the bureaucratisation of action. The formality of rules and regulations causes good ideas to atrophy and slows the process of change.
- ▥ *Radical*. The politicisation of implementation frames institutional change. Power, resistance and empowerment are used to champion the cause of marginal or disenfranchised social groups. Procedure and regulation are overtaken by critical consciousness, action and outcomes.

K. Young (1989)

- ▥ *Regulative*. Regulative discourses are concerned with the conformity of systems and behaviour to an acceptable level. Thus challenging institutional discrimination, discrimination in the workplace, and the training of staff to increase their capacity to ensure awareness, are three modes of regulatory behaviour.
- ▥ *Distributive*. Distributive discourses tend to view equality in terms of increases in resources such as jobs, low inflation, increased pay or new sports co-ordinators in schools that have a trickle-down effect on everyone and therefore everyone benefits. It does not discriminate in any way and there are no obvious 'losers' where these resources are being distributed.
- ▥ *Redistributive*. Redistributive discourses are often seen as ways to target marginalised populations in communities and are often measured in quantitative terms, unlike regulatory policies. For example, employment is often a way to redistribute key resources in a bid to ensure diverse sensitive provision.

A. Swinney and J. Horne (2005)

- ▥ *Gestural*. Organisations described as 'gestural' are generally confident that they are able to be 'fair' without producing any specific Equal Opportunities policies.
- ▥ *Reactive*. 'Reactive' organisations are likely to have equality policies in place. They are likely to sometimes be complacent or confident that they do not have a problem with inequality.
- ▥ *Proactive*. 'Proactive' organisations are likely to be active in systematically challenging racism. These organisations are generally in the minority.

For example, if a sports worker was to adhere to the conditions of the Equality Act 2006, yet members of the community were still excluded, then 'Equal Opportunities' could still be seen to exist, even though it would be ineffective in this instance. However, if the excluded groups were filtered away from the sports worker's sessions because of a lack of transport, of technical equipment, or for cultural reasons, but these gaps were *then* addressed, the sports worker would have moved beyond *just* providing equality of opportunity. As illustrated in Table 4.4 the sports worker would also be providing equality of condition in that considerations other than physical access would have been identified as reasons for a lack of participation by groups in this community. The worker would be moving towards what Cockburn (1989) terms a 'long agenda' rather than a short one. Jewson and Mason (1986) would argue also that the worker is moving from a liberal to a more radical agenda. The long-term implementation and monitoring of equality strategies is complex and involves more than policy statements and rhetoric, as we will see later.

A more radical view of equality in operation might come through the use of equality of outcome principles. Here more positive and explicitly differential provision takes into account some of the larger *structural* inequalities in society. Practitioners and policy makers taking structural differences into account will challenge inequality in sport through new initiatives and strategies. Sports professionals occasionally find it necessary to focus on equality outputs (CRE, 1996) or positive action initiatives to refocus work towards providing more equal and sensitive provision. The Adults with a Disability and Sport survey by Sport England (2002b) suggests one type of positive action through the implementation of leisure credits. It suggested that leisure credits be used as a way to reduce multiple inequalities that affect people with a disability. Therefore this recommendation takes into account inequalities that accrue due to low income and disability thus bringing a direct sporting benefit to disabled people. Women-only sessions, or work with young minority ethnic people, could be viewed as examples of positive action strategies. Positive action, due to the statutes mentioned earlier, can also be applied to recruiting people to work in those areas of provision where they are underrepresented. This basic regulation and distribution of resources is something that has been recognised as one essential aspect of progressive equality policies.

Sport then is not isolated from inequalities in society. Sports development has an endless task if it takes on primary responsibility for reducing social exclusion among people in the UK. Sport's role as *part of* a broader social policy strategy might go *some* way towards contributing to reducing social inequality, increasing community cohesion and acting as a catalyst for social regeneration. The creation of the Social Exclusion Unit and its use of sports development as part of its strategy to increase social inclusion is an indication of, at the very least, the ideological and material significance of sport in society.

EQUALITY AND SPORTS DEVELOPMENT

Certain managerial and political perspectives have informed the practice of equality work since the late 1970s. Taylor's work (1994) encapsulates some of the thinking in this area. Two major competing views in this period have revolved around a New Right ideology which has focused on the primacy of the market as the guardian of individual rights and natural justice. More recently a New Right view has been modified with elements of a social reformist agenda and this has taken a more inclusive stance in public sector interventions. The social reformist perspective encourages a more 'active society' through proactive support mechanisms which encourage community development, capacity building, social cohesion and the reduction of social exclusion. Sport England's Active Communities programme is the closest to meeting these aims, although the cross-cutting agendas now mean that other social objectives permeate school and sport-specific programmes.

Equality in sports development

Ellis (1994) and Escott (1996) have examined positive aspects of working towards equality within 'bottom line' pressures of the commercial sector. One of the major drawbacks of the contracting process as a result of the Local Government Act (1988) was that social objectives or equality targets were not necessarily written into contracts. Equality targets in the political climate of 1988 were seen as non-commercial considerations. The then Sports Council's National Information Survey in 1993 on the first round of Compulsory Competitive Tendering bore testimony to this. It was established that out of many local authorities only a few incorporated social objectives into clauses for contracts that went out to tender. However, more enlightened organisations have tied equality targets into contractor activities by linking them inextricably with quality targets and principles of Best Value. This is likely to be a focus of the Commission for Equality and Human Rights which has taken over a substantial aspect of this work from previous bodies.

In support of this view Taylor (1994) advocates the use of Equal Opportunities policies in any industry, not from a moral perspective (although there is an element of that) but from a business perspective as well (see Etzioni, 1961; CRE, 1995; EOC, 1996; Coalter, 1998). Taylor outlines the major skills a manager needs to be successful in business. Five major considerations to develop management skills in this area are:

- Human rights and social justice.
- Business efficiency.
- Quality management.
- The labour market.
- Legal considerations.

So equal opportunities is not just defined as the exclusive preserve of the social reformist agenda in the public and voluntary sectors, but can be a desirable aspect of the economics of the commercial private sector as well.

Sociological approaches to understanding inequality

An understanding of the social context of sport necessitates some understanding of society itself (Jarvie, 2006). In terms of sports development, enlightened practitioners must embrace this social perspective and its analysis, namely 'sociology'. Only then can they hope to have any significant understanding and impact on the social context of sport. This prospect can seem daunting as society is all-encompassing and the individual practitioner often feels isolated in relation to the scale of it all. But sociology is not just about 'thinking'. Sociology is alive and breathing. Sociology also involves 'doing', and the enlightened sports development worker (whether aware of it or not) can be an 'active sociologist'! Social processes which create inequality, and solutions (albeit with limitations), must be pursued not just in sport but in society as a whole. Let's face it, 'You're either part of the cure or you're part of the disease!'

Introducing sociology

Sociology is the study of society and is committed to developing a greater understanding of society. The 'sociological imagination' enables a deeper, more significant insight into society and how it works (Mills, 1970; Giddens, 2006). Sociology attempts to explain, and sometimes predict, social behaviour. A grasp of sociology will enable the enlightened practitioner to more accurately understand the profound and complex influences which affect sports participation. The following analysis deploys sociological theory and applies sociological perspectives to the study of inequality in sport. For the uninitiated it may initially be challenging or cause mild befuddlement, but 'hang in there', as it may prove quite illuminating! It begins with an analysis of how significant social influences are in determining participation in sport. It will then work towards offering different perspectives to understand Sport for All. It will establish what sociological perspectives are, what they explain and how they interpret society, sport, sports development and then Sport for All. So hang on to your hat!

Influencing participation

Social influences like gender, ethnicity and class, which can act as barriers or gateways to participation in sport, can be considered as 'structures' which permeate society. However, individuals make choices and exercise free will in leisure and sport and this is known as 'agency'. Social structures influence individuals as they make these choices. Structures inhibit total freedom from constraint. As much as individuals perceive themselves to be exercising free choice, they are either consciously or subconsciously constrained by these structures. Social structures can make certain choices more or less likely. They influence individual choices whether we are aware of it or not. So individuals attempt to make free choices in sport grounded in their own unique opportunities and tastes. But these very opportunities and tastes are informed by social structures. So total free choice is illusory! But we are still free to choose, even if we have less control than we think over what our choices are. So choice is constrained by structures outside the immediate influence of the individual. In short, once again, society influences sport, and sport influences society. The combined influence of structure and agency on choice can be described as a 'dichotomy'. Dichotomies, or real contradictions and tensions in policy and practice, are discussed in detail in Chapter 5.

Understanding society

Within sociology, different perspectives have emerged from which to view and understand institutions and social contexts like sport. These perspectives put more or less emphasis on the role of structure and/or agency in determining choice. Furthermore, they offer different interpretations of the entire social world! They may overlap, but some find more strengths in one interpretation than the others; therefore disagreement and argument ensue, and are inevitable. Sociology as an academic discipline is contested territory.

Four dominant perspectives are outlined below as tools that academics and practitioners may use to better understand sport and society. Ideally the four views should be utilised strategically by sports development professionals to interpret processes and practices in sport. Understanding the way people make sense of society, sport, sports development, and Sport for All, enables reflective practitioners to evaluate the relative merits of competing or alternative views more effectively. If an individual was to imagine their day-to-day relationships at work, or at leisure, then just that small group of acquaintances could offer up (from their diverse backgrounds) different, very challenging views on developing Sport for All.

As sociological perspectives consider much more than just sport, the four perspectives will be introduced from a bigger picture, before working progressively towards a more specific consideration of Sport for All. Table 4.5 highlights four key perspectives: functionalist,

Table 4.5 Interpretations of society

Functionalist

Society is based on broad agreement (consensus). This consensus reflects a balance between different interests. The 'social system' regulates the smooth flow of these plural interests (see Loy and Booth, 2000).

Neo-Marxist

Society is based on coercion and consensus. 'Social relations' are dominated by power struggles. The economically and politically powerful attempt to lead, and protect their dominance. People either consent to these arrangements or offer resistance to them (see Coakley and Dunning, 2000).

Feminist

Society is based on male dominance or *patriarchy*. Social relations exist within a gender order. Masculine values dominate society. Traditional femininity prescribes a subservient role for women (see Scraton and Flintoff, 2002).

Postmodernist

Society is fragmented and diverse. There is no universal truth, only individuality and different interpretations of reality. The only certainty is uncertainty! Society is in a perpetual state of change and flux. Traditional structure and order are things of the past (see Rail, 1998).

neo-Marxist, feminist and postmodernist (see Coakley and Dunning, 2000). Tables 4.5 and 4.6 offer simplified versions of society and sport from the four perspectives. The reader can attempt to judge which perspective they find the most convincing. Ideally, you may find that one perspective seems to emerge as more compelling, or you may choose to apply different perspectives at different times. Whichever you choose, the adoption of a socio-logical imagination and analysis offers a critical insight into how society works, (or does not!).

Comparing perspectives of society

Historical relationships help to clarify differences. Functionalism reflects the most traditional view of Western society and sport. It is perhaps the most popular perspective among the political establishment and the wider population. Its ideals tend to be dominant in current sport and social policy. But it is savagely criticised by Neo-Marxism for being at best too 'rose-tinted', unconditionally positive and unrealistic, and at worst for being ideologically divisive, conning the general public into believing in a society which ultimately works against collective interests. Neo-Marxists draw attention to power inequalities and conflicts which functionalists overlook, particularly in the economics of society and of sport. Feminism arose as a critique of the failure of the two previous perspectives to take account of gender divisions and power relations. Feminists promote the influence of gender as the primary determinant of social relations and sport. Postmodernism is the most recent perspective. It criticises all three perspectives for clinging to any form of clear determination in an increasingly unpredictable world.

Table 4.6 Interpretations of sport

Functionalist

Sport is greatly valued, as it has many positive benefits. It contributes to the smooth running of the social system. It acts as a form of 'cultural glue' which helps to hold society together.

Neo-Marxist

Sport can liberate or constrain. It largely serves the interests of dominant groups and institutions. But it can also act as a site for resistance or change by subordinate groups or individuals.

Feminist

Sport reinforces patriarchy and traditional masculine and feminine values. It promotes masculine values over feminine. But it can also act as a site for women, or men, to challenge these traditional values.

Postmodernist

Sport is a paradox. It can be highly significant to individual self-image and lifestyle, but it is ultimately superficial. It can be highly symbolic of society, but it is ultimately unreal. It is in this sense 'hyper-real'.

Neo-Marxism could be seen as adaptable enough to account for the massive changes in current society. Functionalism, on the other hand, could be viewed as oversimplifying the world, as unrealistic and naive. It is the world we would like to live in but do not. Some might say it is blinkered by its naive faith. Neo-Marxism considers the power processes overlooked and ignored by functionalism. Neo-Marxism can also be argued to encompass and account for the concerns of both feminists and postmodernists. Neo-Marxist analysis then takes account of cultural power as inclusive of concerns about gender division, as well as other dynamics such as ethnicity, class and disability. Neo-Marxism interprets post-modernism as a context, not a perspective. It is the times we live in, not the way they should be understood.

Comparing perspectives of sport

Functionalists clearly place an enormous value on sport, but there are other important issues that have been considered in this chapter, yet which carry less significance for functionalists; they are considerations of power. A Neo-Marxist perspective in sport recognises that sport, like society, can liberate: for example, by offering opportunities, and at the same time by constraining, by reducing choice through processes of discrimination. Feminist writers, and practitioners in the field, have also acknowledged power differentials in society. However, in this case the differences are due to a male-dominated or patriarchal system that results in a more oppressive society for girls and women than for boys and men. So gender relations are a primary source of focus here. Other related areas and issues build upon many of the arguments by Neo-Marxist and feminist thinkers. 'Race' and ethnicity, class, disability and age among others are crucial concerns for the enlightened practitioner. These issues are not mutually exclusive in that individuals are identified by, and identify with, combinations of these socio-economic variables.

Comparing perspectives of sports development

Table 4.7 indicates that functionalism is one view which when used takes as its basic premise that broad agreement typifies the way that sport and sports development is structured and functions in society. The ability of individuals and groups to access opportunities in society and sport is based upon combined interest groups. Simply, if something has not been set up or established in society then individuals in society do not see a need for it. If this point is applied to Lottery funding, then if particular groups in society are accessing funding and others are not, the funding should still be going to the right places because some groups are showing interest in terms of organisation and application.

A Neo-Marxist viewpoint accepts that there are constraints at the same time as there is a level of agency in sport and society. Even a local authority which is proactive in its sports equality work may be working against a backdrop of historically inadequate resources which still cause the limitation of choice and opportunities. This is the context for many practitioners and policy makers in sport. This is also a challenge for the development of Sport for All.

Table 4.7 Interpretations of sports development

Functionalist

Sports development polices gaps in provision and participation. It distributes social justice in the face of market trends. It circumvents barriers to participation. It spreads the benefits of sport. It presides over competing plural interests. It advocates on behalf of marginalised interests. It applies the glue to bind diverse strands into an integrated whole.

Neo-Marxist

Sports development reflects conflict between the interests of dominant groups and institutions, and the needs and wants of subordinate groups and individuals. It illustrates social tensions between *structures* and *free agency*. It perpetuates the dominant agenda, and can act as a site of resistance to that agenda.

Feminist

Overall, sports development perpetuates sport as a patriarchal institution. Token attempts are made to incorporate more women into sport without challenging the fundamentally patriarchal nature of its institutions and culture. But it does also offer some limited opportunities for women to infiltrate and reclaim previously masculine territory.

Postmodernist

Sports development reflects an institutional anxiety to exercise control and impose order in an increasingly disorganised world. It attempts to navigate a complex map of diverse sources of provision and motivations for participation. It is prone to a layering of disparate influences at local, regional, national and transnational levels. It is insecure. The only constant is change.

Postmodernists base their views on the development of sport and society on an analysis and description of the speed of change and the fragmentation of society. They reflect upon how technology, structures, processes and practices today no longer resemble the form they had yesterday, for example, the difference between the 1980s and the 2000s. In sports development the multi-agency, cross-departmental work, common in the achievement of Best Value for the customer, is one example of a significant shift in the industry. Another example of the shift in practices is the way that proof of sports development's worth is part of the move towards more accountability. This was not part of its dominant discourse in the 1970s and 1980s.

Comparing perspectives of 'Sport for All' and inclusion

Having taken a theoretical detour to set the scene, let us return specifically to Sport for All. The different ways of interpreting Sport for All in Table 4.8 are starting points to understand why Sport for All's objectives and equality in sports development are rarely acclaimed uniformly across the profession. The reader can analyse the following perspectives of Sport for All and, as before, critically evaluate the worth of each. Subsequent sections of this

Table 4.8 Interpretations of 'Sport for All' and inclusion

Functionalist

In a maturing society, equity and inclusion are ultimately and inevitably achievable. Historical inequities in sport are gradually eroded. Social consensus necessitates inclusion. The social system is committed to a project of inclusion. Exclusion is 'dysfunctional' and undesirable.

Neo-Marxist

Sport for All is unlikely to happen against the backdrop of a capitalist society, which is based on competition and inequality. Sport reflects and reinforces this. Power struggles in sport mirror those in society. Sport is a site of cultural struggle. This struggle includes the vested political and commercial interests of the dominant culture, the diverse self-interests of communities, and the emancipatory interests of the oppressed. The need to redistribute opportunity is paramount to create a fairer society.

Feminist

In recent years, there has been partial success in terms of addressing numerical inequalities in participation. But women are still institutionally excluded from the governance of sport. Ultimately the quality of women's and men's experiences in sport is still vastly unequal. The culture of sport is still male-dominated. Gender equity in sport is impossible in the context of a broader patriarchal society.

Postmodernist

Concepts like sports equality and inclusion are outmoded. There is nothing objectively fixed to determine inclusion or exclusion. Society is increasingly influenced by global processes which lead to the redundancy of traditional boundaries, social structures and inequalities. Class, gender and ethnic boundaries are collapsing. Lifestyle and identity are increasingly individualised and self-determined through consumption, like sport.

chapter will turn more directly to consider policy and practice, but it is hoped that readers will continue to exercise their sociological imagination throughout.

SPORTS POLICY ADDRESSING INEQUALITY

So inequality is a significant cause of social exclusion whereby individuals or communities are unable, for a variety of reasons, to participate with others or in activities. In sports development, unless there is recognition of the needs and aspirations of diverse people in society and among client groups, providers will continue to maintain inequalities in society. An example of a sports equality policy initiative is the Brighton Declaration (1995), which was written by national and international policy makers to develop a sporting culture that would enable and value the full involvement of women in every aspect of sport. The major areas of the declaration revolve around the guiding themes in Table 4.9. Similarly in the conclusion of the UK presidency of the European Commission in 2005 a meeting

Table 4.9 The guiding themes of the Brighton Declaration

- Equity and equality in society and sport
- Facilities
- School and junior sport
- Developing participation
- High-performance sport
- Leadership in sport
- Education, training and development
- Sports information and research resources
- Domestic and international co-operation

of European Sports Ministers supported the recommendation to promote Equal Opportunities and diversity in and through sport at both the national and European levels (EU, 2005).

Research, equality and sports development

The case study at the end of this chapter focuses on the London borough of Greenwich and considers how economic and social objectives can be successfully balanced in a robust and transparent way. Documented experiences of sport and recreation's inability to work consistently towards equality have led writers and practitioners to look in detail at the reasons for this lack of success. Carrol (1993), Horne (1995), Swinney and Horne (2005) and Spracklen *et al.* (2006) have all concluded that a policy implementation gap exists/ emerges between formulation and implementation of equal opportunities strategies. This in itself carries implications for prospects of success in any organisation.

Horne (1995) and Swinney and Horne (2005) have identified three types of local authority provider and labelled them gestural, reactive or proactive (see Table 4.4). *Gestural* authorities included those with a policy or policy statement but did not feel it necessary to go beyond that step, whereas the *reactive* authorities would have a policy but would not have a rigorous and actively monitored plan to work towards equality. In fact they would react to demand from their local communities which might have the effect of 'the louder you shout the more you get'. *Proactive* authorities had policy statements and plans and were actively working towards achieving their goals. Unfortunately, only a few organisations were placed in the proactive category: most tended to react to local community and staff needs rather than plan ahead. When Swinney and Horne (2005) revisited Horne's (1995) work, they came to similar conclusions about uneven practices among sport providers, between their rhetoric and what they implement. Spracklen *et al.* (2006) also revisited a study that considered the impact of racial equality in sport organisations, *Sporting Equals Equality Standards* (Long *et al.*, 2003, 2005). This study arrived at similar conclusions about the symbolic but superficial use of racial equality standards, as nearly all the governing bodies consulted reported little or no change in their organisation's equity policies in the preceding twelve months.

In *Anyone for Cricket?* (1998), research commissioned by the Essex Cricket Association and the London Cricket Association, the task was to find out why black and Asian teams tended not to affiliate to the county association. The research recognised that institutional systems were not enough to effect lasting change, but a critical mass of people was needed to be motivated to change the culture of the sport. In fact the research gave an indication of where to begin but, due to the size of the task, was vague on how it was to be achieved. The English Cricket Board followed this work up in 1999 with further research, *Clean Bowl Racism*, where it reinforced the notion that the majority of those researched (58 per cent) believe that there is racism in the sport (p. 8).

All organisations vary in their ability to implement all-embracing equality initiatives. Hylton (2003) examined three local authorities in England and compared their operational environments. The three authorities varied in size, location, history, industry, wealth, demography, politics and policies, although they were similar in their diversity of local people, especially where 'race' and ethnicity were concerned. Each authority was publicly committed to 'Equal Opportunities'. After further analysis it was found that, through comparing each authority, their political and professional commitment to equal opportunities work was not the same as the rhetoric. Differences in perception and focus on equality of opportunity, local politics and policies and related variables all impacted upon the quality of equal opportunities work in each organisation.

Analysing the impact of strategies in sport can often reveal some of the glitches in what many would see as a rational decision-making process (see Bramham in this edition). Young and Connolly (1984) categorised over a hundred local authorities in order to understand the work that they had conducted towards policy development and implementation in equal opportunities. They stated that there were those who:

- As a matter of political preference set their minds against change and were prepared to ignore the requirements of their (statutory) duties.
- Were reviewing their policies but were moving cautiously forward in a fairly conventional manner but with a willingness to accept the need for change.
- Were aware of a changed social, moral and legal climate presenting a challenge to traditional practices but were not sure of the appropriate response.
- Were testing out the political and legal possibilities and developing approaches aimed at giving a fair deal to people.

If policy approaches were to be considered from the previous sociological perspectives the conclusions in Table 4.10 could be drawn.

Table 4.10 Interpretations of sports policy

Functionalist

There is broad satisfaction with the current organisation of sport, and the value of the role that sport plays in society. There is conservative support for the *status quo* and milder liberal reforms. Minor reform acknowledges 'dysfunctional' exceptions in need of remedy but their extent does not threaten the overall institutionalised arrangements.

Neo-Marxist

Attention is drawn to the institutionalised and unequal distribution of power within sport, how that supports the interests of dominant groups, and how other groups' interests are marginalised or even oppressed. Given the all-pervasiveness of injustice, radical reforms are imperative.

Feminist

There are differences of opinion about the extent to which patriarchy is institutionalised. So whilst there are some arguments for stronger liberal reform to advance 'a level playing field of opportunity', there are also some arguments for a much more radical approach, even separatism.

Postmodernist

The collapse in influence of the traditional institutions is envisaged, and the growth, and importance, of individualised cultural choice is predicted, and championed. So less paternalistic reforms are favoured which empower individuals rather than specified groups.

Addressing inequality in practice

A sports organisation in context

Each sector and organisation has its own unique context, economies of scale and organisational culture which will impact upon the implementation of equality initiatives. The Badminton Association of England (Badminton England) is a national governing organisation that saw a need to implement an equality strategy that would assist the sport in becoming more representative of society. The organisation's staff decided that there was a problem and that the problem itself needed some form of definition. What brought the Association to this point was a series of acknowledgements by the staff. These acknowledgements recognised the following catalysts for action:

- *Image/Profile*.
  Predominantly white male middle class, stuffy, all-white kit . . .

- *Administration/Coaching*.
  Very few black and ethnic minority coaches, women and disabled people.

- *Executive members*.
  Are not close to reflecting the population mix.

■ *No Equal Opportunities strategy or monitoring.*
   Unable to get an accurate profile of coaches and players.

In addition to these internal drivers the external reality for the governing body included a funding mechanism from Sport England whose more recent conditions on funding ensured that there would be consequences for partners that did not adhere to principles of equity. Reactive or gestural organisations would need to consider practices in the light of financial support being reduced as a result of a lack of consideration of social objectives and strategic planning. An understanding of the catalysts for change is important for governing organisations, as change can occur under duress or rely on the enthusiasm of individuals rather than organisational processes. However, if these principles are taken on as part of an individual or an organisation's goals, there is more of a chance of success in the long term. The governing body may need to challenge its existing power structures. This would result in a focus on its dominant practices and processes and enable a robust opportunity for the long-term implementation of proactive equality outcomes.

According to Badminton England some of the explanations for its actions have included the following needs:

■ To develop an understanding of sports equity.
■ To evaluate the benefits of a sports equity approach.
■ To identify exclusionary factors.
■ To identify issues and target groups.
■ To draft an equal opportunities statement.

This has had the effect of shedding light on the practices that the Association had been engaged in for some years. It has also motivated it to draw in related experts to advise on how to make itself more accessible to those 'hard to reach' groups and communities. Badminton England stated that:

> To become a 'Best Practice' example of an equitable National Governing Body of sport by meeting the requirements of the B.A. of E. Equity Policy and making progress towards achieving the targets contained in the B.A. of E. Equity action plan in the areas of gender, disability and race.
>
> (Badminton Association of England, Targets 2003–04)

Using the policy model in Figure 4.1, Badminton England can demonstrate its strategy to define equality problems and as a result identify responses. After identifying responses the next stages after evaluating options are: selection of policy option, implementation and then active monitoring and evaluation of action. Its implementation of targets for 2003/04 included ensuring that 75 per cent of its clubs had an equal opportunities policy. In addition, it is conducting a survey of its volunteer demographics as well as attempting to meet the intermediate level of an equality standard.

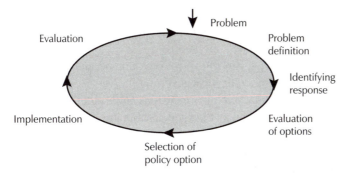

Figure 4.1 The policy life cycle

Jabeer Butt (1994: 77) established in her work that equality strategies needed to have a work programme, a time scale which must be monitored and reviewed. Badminton England has agreed a policy statement on equal opportunities and it can be argued that it is now working towards badminton for all.

Case Study 4.1 shows how the London borough of Greenwich has successfully attempted to balance the social and economic demands of a diverse resident community. In their quest to achieve equality in sport through Best Value Greenwich has managed to satisfy the demands of the external inspectors in this respect, while still leaving itself an ongoing challenge of continual improvement.

CASE STUDY 4.1

PROACTIVE EQUALITY WORK IN SPORTS DEVELOPMENT

The London borough of Greenwich has a population of 215,000 with a significant black and minority ethnic population of 17 per cent. The London Research Centre suggests that there are 10,000 people in the borough between sixteen and twenty-four years old who are registered disabled. As for many multicultural settings there are over one hundred different languages in the borough. The Department of Transport Local Government and the Regions has ranked Greenwich forty-fourth in the Indices of Deprivation, 2000.

The 'vision' for the authority – the council's Community Plan – states that it is: 'The place to live, work, learn, visit and play'.

The values that Greenwich hold are as follows:

- Ensure delivery of high-quality, value-for-money services.
- Protect the vulnerable and promote independence.

- Promote equality in all sections of the community and celebrate diversity.
- Challenge discrimination in our own operations.
- Listen to our communities, especially the voices of young people.
- Provide a model of open, democratic local government.
- Foster high levels of achievement among our citizens and institutions.
- Develop effective partnerships with all the agencies that impact on the lives of Greenwich residents.
- Maximise our impact as a local authority, as a partner with business, the voluntary sector and other public agencies.

The authority's sport strategy for 2001–2006 promises to *harness the transformational power of sport, in all its forms as an instrument for promoting social and economic change in a way that secures lasting improvements to the quality of life of all borough residents, irrespective of their racial or ethnic origin, gender, age, class, disability or sexuality.*

Greenwich was awarded a two-star rating from the Audit Commission (2001) who stated that when compared with similar authorities it is 'a good and improving' local authority. Due to Greenwich managing to balance the business and social objectives of its work the following characteristics of this successful borough have been identified:

- New facilities being opened while the council subsidies have decreased.
- Pricing and programming policies encourage participation from a broad range of customers that reflect the local demographic.
- Innovative partnerships are being developed designed to meet the social and economic objectives of the borough.

The Audit Commission was also persuaded that Greenwich would improve further due to its robust and performance management system and the shared vision that staff and councillors had of sport's potential in the community.

Clearly we should always be working towards equality and Greenwich now aims to improve in the following areas:

- Increase the use of leisure centres from specified target groups to reduce social and health inequalities.
- Ensure partnerships reflect shared objectives and targets.
- Undertake a disability audit to meet statutory requirements.

SUMMARY

This chapter has raised and debated the contemporary relevance of the quest for Sport for All. It has identified continuing inequalities which permeate sport and society, and therefore the failure to realise Sport for All. In drawing attention to the social nature of inequality in sport the chapter has advocated the importance of 'active sociology' to practical sports development. It has considered policy approaches to addressing inequality and finally, aspects of good practice.

Practitioners still occupy distinctive and different roles and responsibilities in the delivery and development of sport. This can cause strategic tensions in provision of sport and recreation, and perennial competition for resources. Sports development can be viewed in a number of different ways by practitioners, policy makers and academics. The significance of sport in society is beyond question. The future of sport and its consequent development in society are also beyond question. Its exact role, however, is in dispute when it comes to developing Sport for All. Concepts such as Sport for All, 'equality', 'social exclusion' and 'equity' are problematic. This exacerbates the complexity of policy decisions and the practices that sports development workers aim to implement. Sports development workers and policy makers have a variety of challenges facing them in the twenty-first century. The continued development of opportunities for people in sport is consistently questioned when practitioners have differing aims, objectives and basic philosophies in their role and place in developing sport and recreation.

It was previously stated that 'sport affects society and society affects sport'. This relationship can be described as reflexive, or symbiotic. Essentially it cuts both ways. Sport and society both reproduce inequality, but they can both challenge it. A fairer arrangement cannot be achieved in one and not the other. So the marriage of sport and social policy is more than just one of convenience. According to the Social Exclusion Unit, social exclusion is constraining the opportunities of members of society, and therefore those in sport should respond accordingly. Sport can play a part in reducing the constraints which exclude social groups. Sports development can help to reduce social exclusion by enhancing community development opportunities, social cohesion, equal opportunities, crime prevention and community safety, lifelong learning, active healthy lifestyles, social and economic regeneration, job creation and environmental protection.

Significantly there is no clear consensus on the importance of unconditionally increasing access for disenfranchised groups in sport. This is due to competing viewpoints and causes. Sociological perspectives should begin to stimulate the sociological imagination to illustrate different ways of seeing sports development and inclusive sport. Effective sports development workers (active sociologists!) should be able to use the appropriate analytical tools and research available to them to ensure that they 'work smart' in trying to address inequality.

REFERENCES

Audit Commission (2001) London Borough of Greenwich Sport and Leisure Provision, November 2001, Best Value Inspection, London: Audit Commission.

Badminton Association of England (2006) Badminton Association of England Targets, http://www.badmintonengland.co.uk/text.asp?section=0001000100110001.

Bagilhole, B. (1997) *Equal Opportunities and Social Policy*, London: Longman.

Blakemore, K. and Drake, R. (1996) *Understanding Equal Opportunity Policies*, London: Prentice Hall.

Butt, J. (1994) *Same Service or Equal Service?* London: HMSO.

Carrol, B. (1993) Sporting bodies, sporting opportunities, in C. Brackenridge (ed.) *Body Matters: Leisure Images and Lifestyles*, Eastbourne: Leisure Studies Association.

Central Council of Physical Recreation (2002) *Everybody Wins*, London: CCPR.

Clarke, A. (1994) Leisure and the new managerialism, in J. Clarke *et al.* (eds) *Managing Social Policy*, London: Sage.

Clements, P. and Spinks, T. (1996) *The Equal Opportunities Guide: How to deal with Everyday Issues of Unfairness*, London: Kogan Page.

Coakley, J. and Dunning, E. (2000) *Handbook of Sports Studies*, London: Sage.

Coalter, F. (1998) Leisure studies, leisure policy and social citizenship: the failure of welfare or the limits of welfare? *Leisure Studies*, 17: 21–36.

Cockburn, C. (1989) Equal Opportunities, *Industrial Relations Journal*, 20(3): 213–25.

Coe, S. (2006) http://www.london2012.org/en/news/press+room/releases/2005/april/2005-04-06-14-33.htm.

Collins, M. and Kay, T. (2003) *Sport and Social Exclusion*, London: Routledge.

Commission for Racial Equality (1995) *Racial Equality means Equality*, London: CRE.

Cunningham, S. (1992) The development of Equal Opportunities theory and practice in the European Community, *Policy and Politics*, 20(3): 177–89.

DePauw, K. and Gavron, P. (2005) *Disability Sport*, Leeds: Human Kinetics.

Desai, M. (1995), *Equality*, London: LSE.

Edwards, J. (1990) What purpose does equality of opportunity serve? *New Community*, 7(1): 19–35.

Ellis, J. (1994) Developing sport through CCT, *Recreation*, 53(9): 31–3.

Equal Opportunities Commission (1996) *Mainstreaming Gender Equality in Local Government*, London: EOC.

Escott, K. (1996) *Equal Opportunities Strategy for CCT*, London: Centre for Public Services Organisations.

Etzioni, A. (1961) *A Comparative Analysis of Complex Organizations*, New York: Free Press.

European Union (2005) UK Presidency of the EU 2005, http://www.eu2005.gov.uk.

Fitzgerald, H. (2005) Still feeling like a spare piece of luggage? Embodied experiences of (dis)ability in physical education and school sport, *Physical Education and Sport Pedagogy*, 10(1): 41–59.

Forbes, I. (1991) Equal Opportunity: radical, liberal and conservative critiques, in E. Meehan and S. Sevenhuijsen (eds) *Equality Politics and Gender*, London: Sage.

Gibbon, P. (1989) *Equal Opportunities in Sheffield: Policies and Outcomes*, Sheffield: Department of Employment and Economic Development and Race Equality Unit, Sheffield City Council.

Giddens, A. (2006) *Sociology*, Cambridge: Polity Press.

Gillborn, D. (2005) 'It takes a nation of millions . . .', in B. Richardson (ed.) *Tell it like it is: How our Schools fail Black Kids*, Stoke on Trent: Trentham Books.

Gratton, C. and Jones, I. (2004) *Research Methods for Sports Studies*, London: Routledge.

Hargreaves, J. (2002) Globalisation theory, global sport, and nations and nationalism, in J. Sugden and A. Tomlinson (eds) *Power Games: A Critical Sociology of Sport*, London: Routledge.

Horne, J. (1995), Local authority black and ethnic minority provision in Scotland, in M. Talbot, S. Fleming and A. Tomlinson (eds) *Policy and Politics in Sport, Physical Education and Leisure*, Brighton: Leisure Studies Association.

Houlihan, B. and White, A. (2002) *The Politics of Sports Development*, London: Routledge.

Hylton, K. (2003) Local Government 'Race' and Sports Policy Implementation, unpublished PhD thesis, Leeds Metropolitan University.

Hylton, K. (2005) 'Race', sport and leisure: lessons from critical race theory, *Leisure Studies*, 24(1): 81–98.

Hylton, K. and Totten, M. (2001) Developing 'Sport for All?' Addressing inequality in sport, in K. Hylton and P. Bramham *et al.* (eds) *Sports Development: Policy, Process and Practice*, 1st edn, London: Routledge.

Jarvie, G. (2006) *Sport, Culture and Society*, Abingdon: Routledge.

Jewson, N. and Mason, D. (1986) 'Race' employment and Equal Opportunities: towards a political economy and an agenda for the 1990s, *Sociological Review*, 42(4): 591–617.

Jewson, N. and Mason, D. (1992) The theory and practice of Equal Opportunities policies: liberal and radical approaches, in P. Braham *et al.* (eds) *Racism and Anti-racism: Inequalities, Opportunities and Policies*, London: Sage.

Jowell, T. (2002) Foreword, in *Game Plan*, London: Cabinet Office.

Ledwith, M. (2005) *Community Development: A Critical Approach*, Bristol: Policy Press.

LeGrand, J. (1991) *Equity and Choice*, London: HarperCollins.

Levitas, R. (1998) *The Inclusive Society? Social Exclusion and New Labour*, London: Macmillan.

London East Research Institute (1998) *Anyone for Cricket? Patterns of Participation and Exclusion in East London and Essex Cricket Cultures*, London: University of East London.

Long, J. (2007) *Researching Leisure, Sport and Tourism: The Essential Guide*, London: Sage.

Long, J., and Hylton, K. (2002). Shades of white: an examination of whiteness in sport, *Leisure Studies*, 21(2): 87–103.

Long, J., Robinson, P. and Spracklen, K. (2005). Promoting racial equality within sports organizations, *Journal of Sport and Social Issues*, 29: 41–59.

Long, J., Robinson, P. and Welch, M. (2003) *Raising the Standard: An Evaluation of Progress*, Leeds: Leeds Metropolitan University.

Loy, J. and Booth, D. (2000) Functionalism, sport and society, in J. Coakley and E. Dunning (eds) *Handbook of Sports Studies*, London: Sage.

McDonald, I. (1998) *Anyone for Cricket?* London: University of East London.

Messner, M. (1992) *Power at Play: Sport and the Problem of Masculinity*, Boston MA: Beacon Press.

Mills, C. W. (1970) *The Sociological Imagination*, Harmondsworth: Penguin.

Mintel Leisure Intelligence (2006) *Leisure Time UK*, London: Mintel Intelligence Group.

Mithaug, D. (1996) *Equal Opportunity Theory*, London: Sage.

Polley, M. (1998) *Moving the Goalposts: The History of Sport and Society from 1945*, London: Routledge.

Rail, G. (ed.) (1998) *Sport and Postmodern Times*, New York: State University of New York Press.

Rawls, J. (1971) *A Theory of Justice*, London: Oxford University Press.

Rheker, U. (2000) *Integration through Games and Sports*, Oxford: Meyer & Meyer.

Rigauer, B. (2000) Marxist theories, in J. Coakley and E. Dunning (eds) *Handbook of Sports Studies*, London: Sage.

Room, G. (ed.) (1995) *Beyond the Threshold: The Measurement and Analysis of Social Exclusion*, Bristol: Policy Press.

Saraga, S. (ed.) (1998) *Embodying the Social Construction of Difference*, London: Routledge.

Schirato, T. and Webb, J. (2003) *Understanding Globalisation*, London: Sage.

Scraton, S. and Flintoff, A. (2002) Sport feminism: the contribution of feminist thought to our understanding of gender and sport, in S. Scraton and A. Flintoff, *Gender and Sport: A Reader*, London: Routledge.

Social Exclusion Unit (2006), http://www.socialexclusionunit.gov.uk/page.asp?id=213.

Sports Council (1993) *Compulsory Competitive Tendering Sport and Leisure Management*, National Information Survey report, London: Sports Council.

Sport England (2001) *Performance Measurement for the Development of Sport: A Good Practice Guide for Local Authorities*, London: Sport England.

Sport England (2002a) *Participation in Sport in England: Sports Equity Index 2002*, London: Sport England.

Sport England (2002b) *Adults with a Disability and Sport Survey*, London: Sport England.

Sport England (2004) *The Equality Standard: A Framework for Sport*, London: Sport England.

Spracklen, K., Hylton, K. and Long, J. (2006) Managing and monitoring equality and diversity in UK sport, *Journal of Sport and Social Issues*, 30(3): 289–305.

Sugden, J. and Tomlinson, A. (2002) *Power Games: A Critical Sociology of Sport*, London: Routledge.

Swinney, A. and Horne, J. (2005) Race equality and leisure policy: discourses in Scottish local authorities, *Leisure Studies*, 24(3): 271–89.

Taylor, G. (1994) *Equal Opportunities*, London: Industrial Society.

Veal, A.J. (1992) *Research Methods for Leisure and Tourism*, London: Longman.

Young, K. (1989) The space between words: local authorities and the concept of Equal Opportunities, in R. Jenkins and J. Solomos (eds) *Racism and Equal Opportunities in the 1980s*, Cambridge: Cambridge University Press.

Young, K. and Connolly, N. (1984) After the Act: local authorities' policy reviews under the Race Relations Act, 1976, *Local Government Studies*, 10(1): 13–25.

CHAPTER 5

COMMUNITY SPORTS DEVELOPMENT

Kevin Hylton and Mick Totten

This chapter examines some of the structural changes in community sports development as policies and sports organisations have adapted over time. It also considers how the inevitability of change over the years has not reduced significantly the necessity for an alternative to mainstream provision. Chapter 4 emphasised how sports development has struggled to engage some social groups and communities and it is often towards community sport practitioners that policy makers turn for answers to this failure. For many involved in community sports development, the experience of cyclical change in policy and practice reinforces the view from experienced practitioners how effectively others have learned from past successes and failures. This chapter aims to uncover the essence of these changes and so explore the fundamental ideals of community sports development. Further, the dynamics of the situated practice of community sports development are considered in relation to divergent forms of community sports development.

Community sports development is a form of practice that conveys a philosophy and spirit which address many themes raised in Chapter 4. It arose as a response to enduring concerns about issues around equal opportunities and participation in sport. An understanding of the precise meaning of community sports development (hereafter most often referred to as CSD) will be developed in this chapter, but a cursory glance would reveal that CSD is more than sport in the community. CSD is also a form of provision which addresses social and political concerns about the nature and extent of inequality, significantly demonstrated by its genesis being concurrent with 'Sport for All?' in the 1970s.

This chapter analyses significant tensions and issues in the theory, policy and practice of CSD. It considers delivery models ranging from 'top-down' to 'bottom-up' and explores CSD from social, cultural and political perspectives. Theoretical concern about policy, process and practice is grounded throughout by specific case studies. We start with an exploration of three key concepts and issues: sports development, community development and 'community' itself. We then examine the complex sectors, levels and partnerships in CSD provision. Next, CSD policy is considered, with a historical overview of the development of community sports policy leading to its contemporary context. Our analysis then shifts to a macroscopic view of different policy models and their rationales. These will be contextualised by a case study of Action Sport located in inner-city areas in the north of England. CSD practice is then critically analysed against a policy backdrop of two further case studies, the Bradford Sports Web project and the Leeds Community Sport Team. In conclusion, CSD will then be reconsidered and re-evaluated by drawing on the concept of hegemony.

CONCEPTUALISING COMMUNITY SPORTS DEVELOPMENT

Community sport is often subsumed under the title of community recreation. This is in recognition that practice often reflects inclusive informal activities which blur the boundary between sport and recreation; some activities at first glance seem hardly to constitute sport at all. Community sport is provided through many different types of organisation. It is not solely the preserve of local authority leisure services or of sports development officers. It is mostly located in the public sector, often also in the voluntary sector, but seldom in the commercial sector. It is practised in youth and community work, social services, probation services, education, and in many other realms as well. Community sport originally arose out of the realisation that traditional participation patterns were dominated by advantaged sections of the population and that an alternative approach was needed. In conceptualising community sport, it must be understood as a contested concept (Haywood, 1994: Lentell, 1994; McDonald, 1995; Coalter and Allison, 1996; Houlihan and White, 2002). With shifting politics and changes in terminology over time, 'community sport' has been interpreted by different bodies, organisations and individuals in substantially different ways.

New community sport networks (CSN) are being established in an attempt to rationalise the fragmented structure of sport into a new 'delivery system for sport' (Sport England Delivery Plan, 2005–08). CSNs are essentially alliances of local providers hosted by a lead organisation such as a local authority. The number of CSNs in England is planned to increase from sixty-one in 2005/06 to 353 in 2007/08. The first evaluation of the CSN system involved Sport Leeds, Gedling Sports and Physical Activity Partnership in Nottingham, Sports Alliance Portsmouth and Cheshire Sport; each have a slightly different approach in its structure, demographic profile and rationale (Sport England, 2005: PMP evaluation). Each works at all levels in its region and operates across local authorities, governing bodies, county sport partnerships, the voluntary sector, education and less so the commercial sector. Each is concerned with the development of sport at all levels and was complimented on its clarity of purpose, roles, commitment and responsibilities. A generic notion of 'community' is being applied here which includes joint working in mainstream provision and the more alternative forms of provision that have more recently been considered under the umbrella of CSD.

To complicate matters further, there are many instances where it is claimed that community sport is practised when in fact it is not. Certain agencies have 'hi-jacked' the prefix 'community' as a flag of convenience because of its perceived 'feel-good' value and currency with policy makers (Butcher, 1993: 3). This has variously been described as deploying community as 'a fashionable label with virtually no recognition that a particular set of practices and values is implied' (Haywood, 1994: 27; SCCD, 2001; CDF, 2001) and as 'often sprayed on purely to lend legitimacy and positive feelings, credence and acceptability' (Plant et al., 1980). Many very senior providers at both a national and local level are prone to such accusations, as are smaller-scale organisations. Not everything which claims to be CSD really is! There are 'frauds and imposters' out there who may be involved in community sport for other reasons than to develop or significantly benefit the community! There are four possible reasons why this might take place: income generation, talent identification, public relations and marketing. Organisations whose primary purpose is mainstream sports participation know that they may be more likely to receive funding or other support if they portray a 'community' or social focus. North West councillor Terry Smith describes one example thus:

> In America storm chasers charge around the country taking pictures of storms and then sell them on. Over here we have SRB (Single Regeneration Bid) chasers who come from outside the community to take what they can from the projects (financially), denying those on the streets any opportunity.
>
> (Cited in Morgan, 2000: 30)

Another more cynical use of the term 'community sport' was revealed in research by the Centre for Leisure and Sport Research about a sports club (CLSR, 2003) which received an 'Awards for All' grant on the premise that it would develop opportunities for black and minority ethnic young people. But there were *no* black young people in the group or in the surrounding catchment area! Like many other projects they received funding because they understood the salience of social goals in sport policy and the attractiveness of community sport in sport-funding mechanisms (Jackson et al., 2003).

Talent identification, public relations and marketing are major motivations behind many projects (though not all) like 'Football in the Community'. Some professional clubs may well go into schools to provide short-term coaching sessions which bring some community benefit, but this operation acts as an opportunity for talent spotters who later may invite only the most talented young people for further coaching. This provision is primarily focused on ability, not need. The Football in the Community schemes are generally aimed at encouraging more people (especially children) to play and watch football; to promote closer links between professional football clubs and the local community; to encourage more people to become interested in and support their local club; and to maximise community facilities and their community use at football clubs. Some football (and also similar rugby) clubs in the community schemes offer free tickets for young people to attend games but only on condition that their parents then buy tickets to 'accompany their child'!

Other examples of marketing ploys would include corporate sponsorship like that of Cadbury Schweppes' (2006) 'Get Active' programme designed to support the training of teachers and to supply schools with equipment, but only if they could generate enough tokens in wrappers bought from sweet packets in another seemingly controversial step into 'community sport'.

Local factors dictate the emphasis of each project as some may have more of a football focus than others that have a closer connection with communities (FA Premier League, 2006). The Football Foundation (2006) has been involved with some Football in the Community schemes that have worked with disabled, anti-racist, anti-crime, healthy lifestyles and tenants-based groups that have built capacity, new skills, empowered and motivated different communities through the game of football.

So in addition to all this good work there are those out there involved in community sport whose emphasis is the development of sport, which may include other externalities, rather than the development of community. However, in order to progress, community sport will be referred to as a form of intervention in sport and recreation provision which in some way addresses inequalities inherent in more established, mainstream, sports provision (see Coalter, 2002).

SPORT, DEVELOPMENT AND COMMUNITY

The term sports development (also taken to include more informal aspects like recreation) dictates that something or someone is indeed developed. This suggests either some form of professional intervention or local voluntary action. Various models have been developed to characterise the nature and intent of these interventions. Chapter 1 illustrated various sports development continua. What each of these continua share is a distinction in type or level of development within sport. They imply a hierarchical progression through levels from participation towards performance and excellence, so the primary focus of development is very much on traditional established sports. In short, they are elitist. However, *community sports development is not solely concerned with the development of sport*. It is not simply 'sport *in* the community'. It also encompasses the realm of 'community development'. Therefore an alternative continuum can be drawn (Figure 5.1).

As this CSD continuum implies, different aspects of practice can be located with different degrees of emphasis at different points on the continuum. At one extreme is pure 'sport' development, or 'sport *in* the community', where the practice of sport is an end in itself. Here practice does not stray beyond the primary focus of participation in sport as sports development beyond participation is best catered for by other mainstream agencies. At the other extreme is sport as 'community development' where sport is simply a means to human development. Coalter (2002) restricts himself to exploring community sport as

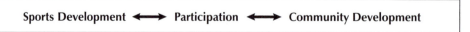

Figure 5.1 The community sports development continuum

kevin hylton and mick totten

sports development practised in areas of social and economic deprivation. Accusations of the use of the term 'community' as a flag of convenience are mainly aimed at initiatives and organisations that fall into the left-hand side of the spectrum (Sports development). Haywood and Kew (1989) are critical of sport in the community; they describe it as 'old wine in new bottles'. It is the same sport as practised in the mainstream but simply repackaged. Community sport implies a much more fundamental adaptation or change of approach and practice. So what does it mean when sport engages in elements of community development?

Community

The term community, like community sports development, is contested and can be interpreted to have multiple meanings. Community implies some notion of collectivity, commonality, a sense of belonging or of something shared. A community can be self-determined by its members or it can be a label externally constructed and defined by some statutory agency. Either way, community can be imagined as much as it can be realised. It can be inhabited, as 'place', a specific locality or a geographical area. It can be an 'experience', through a gathering, an interest or affiliation to a social, leisure or sports activity. It can also be experienced as a shared identity, history or nostalgia, or as an action when engaged in some form of interactive process. It can be 'protective' of a way of being, or 'expansive' in terms of some aspiration (Butcher, 1993; Popple, 1995; Chaskin, 1997; Popple and Shaw, 1997; Brent 2004; Fremeaux 2005).

Analysis of community by place or locality is diminishing in the eyes of many academics, as social relations and society transcend locality due to increased personal mobility. But this narrow model traditionally courts more favour from CSD policy makers and is in greater evidence in working practice. In this approach the state has traditionally taken a leading role in identifying disadvantaged communities and in targeting groups of disenfranchised people. This approach also links with notions of community as shared identity. This deterministic concept of community has connotations of working-class status, shared experiences and living in the inner city. The inner city itself is further characterised by special social needs, high unemployment, high-density poor-quality housing, social disadvantage and concentrations of marginalised powerless groups. Community and community development are of course neither exclusively urban nor exclusively working class but these remain dominant images.

Community development

Community development (CD) challenges passive consumer culture. It is about community consultation, empowerment and involvement in sustainable transformative change. It promotes a participatory democracy (Ledwith, 2005). Work in communities ranges between external agencies imposing their deterministic approaches in a manipulative 'top-down' way and 'bottom-up' interactive models of intervention through community self-help. There is a wide spectrum of approaches between those two extremes (Arnstein, 1969; Haywood *et al.*, 1994; SEU, 1999; Torkildsen 2005). Any individual initiative can be located at a given point on that spectrum. The Bradford Sports Web project (see Case Study 5.1) is an example of a relatively 'bottom-up' approach mutually plotted with enabling professionals, whilst the nationally driven Action Sport initiative (Rigg, 1986) is an example of a more 'top-down' approach. Booth (1997) informs us that the CD approach is 'to facilitate the involvement of people in the participative structures. Community development is oiling the wheels of participation. It is 'bottom-up'.

> Community development is about involving the people themselves in the context of the community's overall needs and developing responses for themselves. It is not simply the delivery of services to the community . . . [it] can empower local people to take an active part in defining both needs and solutions . . . [engaging] local people directly in dialogue and partnership.
>
> (Association of Metropolitan Authorities, 1989: 8,11)

Instances of CD practice in sport include the Active Communities Projects (Sport England, 2000; Active Communities, 2002) whose underpinning ideals resonate with the AMA's goals; to encourage empowerment, devolution, self-determination, active citizenship and neighbourhood renewal. Similarly Sports Action Zones (Sport England, 2001) and other such initiatives have brought something new to community sports development.

A classic example of community sports practice is the Action Sport project. It was originally implemented nationally, but in this chapter reference will be largely confined to research on the project based in Leeds (Totten, 1993). During this study, when Action Sport workers were asked how much their work was community work as opposed to sports work, they saw a very large and significant part of their work as community work, due to the high priority placed on community development activity (SCCD, 2001). On balance, they saw sports work as fractionally dominant, though one worker described community sport (conceptually) as a part of community work. All concerned concluded there was substantial overlap and this has been clearly reflected in policy and practice from Policy Action Teams' PAT 9 and PAT 10 recommendations (DCMS, 1999; Home Office, 1999) through to the joint government department guidance to policy makers and practitioners published by Sport England, *Sport: Playing its Part* (2005). As a result of recognition from policy makers and practitioners, community sport is recognised as a valuable tool to pursue community or socio-cultural development (AMA, 1989; Coalter and Allison, 1996; DCMS, 1999; Sport England, 2005). The Community Development Foundation (CDF, 2001) offers the following definition:

> *Community Development* is about building active and sustainable communities based on social justice and mutual respect. It is about changing power structures

to remove the barriers that prevent people from participating in the issues that affect their lives.

(CDF, 2001: 3)

In the interests of transparency and ensuring that community development was indeed taking place, the PAT 10 report on Sport and the Arts (DCMS, 1999: 41) devised a test for sports organisations that purported to be involved in community development. Many mainstream providers, governing bodies and voluntary groups perpetuate sporting inequalities because they are insensitive to some or all of the key principles that underpin working with marginalised or excluded communities. The PAT 10 test included ascertaining if the following are taking place: Valuing Diversity; Embedding Local Control; Supporting Local Commitment: Promoting Equitable Partnerships; Working with Change; Securing Sustainability; Pursuing Quality; Connecting with the Mainstream.

So CD necessitates social transformation and anti-discriminatory action against broader social inequality. CSD does not exist in a 'sports bubble' as it requires an engagement with social justice. One consequence of practitioners and policy makers not considering community development principles was outlined by Ledwith (2005) who describes the pitfalls of 'thoughtless action' and 'actionless thought'. 'Thoughtless action' would include attempts at CSD which failed to engage with underlying social issues. 'Actionless thought' would be recognition of social issues but no plan for change. Clearly, when it comes to CD, CSD must represent a form of 'thoughtful action'! Thoughtful action is clearly ener-gised when CSD is planned in a holistic way that incorporates the needs of all parties without recourse to short-term gains. Coalter's (2002: 32) summary of best practice in planning community sports development encapsulates issues to consider on that journey to *thoughtful action* (see Table 5.1).

COMMUNITY SPORTS DEVELOPMENT PROVISION

Most CSD does not take place in isolation. Any understanding of why specific activity takes place (or doesn't!) at a local level necessitates an understanding of what influences have been brought to bear from a wider policy context. Understanding how CSD works and why it does what it does at the delivery point to clients is part of a more complex picture of how policy makers and funders influence the scope of activity. This in turn is mediated by factors at a community-engaged level. Overwhelmingly, CSD is framed within policy and funding contexts which are determined by larger organisations remote from the community itself. Their influence and motivations can be tracked, analysed and under-stood through the use of certain models. Subsequent sections will introduce and explain these models, building towards a more holistic analysis of who and what determines practice and why. By selecting organisations and applying them systematically through these models the reader can uncover some of the answers as to why organisations do what they do and who influences them.

Table 5.1 Good practice in community sports development planning

Partnerships and agreed aims

It is not enough for partners and stakeholders to have mutual agendas but they must also have mutually *agreed* ones too. There needs to be empathy between partners and clear commitment to, and understanding of, what they are setting out to achieve.

Aims and objectives

Transparency is important here. Do those setting the aims have a clear idea of community needs? What are the aims, objectives, inputs and outputs for the project? Where is the proof?

Staffing

Whenever staff join a project they should be fully involved and conversant with strategy development and its underpinning philosophies.

Identity and status

For CSD work to be taken seriously it needs to establish a professional identity and be recognised as a significant contributor to mainstream sports development (Skills Active, 2006).

Long-term commitment

Community development is a long-term process and as such partners should be aware of this ongoing commitment to development processes taking priority over short-term gains (Sport England Performance and Measurement, 2001b).

Innovation

Innovation is the cornerstone of CSD, as it often offers unconventional approaches to what should be mainstream issues. A plethora of good practice has emerged in sports development from new approaches adopted in CSD (Hylton, 2003).

Empowerment and ownership

Most commentators on CSD and community work support the notion of empowerment and capacity building where responsibilities are devolved to the community so that control and confidence are substantive not tokenistic (Home Office, 1999).

Source Adapted from Coalter (2002: 32).

Levels of provision

CSD provision operates at different levels; local, regional, national and even transnational. The lens that is taken to view CSD must also take into account different economies of scale, tensions, organisational and personal demands that the different levels must impose on any CSD organisation.

- *Transnational*. Transnational refers to organisations and processes which occur across or beyond national boundaries. The clearest example of this for CSD is the increasing influence of the European Commission (EC) on policy and practice. This is especially true in relation to the funding of projects and initiatives. For example, EC funding work with priority initiative areas often ties in with areas that have been identified in the UK as areas of social and economic deprivation. Therefore the EC funding in some settings for CSD can be seen as the difference between failure and success. The European Year of Education through Sport (EYES, 2004) had a budget of €6.5 million and contributed 50–60 per cent of the overall cost of projects. Approximately 185 'community' projects were operating at local to transnational levels to target a variety of educational and social outcomes through the use of sport.

- *National.* Nationally, the Department for Culture Media and Sport (DCMS), the Department for Education and Skills (DfES), the Department for Communities and Local Government (DCLG) and the Home Office are four leading government departments involved in setting influential policy direction for CSD. Further, Sports Action Zones (SAZ) have concentrated government support for CSD activity in under-resourced or disadvantaged areas (Sport England, 2001). The impact of the DCMS on sport in particular through the 'Active Framework' (which includes the 'Active Communities' initiatives) is crucial in understanding the range of influences on CSD in the UK.

  National governing bodies (NGBs) and non-departmental public bodies also have a major influence on sport in the UK. There are approximately 112 sports recognised by Sport England and nearly 400 NGBs, ranging from the All England Netball Association to the Yachting Association (RYA) and the forum for NGBs; the Central Council of Physical Recreation (CCPR). This gives an indication of a significant part of the policy community that makes and affects CSD policy at all levels.

- *Regional.* Governing bodies and non-departmental public bodies tend to set policy at a national level. However, specific policy implementation strategies occur regionally, as can be seen with the Regional Sports Boards and County Sports Partnerships and in some regions the Community Sport Networks. sports coach UK serves coaches and recreation consortia such as Regional Sports Boards which co-ordinate work at a regional level. They are also examples of organisations that operate at different levels.

- *Local.* Ultimately CSD is most often delivered at a local level and often in a specific geographical area. At this point there are greater differences in delivery as CSD focuses and sets priorities to support specific local needs. Policy may have trickled down from organisations working at wider levels, but practice and micro-policy are generally adapted to suit those specific needs. There are also organisations and individuals who work at a purely local level like the Langley Youth Project (Morgan, 2000) or a local youth worker or CSD officer. CSNs are likely to take a more significant role at this level as they develop.

Levels of provision

Different levels of provision and different organisations can be plotted as a continuum, as shown in Figure 5.2. But a continuum indicates that organisations can be located or positioned beyond and in between the four levels reflected by their scale of operations. Readers might consider where other organisations they are familiar with could be plotted.

The mixed economy of provision

Another important aspect of CSD policy is that it occurs in all three sectors of the economy: commercial, public and voluntary. Some organisations operate exclusively in one single sector. But when it comes to specific projects, they are more often linked with organisations from more than one sector. Public sector links are more likely to create national and local public policy influences. Commercial sector links are more likely to create some form of marketing opportunity for the indirect generation of profits. Voluntary sector links are perhaps more likely to operate more flexibly and freely, as they are subject to less political scrutiny, accountability and interference. Figure 5.3 incorporates the three sectors of provision as well as levels of provision. Organisations from specific sectors have been shown on the diagram. Once again the reader might consider where other organisations would be plotted.

Partnerships

Specific initiatives involve partnerships and incorporate involvement from organisations from different sectors. A hypothetical initiative, X, with equal involvement from all three

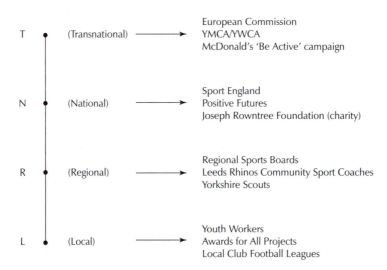

Figure 5.2 The levels of provision continuum

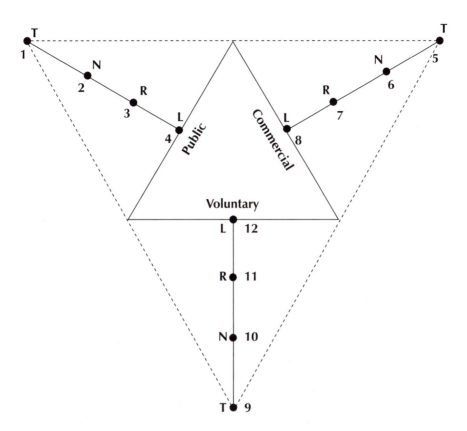

Figure 5.3 The sectors and levels of provision framework

1 European Commission (transnational, T). *2* Sport England (national, N). *3* Regional sports boards (regional, R). *4* Youth workers (local, L). *5* McDonald's 'Be active' campaign (T). *6* Sainsbury's 'Active kids' vouchers (N). *7* Leeds Rhinos community coaches (R). *8* Local business sponsorship (L). *9* YMCA, YWCA (T). *10* Joseph Rowntree Foundation (N). *11* Yorkshire Scouts (R). *12* Local club football leagues (L).

sectors is shown in Figure 5.4. The hypothetical initiative is placed at the centre of the diagram. An initiative with more emphasis from one sector would be placed closer to that particular axis. Another hypothetical initiative, Y, is placed to demonstrate stronger involvement from the public and voluntary sectors, with only partial involvement implied from the commercial sector.

The diagram can be used to reveal how ultimately any initiative's operations are the product of complex interrelationships with a variety of partners. Most initiatives owe their mode of operations as an outcome of complex networks of influence. The reader may choose to consider an initiative they are familiar with or wish to understand a little better. First identifying partners and then using the diagram, the reader can weigh and assess contributory influences upon the project overall and locate where the balance of power falls.

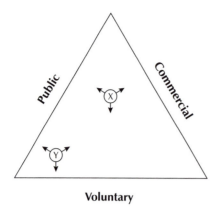

Figure 5.4 Partnership domain framework

Structure and organisation of provision

Any ideal model should incorporate elements of each of the previous diagrams. Such a model would enable a vigorous analysis of the structure of CSD policy provision, and enable comparative analyses of organisations, initiatives and partnerships. Such a model, the 'CSD matrix', is shown in Figure 5.5.

To follow the matrix the reader should recognise that a 'Toblerone'-type hybrid has been assembled from the previous diagrams. An appropriate metaphor would be 'origami'. Imagine the base of the matrix is the 'partnership domain framework' diagram, which can also be seen as the central triangle in the 'sectors and levels of provision framework'. Next, three squares of the models are folded up to form external walls. Thus in '3-D' the partnerships domain permeates every point, top to bottom along the continua, like the message in a stick of seaside rock.

As digital technology and communications develop the reader may have access to this book and this model through virtual reality. One could explore the matrix as though excavating one of the ancient pyramids! Different CSD organisations and initiatives could be understood, or located, at different points and levels in three dimensions. The matrix offers a holistic way of understanding each of the previously discussed elements of structure, provision and policy. So, despite the limitations of a one-dimensional text, it is perhaps worthwhile to consider where further analysis would locate other initiatives on this matrix.

Any consideration of the complexities of CSD will emphasise ambiguities. Utilising the models enables sensitivity to generic issues that must be considered if CSD is to be critically examined across sport and disparate settings. Applying models necessitates a rigorous analysis, which in turn develops a deeper understanding of practice.

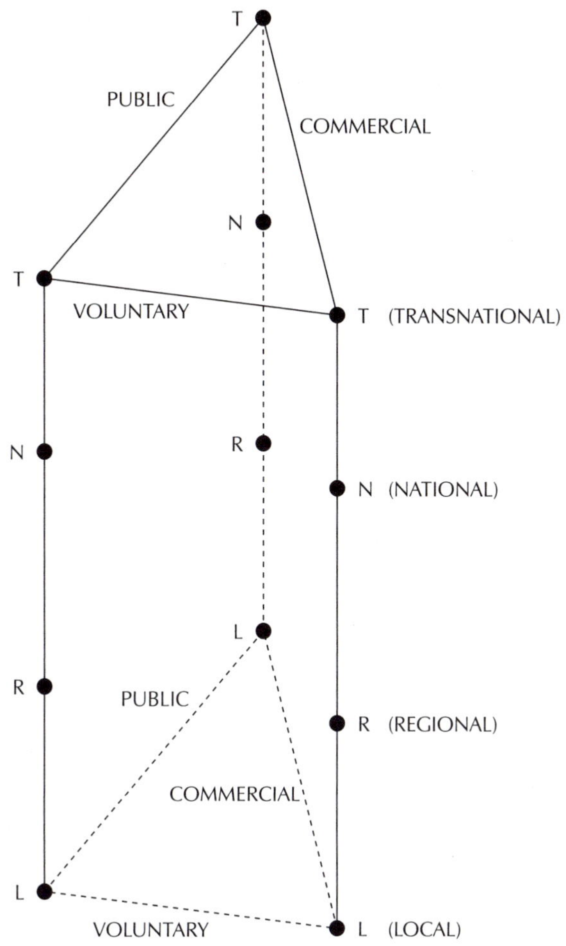

Figure 5.5 CSD matrix

Source Adapted from the 'structural dimensions of provision' matrix in Hylton and Totten (2001: 74).

Factors affecting 'situated practice'

There are many unique differences across CSD projects, due to individuals, organisations, networks, partnerships and stakeholders operating at different levels and within sectors. These characteristics can be considered further using the Situated Community Sports Development model (Figure 5.6). This model illustrates how CSD will operate in different ways as individual practice will differ due to particular circumstances and how personnel interpret the priorities for their project. In addition, the project (or organisation linked with a project) may have resources, policies or practices that will have some bearing on how service development and delivery then operates. This may be further exacerbated by other political and environmental factors that might include stakeholders, funders, client groups and communities. The outcome of these influences is the *situated practice* of CSD which may explain idiosyncrasies demonstrated in the same projects but in different settings and contexts. As a dialectical model, each factor affects the other in a dynamic

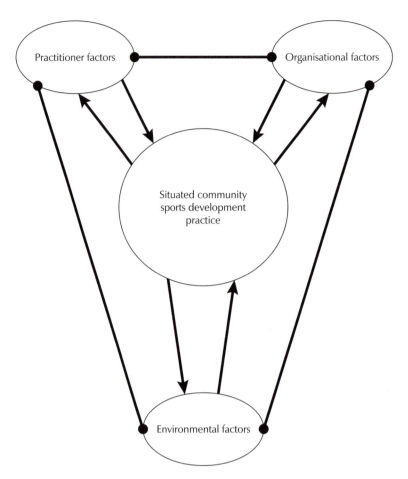

Figure 5.6 Situated community sports development practice

Source Adapted from Hudson (2004).

fashion: for example, changes to staffing, policies or stakeholders will have a relative effect on the practice of CSD in each project.

COMMUNITY SPORTS DEVELOPMENT POLICY

Historical overview

Community sports development is a practice, a policy direction and in particular a philosophy of provision which has developed since the late 1970s. News of its death in the early 1990s (see Lentell, 1994; McDonald, 1995) was premature! CSD persists and thrives in a number of diverse settings and contexts. Despite the political shifts in the 1990s which made CSD policy seem less fashionable in some quarters, continuity existed elsewhere. In difficult times the CSD torch was often carried by other non-sports-specific practitioners like youth workers or by specific sports initiatives at a very local level. One idea that CSD occurs only in local government sport and recreation departments is an error easily made as the most prominent face of CSD is local and often visible in that public sector context. However, this is a narrow view of CSD. More recent developments around neighbourhood renewal, social exclusion and the Policy Action Teams' activity have led to a closer melding of government department agendas. This has meant that community sports development is now but one tool to be used in tackling a range of social issues (DCMS, 1999; Home Office, 1999). There is a need to sketch a bigger picture for practitioners and students alike. Awareness of the way people and organisations work in this policy network is often how good practice gets communicated. In some cases these links might seem as though they have cut across unconnected parts of the service sector, when in reality there is much more in common than at first glance.

CSD was initially seen as a challenge to traditional ways of approaching provision for disadvantaged groups; it was almost a counter-culture. The emphasis on community practice in public services is almost a paradox as the turn to community approaches is often a tactic to ameliorate failures of mainstream provision. It is apparent that in policy systems that are dysfunctional in some way it becomes necessary to offer remedial treatment. In a way community sports development is a side effect or 'by-product' of sports development. The change in emphasis from facility-based sport to community sport and recreation has proved to be effective. In the past this shift persuaded many to 'take on board' ideas by mainstreaming projects, and/or project philosophy into more established units. Consequently, in recent times demarcations between established and what were emergent ways of providing sport and recreation opportunities for most priority groups in society are much less obvious. In reality the current use of the term 'community sport' is almost as ubiquitous as the term 'community' in other areas of social provision. It invokes positive images of considerate client-orientated practice. When **sport**scotland considered sport they considered both community recreation, which they see as the 'informal world of sport', and sport development, which is part of the 'more formal world of sport' (Scottish Sports Council, 1998). The validity of both forms of provision is now unquestioned and they are characterised as 'co-dependent', which is both pragmatic and redolent of the way community sport and community recreation are practised today.

Community sports development grew out of the roots of post-1975 Howell angst which was critical of massive local authority and Sports Council-driven facility build throughout the country which was felt to be to the detriment of more personal community provision. 'People, not bricks' was an ideal which came through quite clearly in London, where it transpired that the major users of facilities, like the Brixton Sport Centre, were mainly white middle-class males from outside the area. Many of the local community felt the centre to be unwelcoming and not a facility they could identify with (Murray, 1988).

Lessons like those learnt in Brixton were occurring all over the UK. However, it took a dramatic series of events culminating in severe social disturbances and a reaction from the government before massive resources were poured into what many practitioners saw as the first recognisable community sports projects. It was no coincidence that young people were targeted in the rush to reduce actual and perceived threats of crime and antisocial behaviour. Ironically, a closer look at the areas affected by the urban unrest showed that they were, in reality, deprived of most social welfare services. The Midlands and London were chosen as areas for the pilot projects of Action Sport to see if there was a way for sport to defuse tensions in inner-city areas which had been scenes of civil unrest in the early 1980s. At that time, the use of focusing on target groups achieved prominence, although, for practitioners involved in good practice, this came as no surprise. Young people, the unemployed, women, black and other minority ethnic groups, disabled people and the elderly were targeted in a combination of partnerships between local government and central government.

The success of the pilots was such that they became national projects wherever partnerships, like those with Action Sport, could be formed. Indeed, evaluations of Action Sport nationally and regionally were very positive (Macintosh and Charlton, 1985; Rigg, 1986). Overall, researchers were unanimous in commenting that leadership skills, outreach and active consultation resulted in successful ways of identifying low and non-participants and ensuring regular sports participation. National demonstration projects built on the success of the Action Sport and Community Recreation initiatives. Target groups were strategically mapped on to each initiative in an effort to reproduce the success of these projects in different contexts. The Coventry Active Lifestyles project, the Solent Sports Counselling initiative and the Scunthorpe Black and Ethnic Minority project are three examples of the evolution of CSD policy, process and practice (Sports Council, 1991).

Community sports development, or community recreation, as it has been known, went through a period of enlightenment in the 1980s, where new forms of knowledge and ideas about community recreation and CSD were tried and the results disseminated. As Lentell (1994) and McDonald (1995) attest, the 1990s were not a constructive time for mass participation and Sport for All as the Conservative government became more focused on school sport and excellence. The devolution of mass participation goals to local authorities meant a lack of leadership nationally on inclusive sport which was clearly successful, if resource intensive, but politically not a vote winner for the struggling Conservatives (Houlihan and White, 2002). Further, the pressure on local authorities to be more competitive and more accountable for their sport and leisure provision meant a withdrawal from more traditional areas of provision that had been the safety net for infrequent participants and those in a pre-contemplation stage of participation (McDonald, 1995).

A corollary of this timeline is that post-1997, with the election of a Labour government, and through the 2000s to date, community sports development has become higher profile and better supported. There has been a sharpening of ideas around core issues that have challenged many in community sports development. Social exclusion, community cohesion, social networking, and sustainable community development, the development of communities through sport and the development of sport through communities are policy slogans that have made prominent appearances in substantive sections of national-level

kevin hylton and mick totten

policies (DCMS, 1999, 2001; Cabinet Office, 2002; Sport England, 2004). More significantly, many of these dimensions of sport and social policy have been supported by resources and political will. Community sports development is now on the agenda in a more comprehensive way than ever before and although CSD has 'never had it so good' there is sufficient evidence to demonstrate that this is just the start that practitioners and policy makers need to capitalise on.

Community sports development settings

The overwhelming majority of community sports initiatives have been funded by the state. This has been directly from central government, indirectly through non-governmental public bodies, and most often by local government. The former Sports Council has played a role as a lead body developing policies and directing provision. Community sport has operated as an arm of the Sports Council's aim of 'Sport for All?', but community sports provision has seldom been funded in its own right and has been legitimated for more instrumental reasons (Houlihan and White, 2002; Collins and Kay, 2003). Sport has been viewed largely from the standpoint of the social function it fulfils, and is as much a part of social policy as it is of sports policy. Nationally, Action Sport has been a demonstrative project which has legitimated the role sport can play in urban regeneration by 'super-concentration' on a few streets (MacIntosh and Charlton, 1985; Glyptis, 1989). This social agenda for community sport has been particularly well documented (Sports Council, 1982; MacIntosh and Charlton, 1985; DoE, 1989; Haywood and Kew, 1989; Yorkshire and Humberside Council for Sport and Recreation, 1989; Houlihan, 2002; Collins and Kay, 2003). Whilst more recently Sport Action Zones and Active Communities projects have progressed more unconventional but innovative and successful techniques further.

The public, commercial and voluntary sectors all have influenced the paths CSD has taken. Voluntary groups, clubs and societies are often the independent face of community sports development. The scale of voluntary sector organisations is such that they range from small local organisations, such as a new 'Little London Baseball Club', to national/internationally linked organisations such as the YMCA and YWCA. The Sports Volunteering in England survey (Sport England, 2002) clearly outlined how voluntary clubs provide a safety net for people who engage in activities which tend to be niche-orientated. This means that the private sector does not see a profitable market there nor can the public sector provide a coherent rationale for supporting those specialist activities. Even in the area of volunteering, the Institute for Volunteering Research (2004) are adamant that those responsible for sport have a challenging task to reduce inequalities.

Commercial sector CSD is often a more extrinsically driven affair where organisations such as professional football and rugby clubs work with schools, and other breeding grounds for talent identification, talent development, income generation, marketing and public relations. Some clubs have, in addition, also established community units as charities which then allow them to draw on the tax concessions and economies that this mode of operating affords to its owners. For example, West Ham United Football Club have added their support to the West Ham Asians in Sport project which should generate a number of positive outcomes for the club through reinforcing community links and widening its search for local talent in underrepresented communities (Active Communities, 2002). Leicester City Football Club has also used its community links to promote an anti-racist message through its support of the Foxes Against Racism (FAR) group. Such links with minority ethnic communities for professional clubs have been successful in forging close relationships but can also be seen as effective comprehensive marketing opportunities.

The public sector, where most CSD work occurs, is often actively implemented at a regional and at local level. Still, the range of interested parties is diverse. The Office of the Deputy Prime Minister's (2004) report into the joint working of sports organisations and those working in neighbourhood renewal gives some indication of the possible range of parties interested in CSD. The ODPM's agenda has identified what people in sport have known for some time, that there is a problem regarding sport participation in deprived areas and that there needs to be a more creative or radical approach. Recreation from a sport-specific view, but with a complementary social policy focus, may emanate from youth work, community work, housing, policing, sport, lifelong learning and recreation departments, arts workers, education, health services and related organisations.

MODELS OF COMMUNITY SPORTS DEVELOPMENT POLICY

Community sports development can be understood as a form of 'socio-cultural' intervention. Different policy models have characterised this mode of intervention. Subsequently five models will be explored: two 'social' models which illustrate the 'instrumental' use of sport, *social control*, and *social welfare*; and two 'cultural' models which illustrate attempts to extend the participatory franchise; *democratisation of culture*, and *cultural democracy*. A fifth political model which characterises the political motivations of some practitioners will also be explored, *radicalism*. It is the intention not for these models to be contrasted against one another exclusively but for them to be seen as operating simultaneously, and exhibiting varying degrees of influence. Individual projects are subject to different policy rationales and power struggles. Often they will feel pulled in different directions as they juggle different policy aims of partners, funders and policy makers. In this respect they reinforce the notion of CSD as a 'site of cultural and hegemonic struggle' (Hargreaves and McDonald, 2002) rather than one of static consensus. (The processes of hegemony and ideological consensus will be discussed later.) The state is able to form a coalition of support for its policies and unite diverse interests behind a dominant project. This approach offers an 'economy of remedies', a single solution to a variety of issues, all within one policy, with a broad base of support (Coalter *et al.*, 1986: 92).

Social control

Social control is performed by the state directly and indirectly, through organisations and institutions. The state intervenes directly to legislate for and against particular leisure forms. Sport is used explicitly as a form of social control. The Sports Council (1982: 3) openly believed 'Young people in sport don't throw bricks' and still does! This philosophy also continues within Positive Futures, which was established as a vehicle to use sport to reduce antisocial behaviour, crime and drug use among ten- to sixteen-year-olds in local neighbourhoods (Sport England, 2002). There are many local examples like the Bradford Sports Web project (Hylton, 2003), Hackney's Midnight Basketball (Sport England, 2002) and Wolverhampton's Midnight Soccer Leagues (Football Task Force, 1999) where sport is used to combat crime. Research reveals that the sports player tends to be conformist in nature (Coalter, 1991). The police have taken an open interest in involvement in community sport (Morgan, 2000). So much so that Carrington and Leaman (1983: 10) state, 'Community policing and community sport would appear to share an identical logic and perform an identical ideological function.' Sport is used as surrogate violence, channelling aggression into a socially acceptable activity. Hargreaves (1986) describes how community sport targets various categories of potential user, but it is clear that the main concern is the 'potentially troublesome'. Hargreaves goes on to argue how a cadre of sports leaders are developed, who are 'co-cultural' with users to enable infiltration and the exercise of influence by the dominant culture.

The final Cantle Report (2006) on the civil disturbances in Oldham made recommendations to develop sport and leisure services further to ease tensions and to enhance community cohesion. Similarly, the salient impetus for Action Sport nationally had been a response to the urban riots of the 1980s (Totten, 1993). The Action Sport workers from inner-city Leeds were overwhelmingly in agreement that they owed their existence to the riots there. One worker commented ironically that if there was another riot their budget would be doubled and applied the following metaphor, 'We act a little like community policemen . . . We walk the beat. We go back to our station house and fill in our forms.' Another worker said he felt responsible to motivate people to get a job. Yet another said that because Chapeltown (in the inner city) is known as a racially black area, politicians were responding in an institutionally racist way: by providing community sport *because* they were 'black'! Despite a clear awareness of their use as potential instruments of social control, Action Sport workers were uncomfortable with this role and recognised their own ability for resistance and to pursue and realise their own objectives; 'We're not just a bunch of "jolly non-whites" doing the bidding of faceless bureaucrats!' One worker pessimistically pointed out that drug pushers went back to their trade after doing their sport (a rather poignant failure of control over individual agency). Despite the fact that Action Sport workers were insistent that they promoted sport purely for fun, one worker observed, 'We may have far less freedom than we think.' Conscious of the controlling role of the state, and the role of Action Sport in that process, he commented that for community sport in the social context of the community as a whole, 'There are certain ways of behaving and attitudes towards people that have to be fostered, that are of paramount importance to the survival of the community, survival of the people.'

Social welfare

Sport England, and other government agencies, have often sought to integrate sport and social policy with much attention drawn to the importance of community sport as a form of social welfare (Lentell, 1994; Collins and Kay, 2003). Bernard Atha, when Vice-Chairman of the Sports Council (1978: 14), stated:

> Deprivation takes place in many forms – social, educational, cultural, housing, emotional, and recreational to mention just a few. This deprivation exists at great cost to our society, a cost most easily seen in terms of crime and vandalism, but more serious in terms of loneliness and alienation.

In similar mood, Glyptis (1989) points out that the 1975 White Paper on Sport and Recreation (HMSO, 1975) heralded a shift from policies of 'recreational welfare' to the use of 'recreation *as* welfare'. Dennis Howell (cited in Coalter *et al.*, 1986, when Minister of Sport) declared that without a social purpose sport would be irrelevant. The Association of Metropolitan Authorities (1989) viewed community sports as vital to community development. And as the new millennium dawned, nothing much had changed. As Chris Smith (1998), Secretary of State for Culture, Media and Sport, stated:

> Sport offers direct economic benefits. It contributes to the regeneration of towns and cities, improving health, productivity and quality of life. It contributes to savings in the cost of health care and leads to a reduction in crime and vandalism. It offers local environmental benefits that can change the image of a city or community and lead to increased inward investment.

Echoing this point in 2005 was the Chief Executive of Sport England, Roger Draper, who added the contribution that sport could make to quality of life, stronger, safer communities and the economy.

The value of sport is often trumpeted (Coalter, 2001), and often too optimistically and uncritically (Long and Sanderson, 2001; Collins and Kay, 2003), but nevertheless it continues to prompt considerable swathes of policy. Action Sport workers have paid great attention to the value of their work in terms of social welfare and the contribution it could make to the quality of life of their users (Totten, 1993). Workers described how people gained a sense of achievement and self-determination which they could apply to other areas of their lives. People were able to enjoy themselves, to self-actualise and increase their feeling of self-worth. Action Sport workers agreed that they were facilitating people's right to the opportunity to participate. Community sports initiatives certainly have the potential to bring about change in people's lives, but individual projects are more likely to stimulate personal change than effect any structural change.

Democratisation of culture

The democratisation of culture model is most commonly talked of in relation to community arts but can equally be applied to CSD. The concept of the democratisation of culture presumes a single national sports culture. This culture, though not fully appreciated, understood or participated in by large sections of the population, can be spread from the top downwards. This process can be described as the demystification, or clarification, of the value of participation (Totten,1993). Sport is promoted as a source of national pride. CSD can act as a tool to overcome social and perceptual barriers, and in some cases to demystify negative perceptions or limited knowledge of sport and recreation, through participation. Some community sports initiatives are premised on the idea that communities are a homogeneous entity and aim to integrate those unattached into participation (Hargreaves, 1986; Fremeaux, 2005). By extending the franchise to participation through CSD and its 'soft' integration into sport, the then enlightened participant can cultivate the sports habit. Continued participation might then lead participants towards mainstream provision. Examples of this would include the Cities Tennis Programme in Liverpool (Morgan, 2000) and many Football in the Community projects whereby mainstream organisations venture into the community attempting to improve 'sporting literacy'. They present established forms of sports that are largely the same as practised elsewhere. Freedom to choose is presented here with an implicit constraint. As such they propagate the dominant culture of institutionalised sport. This resonates with the 'old wine in new bottles' argument (Haywood and Kew, 1989) referred to earlier.

Two Action Sport workers in Leeds felt that it could be a 'stepping stone' or 'foundation' towards integration into mainstream sport (Totten, 1993). Another example would be the way Sport England gives preferential treatment to approving certain sports for funding, like the Outdoor Basketball Initiative. In macro-policy terms, this has the overall effect of lending greater legitimacy to some forms of sporting activity than others.

Cultural democracy

The model of cultural democracy is in part a critique of the democratisation of culture, which is seen as a paternalistic and elitist idea (Simpson, 1976a; Parry, 1986). The democratisation of culture can thus become 'a foredoomed and wasteful effort to graft an alien culture on to tissue where it cannot thrive' (Simpson, 1976b: 50). Cultural democracy describes a more fundamental challenge to the means of provision. It interprets provision as going beyond the consumption of traditional institutionalised forms of sport. Sports like rugby league have been adapted for wheelchair users and judo for blind participants. Judo was also adapted by Armley Disabled Judo Group, in Leeds, when young people with differing disabilities adapted the sport so that techniques with a lowest common denominator were incorporated into their own tailor-made more inclusive grading system. Cultural democracy also advocates devolution of power away from centralised agencies and back to the people. It argues for a plurality of access to means of provision and against passive consumption. The Armley group were not affiliated to any mainstream judo body and functioned quite happily on their own. There are 'gay football' networks which operate semi-autonomously from the FA (Stonewall, 2006) and similarly organised 'Asian cricket leagues' (Carrington and McDonald, 2001).

Cultural democracy supports the finding of the 'Leisure and the quality of life experiments' (DoE, 1977: 161) that:

> The lessons of the experiments may be that a true community applies its development opportunities across the whole spectrum of interest groups rather than in trying to provide a homogenised mass leisure.

It is in recognition of the special needs of subcultures and sub-groups that a cultural democracy is proposed. It calls for a decentralised and more democratic and representative structure of sport and leisure management, allowing effective participation in decision making by the community (DoE, 1989). Devolved strategies promote ownership by, and co-authorship with, the community.

Action Sport workers described how they have provided an organisational framework for the community and have employed animation techniques to give people 'the drive to get up and go', a 'sort of injection' (Totten, 1993). One worker described Action Sport as a 'local sports council'. Workers were critical of the notion of a homogeneous national culture and of policy which was over-prescriptive. A worker pointed out that integration could be oppressive for some Asian women who could see it as infringing their right to their beliefs. 'People should be aware of others' cultural needs. If people were aware of those differences it helps, not just sport, but many other things as well.' Workers described how over time the project has become much more community-led. Representation has been valued, particularly in relation to ethnicity and gender, and has been promoted in appointments, decision making, programme planning and activity leading. In this way the project strives to remain co-cultural with its community.

Radicalism

In contrast to the four previously state-sanctioned models of community leisure, radicalism represents an intervention in the community which is politicised *against*, rather than on behalf of, the state. Whereas cultural democracy emphasises a challenge to cultural values, radicalism emphasises a challenge to social and political values. One sustained attempt to implement a radical cultural agenda by the state was that of the Greater London Council between 1981 and 1986 (Bianchinni, 1989). This was extraordinary cultural action by the local state in defiance of the national state, although smaller conflicts of interest between national and local government are still widespread in an era of excruciating and centralised accountability. Radical cultural agendas in Britain have mainly been carried out by small groups or individuals within larger organisations. Frustrated by conventional approaches with their enslaved accountability to political masters and an inherent bureaucracy, some CSD workers will act outside the view of those authorities. The 'Street Sport' project, Stoke on Trent (Morgan, 2000), employs innovative and unconventional methods to bypass conventional restrictions. Also an Action Sport worker saw himself as infiltrating with an agenda to change (Totten, 1993). He was conscious of his ability to resist and interpret 'top-down' policy and carry out his own mission, saying, 'the bosses don't visit the coal face'. Basically he would 'do his own thing' beyond surveillance. At a later interview, he corrected, 'It's not radical at all. It's very liberal.' He went on to say that there was a potential for radicalism but it can't be made public! He described using 'dual language' as 'one for bureaucrats and one for practitioners'. Action Sport illustrated a potential for opposition to the dominant hegemonic order, but also highlighted the difficulties of resisting assimilation as well as risks of marginalisation or expulsion.

There is a history of radicalism in community arts which is not equalled in the history of community sports (Kelly, 1984). This does not mean that there is no potential for radical action in community sports. Such activists exist in CSD, but their profiles are predominately covert. Sport does not share the historical tradition of protest that the arts have. Many still believe sport and politics do not mix. So activists in CSD may jeopardise their longevity if they raise their heads too high above the parapet. For many it is about infiltration and subversion rather than revealing their true colours. So for a theoretical framework from which to view radicalism it is more profitable to consider community arts.

Kelly (1984) maintains that the role of community arts is to 'topple capitalism'. Kelly advises that community artists should explore alternative modes of cultural production, distribution and reception, and have a clear analysis of their work as part of a revolutionary programme committed to cultural democracy:

> Storm the citadels, and tear them down brick by brick; to demolish the oppressive and imperialist structures and to build in their place a series of smaller haciendas where activity and participation are encouraged and welcomed, and the only activity which is prohibited is the building of citadels.
>
> (Kelly, 1984: 138)

Kelly's analogy applied to sport implies a programme of infiltration by practitioners with political motivations, and subversion by those workers and participants against the domi-nant institutional culture within sport. Namely they might seek to undermine conservative practices and values inherent in organisations governing sport. Ledwith (2005) advocates 'radical community action' as necessary to redress inequalities inherent in current society. She cites Chomsky (2003: 236) to convey the need to be 'challenging the reigning ideological system and seeking to create constructive alternatives of thought, action and institutions'.

Although all CSD workers are involved to varying degrees with disadvantaged groups, radicals embrace a more overwhelming ideological commitment to social change than others. Examples would include Marxists committed to the redistribution of sporting resources towards the working class, feminists committed to working with women towards challenging the prevailing gender order in sport, and also black activists committed to the advancement of black culture, representation, and countering racism in sport.

There are also examples of 'radical networks' which operate outside the sight and control of mainstream provision. In football, teams like the Easton Cowboys (2006) in Bristol, the 1 in 12 Club (2006) in Bradford and Republica Internationale (2006) in Leeds are anti-capitalist organisations. They have stronger allegiances with other like-minded European organisations like Sankt Pauli Football Club (2006) in Hamburg and events like the Anti-racist World Cup (2006) than they do with the English Football Association or more commercialised non-political events. Radicalism may be well hidden or even obscure but it is out there!

COMMUNITY SPORTS PRACTICE

Community sports development is characterised by its approach to service planning, delivery and practice. CSD is a movement away from mainstream or dominant sports provision with their focus on performance and excellence and historical failure to reach all. CSD focuses on the initial threshold to sports participation. CSD is a reaction against elitism and inequality; it is person- or community-centred. There is recognition of the structural barriers to participation discussed in Chapter 4 and access and inclusion are promoted. Disadvantaged groups are identified and prioritised or targeted. Haywood and Kew (1989) emphasise the flexible, proactive style and process of community sport. Community sport is more empathetic and focuses more on the participant and partic-ipatory processes. As such sport is often merely a means towards these developmental aims. Consultation is valued to determine and be responsive to expressed needs and wants, and so to extend the participatory franchise. In that sense community sports development tends to adopt a distinct, less formal, more flexible management style. It is a movement away from 'top-down' deterministic models of provision towards 'bottom-up' community-led provision. Decision making is more devolved to enable community participation. In that sense the community and provider may become co-authors of destiny or partners in policy and practice. In the main, community sport workers attempt to empower through advocacy, facilitation and enablement.

From the early 1980s Action Sport conformed fairly comfortably with this common understanding of community sport (Totten, 1993). It promoted a sense of informality and a feeling of ownership among participants. A worker explains 'We try to cater for people on their own terms.' Action Sport started offering established mainstream activities, but left space and has successfully provided for other activities like chairobics and kabbadi. These principles are still identified as characteristics of best practice in CSD and have been identified by Coalter (2002) in his summary of good practice in planning, delivery and participants in CSD. Action Sport is about enjoyment. Fun is stressed repeatedly as the bottom line. Workers were critical of serious participation. Using their own conceptions of 'community' they described how community sport brings people together, contributing, in a general sense, to community spirit. Workers saw Action Sport as promoting socialising and interaction, and making people happier. Action Sport is concerned with the development process from start to finish, although participation is most important as ultimately that determined if people came back again. The basis of Action Sport is social and the consultation process is important in developing the sense of ownership. Action Sport provides an organisational framework sometimes lacking in a local community. It emphasises an initial pitch of low-ability requirements as the threshold to participation. Any ability fostered towards excellence is channelled towards other forms of provision. Through their unconventional, proactive, outreach work Action Sport and other such initiatives bridge the gap in participation between people and facilities. The challenge for CSD is to promote a philosophy that participation in sport and recreation is positive, and to extend the participatory franchise within the local community.

Bradford Sports Web

The Bradford Sports Web (Hylton, 2003) initiative gives a picture of a CSD context which can be considered in the light of the previous 'CSD Matrix'. The partners involved are: (1) *public sector*: the Department of the Environment through SRB funding, Bradford City Council's Sport and Recreation Division Sports Development section, as well as the Education Department's Youth and Community Youth Sports Development Project, and the West Yorkshire Police linked with the diversionary 'Dynamo Project', (2) *voluntary sector*: the Manningham area community.

CASE STUDY 5.1

BRADFORD SPORTS WEB PROJECT

The Bradford Sports Web Project is a partnership between the West Yorkshire Police, Bradford Recreation Service, Youth Sports Development Project and ostensibly the local Manningham Community.

Manningham is a multicultural area with a high minority ethnic population. The project is part of a Single Regeneration Budget (SRB) bid which focuses on areas of disadvantage.

It is intended to use sport here as a tool for social regeneration and inclusion in what is planned to be a long-term strategy and commitment by a number of key agencies in the managing and development of sport in Bradford.

Main objectives

- To plan, deliver and develop a *sustainable programme of sport, recreational and diversionary activities* which is appropriate and accessible to the whole community and *delivered by the community*.
- To consult and provide support to the community (Manningham, Bradford) to ensure that its sporting needs are catered for.
- To promote new and innovative lifestyle messages within the local community.
- To encourage the provision of educational and training opportunities in sport and recreation within the local community.
- To ensure equality of opportunity for everyone but particularly to target young people from excluded groups.

Consultation

The project partners intend to consult local people with an overview of the project. Outcomes include identifying local people to (a) run sessions where they have the skills, (b) be trained up where they do not have the skills, or (c) there are personal development issues.

Outreach

The Sports Web project plans to use the techniques of outreach working which has always been seen as effective in sports development. Outreach working in geographical areas has been seen as most successful and cost-effective where local facilities, services and people are utilised as often as possible. This has the added benefit of less formal systems and pricing policies being introduced which are conducive to flexible working and positive local word-of-mouth promotion.

The police intend to direct young people on to the programme where they have been convicted or are on probation as part of a subsidiary 'Dynamo' project. These young people will be counselled into the project as participants and, where they show potential, eventually as motivators and leaders.

Further, the *levels* of involvement could be explained using the idea of the project's complementary social function where one key objective is that of social regeneration and inclusion. The issue of social regeneration through sport is an ideal which has come through the sports policy community strongly from the *transnational* European Community, especially through European Social Funding (ESF). *Nationally* a key policy influence in this case study has come via the government's social exclusion policies and *regionally* through the inclusion of West Yorkshire Police in the *local* (Bradford) Sports Web project.

So the Bradford Sports Web can be contextualised as a local community sports development project with local, regional and national partners, mainly drawn from the public and voluntary sectors. Similarly, influences for the project can be logically traced back to the EC.

For many years CSD has been subject to pointed questions concerning the utilitarian way in which key agents approach provision. Queries which suggest that CSD engages in *ad hoc* and piecemeal provision might be given some credence here where the objective of working towards social regeneration through one sole project, in an area of high social and economic deprivation, would seem beyond their sole responsibility. In addition, diversionary projects are regularly asked to prove how they have enhanced the capacity for young people to move away from crime or local trouble. This has often been seen to be very difficult for most!

Community sports development for the Senior Outdoor Development Manager in Bradford's Sports Web is about empowering the community to take control of its own needs. This is done by training members to run activities for themselves or at the very least to develop a healthy lifestyle as a result of contact with the project. The notion of redistributing power and quality-of-life benefits is an important aspect of community development which sometimes provides the common ground for multi-agency working. Liddle (1988: 199) develops this point when giving an overview of youth and leisure services in Avon County Council.

The idea of sustainable sports programmes has come through good practice in CSD from the very first Action Sport programmes in the early 1980s through to the more recent Sports Action Zones and Active Communities Project. What programmes like Action Sport failed to do was to make individuals and sessions independent quickly enough. This often meant that the overall input of resources needed to work towards this objective was very high and many organisations found they could not sustain the level of commitment needed, even though many successes were evident.

The Community Sport Team, Leeds

In this case study of the Community Sport Team, CSD is very much local government-orientated. Partners in other sectors and at different levels are drawn upon according to the specific needs of a local community. CSD here involves a mixture of objectives, in particular opportunities for young people across the city and, in addition, black people in the inner urban areas. The scale of the Community Sport Team in Leeds is much larger than Bradford Sports Web in that it is a city-wide, mainstream unit, building upon the vast experience of its Sports Development Unit and Action Sport. Both have a long history of work from sports-specific development to community development through sport and recreation.

THE COMMUNITY SPORT TEAM, LEEDS

The Learning and Leisure Department in Leeds is split into eight divisions to deliver its services including: arts and heritage, libraries, parks and countryside, sport and active recreation, early years, jobs and skills and youth support. It has three groups of services and these are the Recreation group, the Libraries Arts and Heritage group, and the Learning group. Within the Recreation group is Sport and Active Recreation, which is also split into three sections:

- Facilities section.
- Business and Service Development.
- Sports Development.

The Sports Development Unit (SDU) works with local communities, schools, voluntary sports clubs, national governing bodies and public sector agencies to support the development of sporting opportunities from grass roots through to excellence. The Community Sport Team is part of the SDU.

The Community Sport Team in Leeds is an important part of the overall sports strategy. The team enhances the link between the SDU, which has a broad remit to develop sport from the grass roots and to increase participation. Leeds is a city in the north of England with a diverse population of 750,000 who are split into five public service 'wedges'. The wedges cover inner urban areas to rural ex-mining villages. This range of areas and priority groups means that each CSD officer in each wedge must be very sensitive to local demands and needs.

Main aims

- Co-ordinate activities in the community with other key partners.
- Support and advise voluntary sports clubs and other locally based groups.
- Work with the School Sports Partnerships to develop new opportunities for children and young people.
- Advise organisations about funding.
- Develop volunteering opportunities and organise Sport Leadership courses.

When the Community Sport Team started, the CSD Officers spent twelve to eighteen months gathering information about the Leeds communities. CSD officers were given the remit to 'know their area' so that plans and strategies would be informed in consultation with local communities and meet local needs. There was seen to be no 'quick fix' for success and it was accepted that there were similar projects in the past which have almost been panicked into producing results immediately, therefore not having a solid foundation for long-term development. The Community Sport Team has taken on board evaluations of good and bad practice and has moved forward confident that its information and plans have a grounded rationale.

Recent work

- *Developing clubs*. Coach education and funding support for local clubs.
- *Developing volunteers*. Outreach coaching courses for volunteers to help empower communities and ensure sustainability.
- *Developing events*. Holiday, taster and sports programmes are run at different points of the year for a range of social groups.
- *Developing Projects in the community*. The Community Sport Team staff run the Positive Futures diversionary sport and educational programmes for the most at-risk young people.
- *Developing Leeds*. Priority resources have been reserved for women/girls, black and minority ethnic groups, the disabled and those most at risk of social exclusion.

The Community Sport Team has been involved in other projects aimed to encourage more people to take part in sport and physical activity. Two examples of these are:

- Cross Flatts project in Leeds for young people and adults using the newly developed park facilities. Local partners supported the project, which encouraged hundreds of children from Beeston and the surrounding areas to take part in a range of sports activities (Council Area Committee and Neighbourhood Renewal funding).
- The West Leeds Project, which facilitated a closer working of sport, the police and the youth service to engage young people aged thirteen to nineteen (Active Community Development Fund).

We acknowledge the support of Paul Senior, the Community Sport Team Development Officer, in compiling this summary.

The Community Sport Team in Leeds is influenced at all levels and across all sectors in diverse ways according to the setting of the activity/initiative in the city. The imperative for joint working for the Community Sport Team means that it needs to be able to work with voluntary, commercial and public sector agents to fulfil the needs of its communities.

Shared practice

Notions of sport and recreation are problematised in both case study organisations in Leeds and Bradford. Both take a wider emancipatory view of purposive leisure activity, and diversion where young people are concerned. This generates another accusatory chorus against CSD workers as acting as 'soft police' – indeed, policing on behalf of concerned citizens and controlling the way young people behave and act. In the past, providers have argued that giving people the opportunity to play sport as a diversion from their daily activity allows them to do something constructive and yet different in the time. However, doubts are expressed that this will alleviate crime, or act as a palliative for negative social and economic conditions. In 1977 this functional view was adopted in a Department of the Environment report on recreation and deprivation in inner-city areas and it was a message coming through clearly from the government in 1999 when community sport was being seen as a way of tackling serious social problems (Banks, 1998). Indeed, Glyptis (1989) suggested that this view has been prominent in sport for a number of years:

> The promotion of opportunities for enjoyment has long been paralleled by a belief that recreation opportunities can help to contain urban problems, to build a sense of community, and to overcome class and other social conflicts.
>
> (Glyptis, 1989: 42)

What has been missing from similar claims is evidence of causal relationships between project aims and activities, and any significant change (See Hylton and Totten, and Long, in this edition). Chapter 4 discussed the merits of qualitative information gathering as a means of understanding the collective experience of individuals and community members. Here information can be gathered to test ideals like active citizenship, social regeneration, social cohesion and capacity building. CSD practitioners and policy makers who move beyond sport's reliance on quantitative measurements will have a more rounded view of the success of projects which carry such ambitious objectives. These points were endorsed by the recommendations on sport and social exclusion in 1999 (PAT 10): qualitative measures were advocated as ways to understanding the impact of projects from the experience of participants. They were seen as an essential part of the monitoring of active community initiatives.

Will measuring throughputs enable the Cleveland 'Reach for Success' basketball project to claim that they have reduced levels of boredom, vandalism, peer pressure and intimidation as stated in their aims? The project is attempting to get 20,000 young people to play basketball in five years. Will they be able to support claims unless they use qualitative means of gathering information? The Policy Action Team (10) might argue otherwise and clearly this is a challenge for all sports development professionals to grasp (Freeman, 1999: 13).

Both the case study organisations above espouse a 'bottom-up' way of working or client-led delivery and facilitation. The imperative on both organisations to consult and work in tandem with local people is paramount. In each case active citizenship means people in Leeds and Bradford claiming or reclaiming access to resources for sport and recreation. It also means taking ownership of their own and other people's sport and recreation opportunities and working towards addressing quality-of-life and lifestyle issues in a bid to enhance social inclusion and cohesion. Is it enough to gain an understanding of this personal and social change through collecting statistical data?

In summary, both case studies have different pressures on them. What is clear from the 'CSD matrix', however, is that when professionals discuss community sports development there is now a clear need to clarify whether it is policy, process or practice which is the precise focus of discussion. In addition, the scale, context and levels are all important factors in the way organisations and individuals operate in community sports development.

RECONCEPTUALISING COMMUNITY SPORTS DEVELOPMENT

This chapter has discussed key concepts and considered key dimensions to provision, policy and practice. In so doing it has revealed a complexity in pinpointing exactly what CSD is, how it works, what it does and who does it. Having already explored some of these issues, the remaining section will endeavour to pull these often divergent strands together into a coherent whole. To do so it will employ the concept of 'hegemony' as central to the analysis of CSD.

As highlighted earlier, there are various key themes which must be accounted for:

- CSD is a 'contested concept' which has sometimes been used solely as a 'flag of convenience'.
- The CSD policy community ranges from local to regional to national and even transnational.
- Provision is often founded on a partnership between organisations with different motivations.
- There is a capacity for different individuals engaged in the same work to have politically diverse and opposing motives.
- Policy and provision can be orchestrated either as 'top-down' or 'bottom-up'.
- There are tensions between social welfare and social control, community empowerment and soft policing.
- There are tensions in social and cultural policy between community development and sport development.

Hegemony

Hegemony is a socio-cultural process which also takes account of political and economic processes (Hargreaves, 1982). It is central to theorising around CSD and community development (Ledwith, 2005). Hegemony encompasses cultural relations and implies some form of dynamic or dialogue of power relations between and across people and organisations. Hegemony can occur 'vertically', between the powerful and weak, or the dominant and subordinate. For example, between the service provider and the community, or between Sport England and the national governing bodies or between the local authority sports development unit and individual CSD workers. But it can also occur horizontally, across governing bodies, between departments in the same organisation or, indeed, between workers within the same initiative. Hegemony is a 'lived system of meanings and values . . . It thus constitutes a sense of reality for most people in society, a sense of absolute "because experienced" reality. It is, that is to say, in the strongest sense a "culture" which has also to be seen as the lived dominance and subordination of particular groups' (Williams, 1977: 110). As a socio-cultural process, hegemony permeates all aspects of the theory, policy and practice of CSD.

Hegemonic groups

There are different types of hegemonic groups who represent different interests in CSD and who have varying degrees of influence. McDonald (2002) is clear that it is not a simplistic struggle of powerful elites shaping sport into something only they wish to see. In recognition of these complexities, Raymond Williams (1977) categorises hegemonic groups as dominant, residual and emergent. These groups in turn can be evidenced either as traditions, institutions or formations. These provide a useful starting point for the analysis of the dynamics of CSD policy and practice. The notion of hegemonic groups or influences could be expanded to incorporate other aspects such as policy formation and agenda setting.

The reader might use the previous 'Sectors and Levels of Provision Framework' to identify hegemonic players. It is important to consider the following questions. Who works at what levels? What partners are organisations involved with? What is the precise role of the local community? (Even when it is historically marginalised, a notable absentee from much of the policy-making process!) What different priorities and agendas do organisations and individuals have? Who wields power and influence? The answers to these questions will allow you to begin your hegemonic analysis; to consider how power and hegemony can be experienced between organisations, within organisations and by community members.

Power, freedom and control

CSD works against inequality and discrimination. Any such work necessitates an analysis of who influences hegemonic power and how it can be challenged (Ledwith, 2005). Change will be sustainable only if communities are close to networks of power. This entails empowerment, 'power to the people'! Giving power to the community means taking it away from somewhere else, normally the providers (Taylor, 2000).

CSD is a paradoxical combination of control and planning through state intervention, and freedom, as expressed by the individual in sport or 'at leisure'. Sport is one discrete aspect of life over which people are believed to exercise considerable autonomy and freedom. If not, is it sport at all? This interpretation of sport as freedom is usually at odds with notions of state planning and control. There is an ambiguity of rights to participate in sport in coexistence with more prescriptive concerns to use sport more instrumentally. Long (1981), Gamble (1981) and Coalter (1989) have all described how all leisure, including sport, operates as a dichotomy riddled with *conceptual couples* such as 'liberation and control', 'freedom and constraint', 'the public and private sphere'. Long (1980) was satisfied that a coherent theory should be able to encompass dichotomies; so sport can be 'both a tool for community development and an opiate' which ameliorated deprivations. The sophisticated hegemonic state is quite aware of this dichotomy and does not hesitate to take cunning advantage of its utility. So it aims to exercise *control* over sport, and to promote *freedom* to participate in sport at the same time!

Community sports development must be understood in the context of both structure and agency as described in Chapter 4. Social structures influence the social context of sport even where individual human agents appear to 'choose' their own sports. Structure and agency work with and against one another to influence outcomes. CSD is sensitised to the needs of the community as perceived by the providers and as expressed from within the community. CSD is influenced structurally by provider organisations like Sport England or a local authority recreation department, and also by wider social reality, but it is flexible to adapt and respond to human agency determined by communities.

Hegemony accounts for those inherent contradictions, or dichotomies, apparent in the policy and practice of CSD. It acknowledges the role of both structure *and* agency (McDonald, 2002) implicit in the 'sphere of exchange' (Bennett, 1981a) between the provider and the community. It reconciles the situated practice between planning *and* participant autonomy in practice. It also describes a dialogue between 'top-down' and 'bottom up' dimensions of provision. CSD is complex; it simultaneously spans different intervention policies, and so achieves an 'economy of remedies' (Coalter *et al.*, 1986). This combination of rationales demonstrates the hegemonic power of dominant groups like Sport England, Regional Sports Boards and Community Sport Networks.

Previously cited models of CSD policy – four of which are most often forms of state-driven intervention (social control, social welfare, democratisation of culture and cultural democracy) – describe attempts by dominant cultures, manifested in institutions like sports governing bodies and local authorities, to influence the sports culture of communities. Historically, the Sports Council(s) have rarely legitimised sport as carefree enjoyment as experienced by most people. It has been preoccupied with externalities like the social order, health and so on rather than the cultural meaning of participation. Hegemony describes sport as a site of cultural struggle. This struggle takes place both independently in each of the previous intervention models and also interactively between them. Dominant culture is contested locally by workers in the field, and by the community itself.

For that reason the radical model of CSD was also introduced, as it can be understood as a hegemonic subculture, oppositional to the dominant order.

This perpetual conflict is acted out in CSD between dominant, residual and emergent cultural traditions, institutions and formations. Community sport can be a concession of power by the dominant hegemonic order. This can be seen as a means towards the incorporation of other more marginalised groups into the dominant culture. This position is supported by Hargreaves (n.d.: 60):

> Leisure is unique in its capacity to provide surrogate satisfaction for an alienated mass audience, while at the same time perpetuating its alienation and functioning as a means of political socialisation into the hegemonic culture.

Dominance, resistance and incorporation

Hegemony describes incomplete attempts by dominant cultural groups to incorporate opposition as well as resistance (Williams, 1977). CSD is sited directly in the midst of cultural struggles whereby the dominant order, like Sport England and Leeds City Council, through projects and initiatives, like Active Communities and the Community Sport Team, attempt to enfranchise dissociated sections of the population. Practitioners are conscious, at times, of being the broker between policy makers and the community. They are conscious of carrying out aims set by policy makers and yet are responsive and supportive of leadership and self-determination from within the community. There is often conflict between what a policy instructs compared to what the community needs.

But dominant groups do not rule society, they merely lead it. Dominant groups attempt to engage the support of others fostered around the dominant values. So Sport England sells 'Active Communities' as a framework for all major providers to work within. And Leeds City Council 'buys' into that, and 'sells' the Community Sport Team to its own local co-providers. So dominant groups mainly lead by consensus rather than by coercion. But they can resort to more overtly directive forms of coercion or social control by exercising their power. To *support*, or not to support? To *fund*, or not to fund? . . . that is the question. The state shapes and directs national culture and so enables the construction of a specific dominant culture. Popular cultural forms, alternative to the dominant culture, are incorporated through market forces such as commercialisation, or directly by the state itself (McDonald, 1995).

> Hegemony works through ideology but it does not consist of false ideas, perceptual definitions. It works primarily by inserting the subordinate class into the key institutions and structures which support the power and the social order of the dominant order. It is above all in these structures and relations that a subordinate class 'lives its subordination'.
>
> (Gramsci, 1971: 164)

kevin hylton and mick totten

The tendency of dominant groups to structure or frame the conditions for CSD practice does not enable them to dictate results. So 'we operate, within constraints, which we are free to change, but we are not free to abolish the principle of living within constraints' (Kelly, 1984: 4). Individual agents still ultimately make their own sport by responding to their own situations. Resistance is as much a part of hegemony as are conformity and control. Capacity for interpretation and reaction, agency itself, is dependent upon the situation. Individuals and groups find alternative, sometimes radical, cultural expression in opposition to the *status quo*, despite the centralising tendencies of sports policy and provision. Sport (as leisure) has provided 'a more negotiable space' for agency than other spheres of life (Hall and Jefferson, 1976). Sport has emancipatory potential, the 'extent to which the politics of the popular provides a point of resistance to bourgeois hegemony' (Hargreaves, 1986: 220).

The state preserves its position as the dominant culture in CSD by pursuing its own hegemonic project and responding to hegemonic opposition. New Labour has been vigorously involved in CSD, but it still regulates the mainstream market in which inequalities in choice occur. It may intervene 'in pursuit of distributive justice' (Roberts, 1978) but without fundamentally changing the mainstream infrastructure. The responsive state is the hegemonic state which incorporates resistance and preserves mainstream order. In relation to community arts, Kelly concedes that a radical programme, lacking co-ordination, has been diluted by assimilation into the arts establishment in a legitimated form, in which radicals have become foot soldiers in their own movement: 'we came as invaders, but without a language of our own we were soon acting and talking like the natives of the citadel' (Kelly, 1984: 29). The same fate has no doubt been met by many of those radical idealists working within CSD. This polemical analysis demonstrates the hegemonic power of the dominant culture to incorporate and disarm even the most radical of opposition. It also illustrates the potential for alternative and oppositional hegemonic cultures to emerge in a subcultural form.

Hegemony: a dynamic process

So hegemony accommodates elements of both resistance and control, and must therefore be seen as a dynamic process. The dominant actors within CSD policy and provision seek to impose control, and subordinate groups offer resistance. CSD is an arena in which this cultural struggle can be acted out (McDonald, 2002). Hegemony is a continual process. It is continually assembled and reassembled, reproduced and secured (and set back!) (Bennett 1981b). Hegemony is never completed; 'it has continually to be renewed, recreated, defended and modified. It is also continually resisted, limited, altered and challenged by pressures not all its own' (Williams, 1977: 112). In hegemonic terms, that position, in limbo, will never be resolved. The struggle is ongoing: top-down control and bottom-up resistance, but also between and across organisations and individuals operating at similar levels. Individual CSD workers are able to discriminate, within certain confines,

on the balance they wish to achieve between these contradictory aims, but hegemony itself is perpetual and all-encompassing.

CONCLUSION

This chapter opened with an examination of key concepts and tensions in CSD. It then offered a vigorous analysis of the complex nature of CSD provision, policy and practice. It has raised many issues and debates about that very nature. It concludes with a theoretical reconceptualisation of CSD which accounts for ambiguities in practice.

The conceptual complexity of CSD is compounded by a diverse range of provision. Its true nature and meaning are therefore contested in theory, policy and practice. For some, the content is very much conventional institutionalised sport. For others, it is a more informal manifestation of sport or recreation and much else that may not be sport at all! For some, the central focus is sport. For others, who may not bear any particular allegiance to sport, the key focus is very much people or community. So CSD practice reflects these tensions between both sport development and community development.

The diverse range of CSD practices, and therefore its policy community, are reflected in the 'CSD matrix'. This model accounts for policy formulated and driven at different levels: transnational, national, regional and local. It draws attention to different styles of the management of provision, ranging from 'top-down' to 'bottom-up'. It plots the involvement of all three sectors of the mixed economy engaged in provision; mostly public or voluntary, and occasionally commercial. It brings attention to the fact that many individual initiatives are often partnerships between organisations from different sectors, perhaps at different levels, which, in turn, are in partnership with local communities. It further alluded to the different types of practitioners who may all share some interest in CSD: SDOs, facility managers, youth workers, education workers, health workers, social workers, probation officers and others.

This broad range of practitioners is reflected in the range of policy interests which rationalise or legitimise provision. CSD is orientated around different and overlapping social, cultural, political and economic concerns (Totten, 1995). It can be analysed from any combination of those perspectives. CSD accommodates a range of different philosophies, policy rationales and practices. They all share similar concerns about inequality, access and inclusion, marginalised groups and exclusion, democracy and participation. So CSD is a form of socio-cultural intervention in mainstream provision, and in the everyday lives of communities. Five overlapping 'policy models' were introduced: social control, social welfare, the democratisation of culture, cultural democracy and radicalism. Each can have some bearing on CSD, and their compound effect is to sustain the broad appeal of CSD to policy makers. CSD is dichotomous; it is about liberation and control. Its agenda ranges from tokenism to manipulation, and radically to emancipation.

All the above complexities underline the crucial fact that CSD is conceptually dynamic, a hegemonic 'cultural struggle' between varied institutions, organisations and interest groups

who all share some commitment to this unconventional approach to provision. Best practice in CSD is varied, but what makes it so valuable and unique is its philosophy of approach or process. Community sports development is a flexible, adaptable, informal, consultative, people-centred approach, aimed at the initial threshold to participation in order to address the deficiencies of mainstream provision.

REFERENCES

Althusser, L. (1971) *Lenin and Philosophy and Other Essays*, New York: New Left Books.

Anti-racist World Cup (2006) http://www.mondialiantirazzisti.org.

Arnstein, S. (1969) A ladder of citizen participation, *Journal of the American Institute of Planning*, 35(4), 216–24.

Association of Metropolitan Authorities (1989) *Community Development: the local authority role*, London: AMA.

Atha, B. (1978) *The Sports Council and Recreation Deprivation in Greater London and South East Council for sport and recreation Quality of Life: the contribution of sport and leisure*, London: Greater London and South East Council for Sport and Recreation.

Baldry, H. (1976) Community arts, in J. Haworth and A. Veal (eds), *Leisure and the Community*, London: Lepus Books.

Banks, T. (1998) Sport: The Strategic View, http://www.coi.gov.uk/coi/depts/GHE/coi8450e.ok.

Bennett, T. (1981a) Popular culture and hegemony in post-war Britain, in *Politics, Ideology and Popular Culture* I, Milton Keynes: Open University.

Bennett, T. (1981b) Popular culture: history and theory, *Popular Culture: Themes and Issues* 2, Milton Keynes: Open University.

Bianchinni, F. (1989) *Urban Renaissance? The arts and the urban regeneration process*, Liverpool: Centre for Urban Studies, University of Liverpool.

Booth, M. (1997) Community development: oiling the wheels of participation, *Community Development Journal*, 32(2), 151–8.

Bothlolo, G. (1986) *A Sporting Chance: the work of the GLC sports sub-committee 1983–1985 and a review of the Brixton Recreation Centre*, London: GLC.

Brent, J. (2004) The desire for community: illusion, confusion and paradox, *Community Development Journal*, 39(3), 213–23.

Butcher, H., Glen, A., Henderson, P. and Smith, J. (1993) *Community and Public Policy*, London: Pluto Press.

Cabinet Office (2002) *Game Plan: a strategy for delivering government's sport and physical activity objectives*, London: Cabinet Office.

Cadbury Schweppes (2006) http://www.bitc.org.uk/resources/viewpoint/cadburygetactive.html.

Cantle, T. and Institute of Community Cohesion (2006) *Challenging Local Communities to Change Oldham*, Coventry: ICC.

Carrington, B. and Leaman, O. (1983) Sport as community politics, in L. Haywood (ed.)

Sport in the Community – the next ten years: problems and issues, Ilkley: Leisure Studies Association.

Carrington, B. and McDonald, I. (2001) Whose game is it anyway? Racism in local league cricket, in B. Carrington and I. McDonald (eds) *Race, Sport and British Society*, London: Routledge.

Centre for Leisure and Sport Research (2003) Awards for All: an impact study evaluating sports projects in the Awards for All programme, unpublished report to Sport England.

Chaskin, R. (1997) 'Perspectives on neighbourhoods and communities, *Social Service Review*, 71(4), 521–47.

Chomsky, N. (2003) *Hegemony or Survival*, New York: Metropolitan.

Coalter, F. (1989) *Freedom and Constraint*, London: Routledge.

Coalter, F. (1991) Sports participation: price or priorities? *Leisure Studies*, 12, 171–82.

Coalter, F. (2001) *Realising the Potential of Cultural Services: the case for sport*, London: Local Government Association.

Coalter, F. (2002) *Sport and Community Development: a manual*, Edinburgh: **sport**scotland.

Coalter, F. and Allison, M. (1996) *Sport and Community Development*, Edinburgh: Scottish Sports Council.

Coalter, F. *et al.* (1986) *Rationale for Public Sector Investment in Leisure*, London: ESRC.

Collins, M. and Kay, T. (2003) *Sport and Social Exclusion*, London: Routledge.

Community Development Exchange (CDX) (2001) The Strategic Framework for Community Development, http://www.cdx.org.uk/resources/library/docs/sframeword.doc (accessed on 5 July 2006).

Cooke, G. (1996) A strategic approach to performance and excellence in supercoach, *National Coaching Foundation*, 8(1), 10.

Council of Europe (1971) *Planning the Future* VIII, Brussels: Council of Europe.

Department for Culture Media and Sport (DCMS) Policy Action Team (10) (1999) *PAT 10: A Report to the Social Exclusion Unit*, London, DCMS.

Department for Culture Media and Sport (2001) *The Government's Plan for Sport: a sporting future for all*, London: DCMS.

Department of the Environment (1977) *Recreation and Deprivation in Inner Urban Areas*, London: HMSO.

Department of the Environment (1989) *Sport and Active Recreation Provision in Inner Cities*, London: Crown Publications.

Easton Cowboys (2006) http://www.eastoncowboys.org.uk.

EC (2005) European Year of Education through Sport, http://www.welcomeurope.com/default.asp?id=1300&idnews=2518&print=yes.

FA Premier League (2006) http://www.premierleague.com.

Football Foundation (2006) http://www.footballfoundation.org.uk/about-the-football-foundation/case-studies.

Football Task Force (1999) *Investing in the Community*, London: Ministry of Sport.

Freeman, A. (1999) Exclusion zone, *Leisure Manager*, May, pp. 11–13.

Fremeaux, I. (2005) New Labour's appropriation of the concept of community: a critique, *Community Development Journal*, 40(3), 265–74.

Gamble, A. (1981) *An Introduction to Modern Social and Political Thought*, London: Macmillan.

GLC (1986) *Campaign for a Popular Culture*, London: CRS.

Glyptis, S. (1989) *Leisure and Unemployment*, Milton Keynes: Open University.

Gramsci, A. (1971) *Selections from the Prison Notebooks*, New York: Lawrence & Wishart.

Hall, S. and Jefferson, T. (1976) *Resistance through Rituals*, London: Hutchinson.

HMSO (1975) *White Paper on Sport and Recreation*, Cmnd 6200, London: HMSO.

Hargreaves, J. (n.d.) *State Intervention in Sport and Hegemony*, London: Goldsmiths, University of London.

Hargreaves, J. (1982) *Sport, Culture, and Ideology*, London: Routledge.

Hargreaves, J. (1986) *Sport, Power and Culture*, Cambridge: Polity Press.

Hargreaves, J. and McDonald, I. (2002) Cultural studies and the sociology of sport, in J. Coakley and E. Dunning (eds) *Handbook of Sports Studies*, London: Sage.

Haywood, L. (1983) *Sport in the Community – the next ten years: problems and issues*, Brighton: LSA.

Haywood, L. and Kew, F. (1989) Community sports programmes: old wine in new bottles, in P. Bramham *et al.* (eds) *Leisure and Urban Processes*, London: Routledge.

Haywood, L. *et al.* (1994) *Community Leisure and Recreation*, London: Heinemann.

Home Office (1999) *Report of the Policy Action Team 9 on Community Self-help*, London: Home Office.

Houlihan, B. and White, A. (2002) *The Politics of Sport Development*, London: Routledge.

Hudson, K. (2004) Behind the rhetoric of community development: how is it perceived and practised? *Australian Journal of Social Issues*, 39(3), 249–65.

Hylton, K. (2003) *Sportsweb: An Evaluation*, Leeds Metropolitan University: Centre for Leisure and Sport Research.

Hylton, K. and Totten, M. (2001) Community sports development, in K. Hylton, P. Bramham *et al.* (eds) *Sports Development: policy, process and practice*, 1st edn, London: Routledge.

Institute for Volunteering Research (2001) *Volunteering for All? Exploring the link between volunteering and social exclusion*, London: IVR.

Jackson, D., Totten, M. and Robinson, P. (2003) Evaluating sports projects in the Awards for All programme, *Yorkshire and Humber Regional Review*, 13 (3), 27–8.

Kelly, O. (1984) *Community, Art and the State*, London: Comedia.

Kingsbury, A. (1976) Animation, in J. Haworth and A. Veal (eds) *Leisure and the Community*, Birmingham: CURS.

Ledwith, M. (2005) *Community Development: a critical approach*, Bristol: Policy Press.

Lentell, B. (1994) Sports development: goodbye to community recreation, in C. Brackenridge (ed.) *Body Matters: leisure images and lifestyles*, Eastbourne: Leisure Studies Association.

Liddle, D. (1988) Youth and community services as part of local authority leisure provision (pp.199–205), in J. Benington and J. White (eds) *The Future of Leisure Services*, Harlow: Longman.

Long, J. (1981) Leisure as a tool for community development and the opiate of the masses, in A. Tomlinson (ed.) *Leisure and Social Control*, Brighton: Leisure Studies Association.

Long, J. (1991) *Leisure Health and Wellbeing*, Eastbourne: Leisure Studies Association.

Long, J. and Sanderson, I. (2003) The social benefits of sport: where's the proof?, In C. Gratton and I. Henry (eds), *Sport in the City*, London: Routledge.

MacIntosh, P. and Charlton, V. (1985) *Action Sport (MSC): an evaluation of phase one*, London: Sports Council.

McDonald, I. (1995) Sport for All: RIP? A political critique of the relationship between national sport policy and local authority sports development in London, in S. Fleming, M. Talbot and A. Tomlinson (eds) *Policy and Politics in Sport, Physical Education and Leisure*, Eastbourne: Leisure Studies Association.

McDonald, I. (2002) Critical social research and political interventions: moralistic versus radical approaches, in J. Sugden and A. Tomlinson (eds) *Power Games: a critical sociology of sport*, London: Routledge.

McIntosh, P. and Charlton, V. (1985) *The Impact of the Sport for All Policy*, London: Sports Council.

Morgan, D. (2000) *Sport versus Youth Crime*, Bolton: Centre for Sport and Leisure Management, Bolton Institute.

Murray, K. (1988) The Brixton Recreation Centre: an analysis of a political institution, *International Review for the Sociology of Sport*, 23(2): 125–38.

Office of the Deputy Prime Minister (ODPM) (2004) *Teaming Up: how joint working between sport and neighbourhood renewal practitioners can help in deprived areas*, Wetherby: ODPM.

Parry, J. (1986) The Community Arts: an arts revolution incorporated, in J. Parry and N. Parry (eds) *Leisure, the Arts and Community*, Brighton: Leisure Studies Association.

Plant, R., Lessen, H. and Taylor-Gooby, P. (1980) *Political Philosophy and Social Welfare*, London: Routledge.

Popple, K. (1995) *Analysing Community Work*, Buckingham: Open University Press.

Popple, K. and Shaw, M. (1997) Editorial introduction: Social movements: Reasserting 'community', *Community Development Journal*, 323(3), 191–8.

Republica Internationale (2006) www.republica-i.co.uk.

Rigg, M. (1986) *Action Sport: an evaluation*, London: Sports Council.

Roberts, K. (1978) *Contemporary Society and the Growth of Leisure*, London: Longman.

Sankt Pauli FC (2006) http://www.fcstpauli.de.

Scottish Sports Council (1998) *Sport 21: nothing left to chance*, Edinburgh: Scottish Sports Council.

Simpson, J. (1976a) *Towards Cultural Democracy*, Strasbourg: Council of Europe.

Simpson, J. (1976b) Notes and reflections on animation, in J. Haworth and A. Veal, *Leisure and the Community*, Birmingham: CURS.

Skills Active (2006) *A Summary of the Community Sports Development Research Report*, London: Skills Active.

Smith, C. (1998) *The Comprehensive Spending Review: new approach to investment in culture*, London: DCMS.

Social Exclusion Unit and Department of Culture Media and Sport (1999) *PAT 10: a Report to the Social Exclusion Unit*, London: DCMS.

Sports Council (1978) *Sport and Recreation in the Inner Cities*, London: Sports Council.

Sports Council (1982) *Sport in the Community: the next ten years*, London: Ashdown Press.

Sports Council Research Unit (1991) *National Demonstration Projects: major lessons and issues for development*, London: Sports Council.

Sport England (2000) *Active Communities: an introduction*, London: Sport England.

Sport England (2001a) *Performance Measurement for the Development of Sport: a good practice guide for local authorities*, London: Sport England.

Sport England (2001b) *Sport Action Zones: a summary report on the establishment of the first 12 zones – issues, successes, and lessons for the future*, London: Sport England.

Sport England (2002) *Positive Futures: a review of impact and good practice*, London: Sport England.

Sport England (2004) *The Framework for Sport in England: making England an active and successful sporting nation – a vision for 2020*, London: Sport England.

Sport England (2005a) *Sport: playing its part*, London: Sport England.

Sport England (2005b) *Delivery Plan, 2005–2008*, London: Sport England.

Sport England (2005c) *A CSN Evaluation Summary by PMP*, London: Sport England.

Standing Conference on Community Development (2001) *Strategic Framework for Community Development*, Sheffield: SCCD.

Stonewall (2006) http://www.stonewallfc.com.

Taylor, M. (2000) *Top Down meets Bottom Up: neighbourhood management*, York: Joseph Rowntree Foundation.

The 1 in 12 Club (2006) www.1in12.com.

Torkildsen, G. (2005) *Leisure and Recreation Management*, London: Routledge.

Totten, M. (1993) Birds of a Feather: A Comparative Analysis of Community Sports and Community Arts, unpublished MA dissertation, Leeds Metropolitan University.

Totten, M. (1995) Conceptualising community leisure: unravelling the rationale, in J. Long (ed.) *Nightmares and Successes: doing small scale research in leisure*, Leeds: Leeds Metropolitan University.

Williams, R. (1977) *Marxism and Literature*, Oxford: Oxford University Press.

Yorkshire and Humberside Council for Sport and Recreation (1989) *A Sporting Chance*, Leeds: Yorkshire and Humberside Council for Sport and Recreation.

CHAPTER 6

PARTNERSHIPS IN SPORT

Stephen Robson

> To make our shared vision a reality we must speak with one voice in making the case for Sport. And we must share a common commitment to deliver.
>
> (Sport England, 2004: 2)

Many feel anxious about working with others in professional and organisational life. However, sports development work is such that organisations can no longer expect to be able to function and thrive in isolation. The need for partnerships has been emphasised by the successes of many joint ventures and the failures of many individual pursuits. This has led to an increasing compulsion for sports organisations to perform effectively in concert to obtain cultural, financial and political support, as confirmed by Pettinger (2000: 21):

> No organisation exists in isolation from its environment, the nature and extent of the relationship and interactions must be considered. Organisations are subject to a variety of economic, legal, social and ethical pressures that they must be capable of accommodating if they are to operate effectively.

The range of alliances now in existence in sport and recreation management is immense. They range from major national consortia, preparing and implementing the London 2012 Olympic and Paralympic Games, to local authority sports development professionals, assisting the local netball team in its attempts to attract new players. As a more strategic approach to partnership working develops, the professionalisation of sports development work has witnessed the growth of managerial posts specifically to oversee the partnership process. Operating in isolation still has its merits for many of us in sport, although it is clearly something of the past where it is the only strategy.

Partnership working centres on the idea that agencies make a commitment in terms of what they are able to input to the relationship, on the basis that some or all of the *outputs* will help them to achieve their overall goals. Recently policy makers and practitioners have become interested in *throughputs*, the sustained benefits of staff development when working with other partners. Strategic alliances, relationships with still greater forms of interdependence, are differentiated by their capacity to enhance or foster organisational learning. According to Child and Faulkner (1998), organisations engaged in strategic alliances should grow in competences as they learn from one another; in particular, they should attempt to become competent in the skills valued and provided by another. This concern with mutual benefits permeates the chapter, although examples will also be drawn from selected partnerships where the rewards are not always clear or shared.

The purpose of this chapter is to explore both benefits and problems experienced by organisations working together. It provides practitioners and students with the means to analyse and optimise such working relationships by drawing on relevant organisation and management theories. A brief historical perspective details the growth in strategic partnerships encouraged in these 'new times' of more flexible state and government agencies. Partnerships predominantly involving public and voluntary sectors have primacy, as the majority of organisations with a responsibility for developing sport and recreation are located within these sectors. Political and strategic dimensions are intrinsic to much collaboration. These considerations provide practitioners with a critical edge to aid planning, and students of sport and recreation with the means to develop critical skills. It is useful, initially, to reflect upon accepted definitions of the term 'partnership', and to consider how these may be applied to the world of sports development.

KEY TERMS

Throughout this chapter a number of terms are used interchangeably. Expressions such as 'alliance', 'networking', 'collaboration', 'joint working' and 'working together' carry the same emphasis as the key concept 'partnership'. The *Oxford English Dictionary* (2006: 543) defines 'partnership' simply as an 'association of two or more people as partners', a partner being 'a person who takes part in a business or other undertaking with another person or group'. In the context of sport and recreation professions, this definition accommodates the gamut of alliances to be considered. Thus any coming together of organisations (often through their representatives) or interested individuals to further sport experiences can be considered to constitute a partnership.

Given the possibilities for partnerships within and between organisations across public, commercial and voluntary sectors, it is surprising that the bulk of related literature makes reference to partnerships solely in business and management contexts. However, it is helpful to start with the concept of alliances as provided by business discourses in order to refine definitions. Yoshino and Rangan (1995: 5) assert that characteristics of strategic alliances are that two or more organisations unite in the pursuit of common goals, to share both the benefits and the assignment of tasks. Importantly, as reinforced by Dussauge and Garrette (1999: 2), there is no loss of strategic autonomy; in other words, organisations remain independent of one another. They offer a representation of an alliance for further clarification. Figure 6.1 illustrates that a partnership or alliance is distinct from a merger, where two organisations are replaced by a single new entity. The alliance is constituted

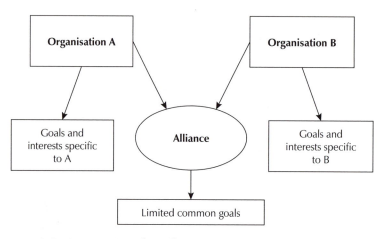

Figure 6.1 Representation of an alliance

Source Adapted from Dussuage and Garrette (1999).

to deal with issues relevant to goals that both organisations have in common; meanwhile each organisation will be engaged in its core work elsewhere.

THE NATURE OF PARTNERSHIPS

Partnerships in sport and recreation take on myriad forms, each one as unique as a fingerprint. This section considers the main factors involved in characterising any given partnership.

The first of these is time scale. A collaborative venture may be temporary or permanent. This may involve a relatively long lead-in and negotiation period or may be instigated rapidly, once a need or common interest has been identified. At the time of writing, the proposed England 2018 bid to stage the FIFA World Cup, for instance, would require a temporary partnership between the English Football Association, government, professional football clubs, local authorities, sponsors, stadium developers and financial organisations. There would need to be many other partners but the planning and implementation phases would need to be relatively long term.

The second factor to consider is the types of partner. These may be drawn from any combination of the public, voluntary and commercial sectors. In a local authority-led alliance legislation demands that there should be a strong emphasis on stakeholder involvement in public policies and their implementation. Citizens of the local area enjoy a dual role as customer and partner of the authority. Elsewhere, organisations such as professional rugby teams and sportswear manufacturers enter into arrangements located solely in the commercial sector.

It is important to recognise that partnerships occur *within*, as well as *between*, organisations. For instance, in the wake of Compulsory Competitive Tendering (CCT) and as a consequence of the development of leisure trusts (see Reid, 2003), local authority sports facilities are often managed according to a client–contractor arrangement where all actors and agents are employees of the same organisation.

Power distribution is the next factor to consider in characterising a partnership. Whilst many alliances are entered into equally by all partners (for example, a high-profile sponsorship deal where the benefits to each partner are tangible and relatively commensurate), others may have a dominant or lead agency. Power differentials can arise organically, often in instances where one agency takes the lead on an initiative. Whilst others are in the process of committing resources to the initiative the lead organisation has to assume a position of authority or little will be achieved. In alliances working across public and voluntary sectors it is important that all stakeholders have opportunities to influence decisions, especially in a public policy climate that encourages social inclusion.

The scale or size of partnerships can vary greatly. There is scope for joint working at every level from a joint venture between a community sports club and the local church to the long-running and deeply controversial Wembley Stadium development where millions have an interest. Partnerships exist at transnational, national, regional and local levels; certain alliances are local or regional manifestations of national partnership projects.

The scale of a partnership is often determined by its aims. Once again, there are as many possible motivations for entering into collaboration with others as there are projects. The *raison d'être* for the majority of sport and recreation alliances is the attainment of some social and educational objectives. However, especially in elite sport, commercial considerations attain increasing importance. Sponsors' profit motives often cross over with political, cultural and social goals at local and regional level, as sports development professionals court commercial support for worthy initiatives. Those responsible for developing 'grass-roots' football may be heartened by the major investment in coaching provided by MacDonald's but may also be troubled by associated moral and ethical issues (FA, 2003). Political agendas also instigate many partnerships from national to local level. It is therefore important to note that not all partnerships are entered into voluntarily, as pragmatism also produces unforeseen and unintended consequences. Some ramifications of enforced partnership working will be considered later.

THE DEVELOPMENT OF PARTNERSHIP WORKING

This section offers a substantial update to the historical overview of sport and recreation partnerships offered in the first edition of this book. The focus here will be on developments in the early part of the new millennium; readers should therefore consult the previous edition for a more detailed breakdown of the development of partnership working in the 1970s, 1980s and 1990s.

Central government's explicit role as a partner in major national sport and recreation initiatives is a relatively recent development. Governmental interest has developed as the sector has gradually become more definable and organised. The extent to which one has been determined by the other is a subject of ongoing debate.

Since its establishment in the early 1970s the Sports Council, through its various organisational incarnations, has indicated a willingness to address the lack of structure and co-ordination in UK sport as evidenced by both mass participation and international performance. As noted in Chapter 4, during the early 1970s the Sports Council promoted the 'Sport for All?' message through a range of organisations. It was apparent that this could not be achieved through traditional structures of national governing bodies of sport. Almost four decades later, Sport England continues to take the lead in determining the structures through which investment into mass participation sport should be channelled.

Hylton and Totten (Chapter 4) outline how the Action Sport schemes of the early 1980s were instrumental in establishing a foothold for sports development at the heart of public sector provision. The Sports Council sought to invest in programmes which would see sporting activities delivered in disadvantaged communities and local authorities were chosen as the mechanism for service delivery. From these schemes sprang numerous full-time, often mainstream funded sports development units, leading to strategic and increasingly refined partnerships formed between the public and voluntary sectors.

Henry (2001) charts changes in approach to public sector sport and recreation provision over this period, highlighting moves towards partnership and advocacy (with local communities as well as other organisations). The mood of economic realism induced by the fiscal policies of the Thatcher government meant that, whilst individuals with the capacity to stimulate others into sport participation were finding gainful employment in the public sector, imaginative and flexible ways of achieving this within a tight budget would become ever more necessary.

Client–contractor relationships under Compulsory Competitive Tendering (see Chapter 9) in the early 1990s regularly served to drive a wedge between sports development professionals and managers of sports facilities that were crucial to their work. Sports development workers had to be ever more enterprising in order to maintain the benefits of these internal partnerships to which they had become accustomed.

Labour's Best Value initiative placed the most explicit requirement yet upon local authorities to operate in a flexible, democratic and collaborative manner. Enshrined in legislation by the Local Government Act of 1999, Best Value was quickly superseded in 2002 by the Comprehensive Performance Assessment (CPA) framework, led by the Audit Commission (Audit Commission, 2006). After a vigorous campaign by a range of agencies, a 'culture bloc' was established within the CPA in order to ensure that cultural services, including sports development, would receive similar scrutiny to housing and environmental services. This offered sports development professionals the opportunity to enhance their strategic status within local authorities and secure future investment, as sport is singularly capable of generating 'good news stories' which can enhance a local council's CPA score.

One key focus of the CPA is that local authorities should negotiate and develop partnerships with the voluntary sector, local community groups, users and non-users. Indeed, local government performance will be in part measured with reference to its ability to develop strategic alliances with related organisations and, crucially, with the local communities they are charged to serve.

Whilst sports development has become firmly embedded in local government structures and countless formal and informal partnerships have resulted, all levels of sport have continued to wrestle with a bewildering and illogical structure that seems to confound all parties rather than offering support. In 2005 Carter bemoaned that there was:

> no clear alignment between local and national sports delivery, nor is there a systematic, joined up approach towards community sport.
>
> (Carter, 2005: 20)

With its leadership status assured by its function as distributor of National Lottery money through the Community Investment Fund (Sport England, 2007b), Sport England has attempted to minimise confusion in England by instigating a Delivery System for Sport (Sport England, 2006). This focuses on sub-regional strategic bodies (County Sport Partnerships) and local delivery mechanisms (Community Sport Networks, CSNs). In theory, all key stakeholders will be represented in one or both of these structures. Investment is channelled through the county mechanism and distributed throughout the county via the CSNs. Experiences of many stakeholders working in sport are such that it would be unwise to hold too high expectations of the efficacy of the new system but it would seem to be a step in the right direction.

Partnership working is now part of the political landscape of sporting governance. Its role has been upgraded from a desirable tactic for the advancement of sports development to its present status as a necessity for prosperity and survival. Given the political and professional significance of partnerships, the paucity of academic material dealing with this area is surprising.

THE BENEFITS OF PARTNERSHIP WORKING

In an atmosphere of obligatory partnerships, it is all too easy to lose sight of numerous benefits gained from collaboration. Prior to the introduction of a regulatory framework demanding that partnerships become the focus of local authority work, many far-sighted practitioners were actively engaged in fruitful arrangements with partners from a wide range of organisations. This section will provide an overview of benefits such alliances have realised, with particular reference to a successful multi-agency initiative at local level – Sport Leeds. Established in 2003 and later to be designated as the Community Sport Network for the city (Sport Leeds, 2006), Sport Leeds is founded on the principle that the benefits of collaborative working far outweigh accompanying inconveniences and difficulties.

The Sport Leeds strategy document *Taking the Lead* was launched in late 2006 (Sport Leeds, 2006) and is a good example of partnership strategies in sport, a phenomenon which has increased dramatically since 2000. Alongside Sport England's drive towards a more coherent delivery system has come recognition that rather than merely acknowledging the value of partnerships within 'stand-alone' sports plans, it is preferable to establish the alliance first before pursuing strategic plans in a more collaborative fashion. City of York Council has demonstrated such vision; the city has been partitioned into four zones under the auspices of Active York, the city's Sport and Active Leisure Partnership (Active York, 2005). Sports development services are delivered by relevant partners according to need in each of the zones.

Pooling of resources

Unprecedented investment in physical education and school sport has led to improvements across the sector (see Chapter 7). However, core funding for local authority sports development remains limited and hard-pressed, so professionals who embrace the prevailing partnership culture should accrue tangible resource benefits:

- *Duplication* in two or more agencies' work can be identified and eliminated. This reduces the financial burden on both organisations, enabling desired outcomes to be realised. This aspiration was identified by the government in *Game Plan* (2002), which expressed a wish for 'less duplication of function between and within sporting organisations' (DCMS/Strategy Unit, 2002: 169). The possibility of duplication and conflict among partners is identified with clarity by Caradon District Council (2006: 4) in Cornwall in its Sports Development Strategy for 2006–10: 'a lack of clarity over partnership responsibilities create[s] tension and often a feeling of dissatisfaction from clubs.' Caradon recognised that role clarification between itself and sports clubs operating on Caradon-owned premises would reduce duplication and ensure that each partner was engaged in activities where it was expert, thereby reducing each partner's work load, whilst achieving a greater number of (mostly shared) objectives in the process. Sport Leeds also expresses the intention that 'duplication and wastage of resources are to be avoided' (Sport Leeds, 2006: 23). This is manifested in the numerous centres of excellence which operate through university sport facilities (e.g. gymnastics and tennis at Leeds Metropolitan University). This obviates the need for other facilities to be developed at great expense and increases the prospects of continued investment.
- *Human resources* can be maximised. Sports development professionals have developed more flexible notions of what constitutes the work force for sport. The Level 3 National Occupational Standards for Sports Development (SkillsActive, 2005) embraces this principle; for example, unit A326 'Involve, motivate and retain volunteers' emphasises that good human resource practice, such as that used to support paid employees, is just as relevant to the voluntary work force upon whom sustainable sport provision depends.

- *Expertise* is another aspect of human resources that can be pooled. In this regard it is proposed that Community Sport Networks such as Sport Leeds will generate positive outcomes on a previously unseen scale. Elsewhere unique partnership initiatives involve the pooling of expertise in new and innovative ways. Rochdale Federation of Tenants' and Residents' Associations (RoFTRA), a body predominantly concerned with campaigning on housing issues for the populace of housing estates in Rochdale, appointed a Sports Development Officer in recognition of the potential social benefits of sport. The officer's sports development knowledge and expertise are coupled with the expertise of key local figures in order to identify and act upon opportunities for community development through sport. It is self-evident that neither party would be in as strong a position to achieve their goals without the other (RoFTRA, 2007).

Pooling influence

Partnership working often facilitates realisation of otherwise unattainable goals. This is important in terms of getting favourable decisions made, such as the approval for projects to go ahead, particularly in the context of sharing vital resources. It is evident from examining the list of collaborators in *Taking the Lead* that Sport Leeds has access, through the representatives of its partner organisations, to some of the key decision makers in Leeds and West Yorkshire as a whole. Influence can be exerted upon key figures in partner organisations in a number of different settings:

- *Personal links* between individuals at similar levels in partner organisations often ease access to other networks. Productive personal relationships lead to mutual commitment to projects, and it is relatively straightforward for those in senior positions to be informed of plans. Barriers of technical language and professional jargon can be overcome by the presence of an advocate within an organisation. The credibility of the intended activity can be enhanced in this way. Many of the host of sport–health alliances now in operation across the UK owe their success to sport development and health professionals setting aside suspicion and doubt in inter-agency working (see Chapter 8 for detailed examples). Once convinced of the benefits of partnership arrangements, key actors are in a position to support a project's merits within their organisation and so take the work forward collaboratively.
- *Political power* can be exercised in ways which have productive or destructive effects upon sport and recreation development. Politics and politicians are intrinsically linked with the management and provision of sport at all levels. It is always desirable, and often essential, to have the capacity to influence politicians, whether they are local authority elected members, executive members in a national governing body or Members of Parliament. Various mechanisms include the formal reporting systems of local authorities and governing bodies of sport, where ratification for activities is sought through voting and lobbying.
- *Lobbying* involves interest groups making representations to politicians in order to

secure support on issues of consequence. Increased investment in PE and school sport is due in part to many years of lobbying by key organisations such as the Youth Sport Trust. Interest groups often take a circuitous route to the key decision makers, and in this instance the Trust worked in partnership with the CCPR and others to send strong and consistent messages to central government. Lobbying also works effectively at a local level, where citizens' groups can combine forces to enlist the support of ward councillors. In the case of RoFTRA, the Association was formed in the early 1980s as a partnership of communities within Rochdale, and with careful planning, collaboration and lobbying was eventually able to expand its operation (RoFTRA, 2007) to include community sport. As with so many projects, this would have been impossible to achieve without political backing and collaborative working.

■ *Key contacts and gatekeepers*. Having access to important people is crucial both at an interpersonal as well as an organisational level. Effective working together means sharing *contacts*, whereby tactical use is made of each partner's professional relationships. This is another example of the ability of alliances to open avenues to resources. Contacts range from community leaders to senior politicians. In order to achieve the goals of *Taking the Lead*, relationships need to be formed at all levels in Leeds from the operational to the strategic. Utilising existing contacts, personnel can act as 'gatekeepers', giving colleagues in partner organisations access to key individuals which may otherwise be denied.

■ *Internal lobbying*. Partnerships can also enable those in less senior but strategically vital positions in organisations to elicit support for their extended work among their own senior managers and politicians – a kind of internal lobbying which embraces the notion that politics takes place in a non-governmental sense within organisations (Kingdom, 2003). In the climate of the Comprehensive Performance Assessment and the requirement for local authorities to demonstrate that they are offering value for public money invested, sports development can contribute by servicing a wide range of partners and their agendas. This is acknowledged in *Taking the Lead* (see Sport Leeds, 2006: 2) and exemplified in Huntingdonshire's holiday activity programmes. These are offered in partnership with local sports clubs (Huntingdonshire DC, 2007), which of itself is quite commonplace; what is significant is that the local authority's own corporate self-assessment for the Comprehensive Performance Assessment explicitly maps this provision to one of its wider, corporate priorities of safe and active communities (Huntingdonshire DC, 2003). That this was published prior to the confirmation of the 'culture bloc' is a reminder that the political influence of sports development has long been recognised by enlightened strategic thinkers in the public sector.

Sport Leeds is a success story of partners pooling influence, which is embodied in *Taking the Lead*, but there exists a plethora of initiatives within and around broader partnerships. Leeds Metropolitan University and Leeds Rugby's pioneering strategic alliance is an instructive example. Leeds Rugby itself is the first 'cross-code' partnership between League and Union clubs and, as well as being a major commercial venture, enables Leeds Rhinos

(League) and Leeds Carnegie (Union) to pool their resources. The university's high-profile and strategic involvement with the rugby partnership has seen the development of new shared facilities and the use of the rugby brands to market the Leeds Met Carnegie identity.

Accessing resources

Many public and voluntary sector organisations in sport and recreation face financial restrictions and, together with the themes of resources and influence, partners with a joint mission can use their combined strength to attract finance for programmes. Indeed, the current financial and political climate dictates that, when it comes to obtaining major funding support, partnership working is a necessity rather than merely an advantage. Sport England's guidance for prospective applicants to its Community Investment Fund expressly requires engagement with partners in terms of the development and delivery of projects (Sport England, 2007b). This applies uniformly at all levels of sport, from participation initiatives at a local level to support mechanisms aimed at developing and nurturing elite performers.

Taking the Lead highlights initiatives which have already been established with the assistance of external investment, such as £7.5 million spent on improving sports facilities, supported by the now defunct New Opportunities Fund (Sport Leeds, 2006: 33). Sport England's funding priorities for Yorkshire include a wish to support 'projects that encourage a partnership approach between sport, health, education and the community' (Sport England, 2007b: 1). In addition to targeting resources which would meet this commitment directly, Sport Leeds is engaged in partnerships with commercial sector investors; for example, the Private Finance Initiative (PFI)-funded New Leaf Leisure Centres project. This involves attracting sufficient private investment to unlock £30 million of government PFI credits (Leeds City Council, 2007) and incorporates the aforementioned links with health, education and the community.

In conclusion, Sport Leeds and thousands of other prosperous ventures are not solely improved by partnership working, they are *predicated* upon it. Sport Leeds would not have taken place without the opportunities presented by the sharing of motivation, expertise, financial and physical resources and influence. There is a powerful case that the vast majority of sports development objectives can be attained more readily, and to a higher standard, through working in partnership.

It would be foolhardy to assume that joining forces with another organisation cannot also generate problems. By acknowledging what can go wrong we can anticipate potential difficulties and take steps to overcome them – 'the true test of a relationship is not that it can solve problems but that it can function *despite* problems' (Drucker 1990: 125).

PARTNERSHIP PROBLEMS

A realistic appraisal of some difficulties encountered through partnerships will be presented, but always with one eye on the overwhelming case in favour of collaborative working. To illustrate that even fruitful partnerships can experience pitfalls, relevant examples from Sport Leeds will be chosen, although emphasis will be given to means of *overcoming* identified problems.

First, consider the point, made at frequent intervals in this chapter, that by no means are all alliances entered into voluntarily. This is often due to the requirement to work collectively to access resources but other factors can lead to individuals and organisations being required to work together. Politicians or managers may demand that a particular initiative is embarked upon or public pressure may be acceded to. Whatever the reasons for their inception, enforced partnerships are inherently problematic, not least in the initial stages.

Enforced partnerships

As two distinct organisations will undoubtedly possess different structures, cultures and methods of operation, so it follows that individuals within and between partner agencies will be inherently different. The experience of countless individuals asked to align significant aspects of their work to that of 'outsiders' bears this out. First consider how these issues are manifest at an organisational level:

- *Organisational priorities* may be very different between the players in the partnership. These conflicts can centre on such factors as financial imperatives, social objectives and political direction. Discord between organisations may be so great that, rather than overcoming the issue, at best, an *accommodation* may be achieved which enables the initiative to move forward. In such instances, what underlies the partnership is the fact that irreconcilable differences exist. For example, the language of partnership is commonly employed in sponsorship arrangements between public, voluntary and commercial sector organisations. Whilst many of these satisfy the needs of all partners, there is a clear dissonance between the sports organisation's social goals to improve the provision of sport in some way and the commercial organisation's profit motive. Manipulation of sports events/rules/protocols, etc. to suit marketeers is now an accepted feature of contemporary sports management, although many of those who consider themselves to be purists are often opposed to such measures. Clashes in domain assumptions and organisational priorities can also occur at local level. With the emphasis in the PE and School Sport Club Links (PESSCL) strategy upon developing and improving school–club links, this tension may permeate sporting landscapes. The educationalists in physical education departments may express discomfort at a basketball club's elitist approach to developing its athletes, whilst the club may simultaneously feel that the PE department is holding back potential players through an over-cautious approach to club recommendation and endorsement.

- *Political obstacles* may also be encountered in enforced relationships. Elected officials may have personal or partisan agendas at the forefront of their thoughts and actions. Contemporary governmental interest in sport has grown and it is inevitable that the political cycle (e.g. approaching elections) will have some impact on decision making. The personalities of those with political influence can also have a major impact on matters. Political priorities currently gravitate towards the 2012 Olympic and Paralympic Games and there is concern among many in sports development that their work may be compromised due to resources being diverted elsewhere. If all politicians continue to attach the prospect of votes to 2012 then it is unlikely that dissenting voices will have much impact in terms of resource allocation in sports development partnerships.
- *Initiative overload* is a real issue for harangued sports development professionals. There has undoubtedly been a concerted effort by Sport England to rationalise the range of programmes they were asking partners at all levels to deliver. The Delivery System for Sport (Sport England, 2006) represents their most thoroughgoing attempt to rationalise structures and funding regimes. Over seventy programmes were reduced to a core of three. Whilst there is still a sometimes puzzling assortment of programmes there is a feeling of more coherence than previously.
- *Culture* is another organisational factor that may differ greatly between partner organisations. Organisational culture can be considered to be 'the way of life in an organization' (Hatch, 1997: 204) or meanings and norms shared between individuals interacting within the workplace. Some national governing bodies of sport were previously criticised for demonstrating cultures of snobbery, social exclusivity and paternalism (Houlihan, 1997; Hylton and Totten, Chapter 4). Many national governing bodies have engaged in modernisation programmes in order to secure Sport England funding through Whole Sport/One Stop Plan mechanisms (Sport England, 2005) and have significantly refreshed their organisational cultures to become more accommodating to external partners. Culture clashes are a perennial aspect of partnership working.

In a major alliance on the scale of Sport Leeds it is inconceivable that issues of this nature should not be encountered at some stage. Historical difficulties between organisations may still have resonance, individual hostility between managers and/or politicians can have an impact on the support offered to partnership initiatives and key personnel changes can have an impact. The previous edition of this book reported how managerial changes jeopardised the working of the Middlesbrough GAP Scheme. The challenge to members of Sport Leeds is to maintain collective commitment to the vision and to focus on limiting potential effects of inter-organisational and interpersonal antagonisms.

Further obstacles may be encountered even in operations between willing collaborators. In many cases, mechanisms for resolving such issues have not been agreed in advance and this can be a further source of difficulties.

Planning problems

Management texts exhort managers to plan rationally and effectively. For a variety of reasons, this does not always occur. *Bounded rationality* (see, for instance, Cherrington, 1989; Bramham, Chapter 2) dictates that individuals make decisions under a number of external and psychological constraints. All relevant information is not available and, even so, decision makers would be unable to process it all, nor would they necessarily choose to. Thus individuals involved in a sports development partnership cannot be expected to plan effectively for every eventuality.

It is however extremely naive to assume that difficulties will not arise. Despite this, in some partnership settings, potential problems are never raised or discussed at the outset, resulting in situations all too familiar to experienced practitioners:

- *Delegation* of the work load should be carefully considered and conducted at the commencement of the relationship. In multi-agency undertakings particularly, the nature and scope of tasks to be performed will be large and complex. Yoshino and Rangan (1995: 126) highlight that some organisations hold back their best people for internal activities, and partnership managers need to monitor carefully this type of activity. Delegation is not merely about overburdening people but should be more to do with empowerment and the development of skills and experience whilst contributing to the overall effort (Green, 1999). This is as true in multi-agency partnerships as it is in single organisations, the crucial distinction being that leaders may not have direct authority over other key individuals, who may have to surrender elements of internal organisational status to benefit the alliance. According to Hogan and Kaiser (2005: 169), 'leadership solves the problem of how to organise collective effort; consequently, it is the key to organisational effectiveness' (2005:169). Those in positions of responsibility within partnerships must use all their influence and powers of persuasion to ensure that work loads are allocated and executed fairly and effectively.
- In the event of problems, individual and organisational responsibility must be negotiated. This may not always be conferred upon the organisation as the lead agency in the partnership. Conversely, if the lead organisation is initially identified, it does not always follow that the lead individual will be drawn from that agency, although such will often be the case. In any event, as and when problems are experienced it is vital to have agreed in advance who will take responsibility and manage those situations on behalf of the partnership. If a positive approach is taken to difficulties, the likelihood of a culture of blame and suspicion will be diminished. This avoids expending energy assigning liability for issues which could be better spent rectifying problems.

Whilst *Taking the Lead* provides a cogent and tangible overall vision for the alliance, as with all large-scale strategic partnerships it is necessary to operationalise wider goals into tangible action plans that can be implemented by different combinations of organisations. This is an intense and demanding process but an essential one in order that every individual at every level knows what is expected of them. Cultural differences and personal animosities need to be set aside if the 'greater good' is to be served.

To conclude, it is as well to restate that it would be unusual for any sport and recreation partnership not to experience some form of obstacle during its life cycle. Consequently, partners can plan for a number of contingencies and tackle them maturely and productively as and when they arise. Relationships built on trust are far more likely to thrive than those where a hidden agenda or a mood of mistrust is allowed to prevail.

The merits and shortcomings of joint working have been presented from a personal professional perspective due to the lack of academic theoretical writing, specifically on the nature of partnerships. It is, however, useful to the student and practitioner alike to consider how generic theoretical analysis may be applied to understanding the dynamics of partnership working.

PARTNERSHIPS AND ORGANISATION THEORY

Numerous disciplines offer themselves for academic scrutiny of sport and recreation partnerships; for example, psychology, sociology, economics and political science as well as fields of study which include management, business studies and policy studies. As Cousens *et al.* (2006: 33) suggest, discourses about partnerships are often vague:

> It appears that the term partnership is used by leaders and managers of local governments to describe virtually all interactions with organisations with which they are involved, regardless of the strength or pattern of the relationships.

This section illustrates how key components of one field of study can be applied to understanding partnerships. Organisation theory has been chosen as the most compelling, as it encapsulates key debates underpinning strategic partnerships and joint working. For those unfamiliar with the field of study, organisation theory boasts an immense body of work. Theories of organisation offer 'abstract images of what an organisation is, how it functions, and how its members and other interested parties interact with and within it' (Hatch, 1997: 7). This notion of organisation theory provides for the study of partnerships particularly at the level of examining interactions between people. Indeed, Thibault *et al.* (2002) argue that organisational and individual values and beliefs are major components for consideration when discussing partnerships. Branches of theory include the design and structure of organisations, management of organisations, operational decision making, culture, conflict and the management of change. All can provide a critical lens through which to view the issue of collaborative working. However, the focus of this section will be on one central issue – how organisations interact with the environment. Although this topic will be dealt with discretely, as with most aspects of organisational life, it is interconnected with a host of other factors.

The organisation and its environment

Every organisation is located within an environment in which are situated all 'other organisations and people with whom transactions have to take place' (Pugh and Hickson, 1996: 52). The organisational environment for a sporting body incorporates national and regional governing bodies, government and other political institutions, the public, commercial and voluntary sectors, current and potential sports participants, suppliers, and so on. The environment is subject to changes (demographic, economic, cultural, technological, political, and so on) to which the organisation needs to be able to respond. Relations with the environment are complex and include ways in which the organisation copes with uncertainty and turbulence; ways in which the organisation seeks to influence the environment; and the extent to which it behaves proactively or reactively (Pettinger, 2000: 195–6). From this it can be inferred that all inhabitants of the environment are potential partners.

Mary Jo Hatch's comprehensive and accessible text *Organization Theory: Modern, Symbolic and Postmodern Perspectives* (1997) tackles this with clarity and vision. Hatch argues that organisations can be characterised as occupying a place within a network of interacting and competing organisations and that managers traditionally perceive their own organisation to be at the centre of such networks. This is represented in Figure 6.2.

Organisational network analysis suggests a variety of systemic questions about the interface between the internal organisation and the external environment. Starting with the

Figure 6.2 The organisation at the centre of a network

Source Hatch (1997: 66). Copyright © Mary Jo Hatch (1997), reprinted from *Organization Theory: Modern, Symbolic and Postmodern Perspectives*, reproduced by permission of Oxford University Press.

stephen robson

manager's viewpoint of the organisation at the centre of the network, like a spider in a web, this allows any groups in the network to provide partnership opportunities (see Figure 6.2). For example, if we take the organisation to be the English Table Tennis Association (ETTA), then the types of relationships which can be developed would include sponsorship deals (perhaps with suppliers), coach development initiatives (with the ETTA's customers) and scientific studies of athlete performance with Leeds Metropolitan University (a special interest group). Equally, the organisation at the centre could be a partnership such as Durham Sport, a conglomerate of public and voluntary sports organisations. All the above relationships could be developed in respect of this wider 'organisation of organisations'. Thus it is possible to view partnerships in the context of one organisation's interactions with its environment or to consider the partnership itself to be an organisational network which connects and interacts within a reconfigured environment. Senior management or dominant coalitions within partnerships or inside organisations can adopt different strategies to achieve long- and short-term goals because of challenges imposed by changes in the external environment (see Ellis and Dick, 2003:151).

As well as the network of organisations, wider forces impact upon the organisation/partnership. These have been categorised by Hatch (1997: 67) as the general environment. Hatch locates both the organisation and network within the general environment as follows (see Figure 6.3).

The partnership manager can conduct an environmental analysis (see, for instance, Crowther and Green, 2004) to assess forces outside the control of the partnership which

Figure 6.3 Sectors of the general environment

Source Hatch (1997: 68). Copyright © Mary Jo Hatch (1997), reprinted from *Organization Theory: Modern, Symbolic and Postmodern Perspectives*, reproduced by permission of Oxford University Press.

may have a bearing on its *modus operandi*. In the case of Durham Sport, salient factors would include:

- *Political trends* towards partnership work, as outlined by government with its injunction to sport and neighbourhood renewal organisations to stop working within their separate 'silos' and on separate unfocused agendas (see ODPM, 2004). The likelihood that partnership will be an ongoing political theme can be recognised and treated as an opportunity by the consortium.
- The cultural dominance of football. This can be embraced by partners to promote wider sports participation, whilst those with an interest in developing other sports could prepare for battle, so to speak, to engage with local dominant cultures and subcultures.
- *Economic trends* should be identified, both locally and nationally. In times of financial restriction, opportunities should be co-ordinated between partners who do not discriminate on grounds of price; cross-subsidisation of partnership activities may be deemed necessary.

A full environmental analysis would clearly involve further contextual elements and much greater depth. The reader is encouraged to attempt this in relation to a partnership with which s/he is familiar. Such an appraisal helps managers to locate the place of the partnership within the environment and to identify issues to be addressed.

Numerous writers have developed theories on ways in which the interaction between an organisation and its environment takes place (*organisation–environment relations*), and these are summarised by Hatch. Early writers on *contingency theory* made an assertion that is now taken for granted – managers should organise in response to the demands of the environment. There are, of course, instances where powerful organisations are able to shape their operating environment (e.g. Nike as market leader in the sportswear industry). However, in sports development the environment usually exerts a powerful influence over organisational activity. There are three principal perspectives within contingency theory detailing the options for *how* to respond to the environment:

- *Resource dependence*. This assumes that organisations are controlled by their environments due to the need for resources such as knowledge, labour, equipment, customers, political support and so on. A resource dependence analysis begins by tracing each of the needed resources back to its source; the levels of dependence can then be categorised. Pfeffer and Salancik (cited in Pugh and Hickson, 1996), who developed this theory, determined that an organisation should attempt to create a 'counter-dependency'; in other words, it should endeavour to render elements of the environment dependent on it. Powerful dominant coalitions inside organisations can shape environments and strategically choose which environment to operate in . . . for example, Microsoft, McDonald's or Nike. Another tactic proposed is to work in partnership with other organisations. From a sport and recreation perspective, the resources upon which organisations depend are not always tangible physical commodities. Political support at local, regional and national levels is crucial for local authority sports development teams. By entering into partnerships with, for example, social workers servicing socially excluded young people a sports development team can deliver on one key aspect of the government's modernising agenda. Such counter-dependence through partnership working helps the team to contain the effects of its own vulnerability to the environment.

- *Population ecology*. This starts from the same perspective as resource dependence theory. The difference is that population ecology evaluates the relative success and failure of all the organisations competing in a given 'resource pool' (Hatch, 1997: 81). The environment has the ability to select from all the organisations competing for its resources. Writers such as Hannan and Freeman (cited in Pugh and Hickson, 1996) see the world of organisations from a Darwinian 'survival of the fittest' standpoint. Specific areas or features within the environment, called *ecological niches*, are examined rather than the environment as a whole. These are resource pools on which groups of organisations depend. The focus of interest is on patterns of survival and not on links between organisations and their environments. Maintaining the Darwinian theme, population ecologists are interested in evolutionary processes of *variation* (the entry of new organisations into the population, or the adaptation of existing ones), *selection* (by the environment on the basis of fitness) and *retention* (the attrition or survival rate of organisations). One implication is that much of what happens to an organisation is the result of chance or external forces. Sport and recreation organisations can be said to be in just such a situation in terms of jostling and competing for external public funding. As well as conforming to the requirement to work in partnership (variation), under the population ecology model, organisations bidding for funds would do well to demonstrate the *strength* and *quality* of the partnership in order to prove their fitness to the environment, thereby increasing prospects of selection (i.e. a successful funding bid).

- *Institutional theory*. Environments impose social and cultural demands on organisations which force them to adapt and so play specified roles and maintain desired outward appearances. The *institutional environment* represents shared values of a society to which certain organisations are expected to conform. Slack and Hinings (1994) investigated Canadian sports organisations from an institutional perspective, identifying increased structural homogeneity (i.e. similar outward appearance) brought about by pressures imposed by Sport Canada (see also his arguments about professionalisation and changing leadership styles).

In summary, these three perspectives offer valuable insights into partnership working from the viewpoint of organisational interactions with their environments. Hatch (1997) emphasises that the greatest benefit to the manager or student is to examine an organisation or partnership through each of the lenses provided and to be prepared for surprises when the findings are collated.

Finally, environmental theory provides for managers to defend the organisation against the uncertainty inherent in most environments. Hatch (1997) characterises the environment as having properties of complexity (number and diversity of elements) and subject to constant change. These factors lead to uncertainty in the minds of managers who lack the information they need to make robust decisions. Arguably, the environment for managers in sport and recreation is highly complex, with a baffling array of structures and organisations, subject to a high rate of change and innovation. Uncertainty occurs when, far from having the required information, the manager does not know what type of information is needed.

One response to uncertainty is *isomorphism*, when the organisation attempts to match the complexity of the environment. Two techniques, suggests Scott (cited in Hatch, 1997: 91), employed by organisations to achieve this involve structural differentiation or reordering aspects of the organisation to deal with specific aspects of the environment:

- *Buffering*. This is usually applicable to manufacturing organisations, whereby certain personnel are assigned to insulate the remainder of the work force from shocks in the environment; for example, resource shortages or increased demand (Slack, 1997). However, this notion can be applied to service-oriented sport and recreation organisations and to partnerships. A manager within a community sports network may provide a buffer between the operational staff delivering coaching and subtle or sweeping changes in the priorities prescribed by Sport England, which would otherwise serve to distract coaches from their objectives. Through an appropriate response to the institutional environment, cosmetic changes can be steered through without affecting service provision.
- *Boundary spanning*. This role is at the heart of partnership. Boundary mechanisms deal with the transfer of information between the organisation and the environment so that in one sense individual members of a partnership are acting in this role on behalf of organisations. The duality of the role is central to joint working – first, the boundary linkage provides decision makers within their organisations with information relating to the environment. If a partnership is to succeed, the boundary spanner must be personally committed. Second, s/he represents the organisation in the partnership setting. In this instance, the image portrayed must be professional and contribute to the *counter-dependence* the organisation wishes to instil in the environment by being a valued party to the alliance.

This section has introduced but one aspect of organisation theory and applied it to the study of sport and recreation partnership working. Those working in the field should be encouraged to read independently and widely around the subject to stimulate a critical awareness of the strategic role of partnerships in modern sport and recreation organisations. The final section draws together the key themes of the chapter through the critical examination of a partnership case study.

WEST YORKSHIRE SPORT

This case study focuses on the *skills* for partnership working which will be developed alongside a discussion of West Yorkshire Sport (WYS), the County Sports Partnership (CSP) for West Yorkshire. The skills element will be considered from the perspective of hypothetical sports development professionals working in the five metropolitan authorities (Leeds, Bradford, Calderdale, Kirklees and Wakefield) which form an integral part of WYS – in other words, the *boundary-spanning* role of sports development professionals will be examined.

Background to WYS

The national network of CSPs was formed partly in response to calls for a more integrated and less confused system for sport and in part to co-ordinate a strategic response to New Labour's agenda for sport and physical activity. A by-product of this process should be that investment is made with greater confidence in its likely strategic impact.

As well as metropolitan authorities, WYS comprises representatives from a diverse range of bodies such as almost twenty School Sport Partnerships (acting on behalf of 800 schools), fifteen Primary Care Trusts, five universities, national governing bodies (representing over 2,000 sports clubs), the police and the commercial sector (West Yorkshire Sport, 2006). As with all CSPs its three core functions are:

- Strategic co-ordination and planning.
- Performance management.
- Marketing and communication.

(Sport England, 2007c)

Note the absence of any responsibility for delivery of sports activities and programmes. Whilst delivery agencies are represented on the partnership the focus is strategic, with delivery to be co-ordinated by the constituent Community Sport Networks like Sport Leeds. To this end WYS directly employs only a small staff team whose roles are principally to service the partnership and to support the work of local deliverers within the regional strategic framework (West Yorkshire Sport, 2006).

The sports development manager's role within WYS

Each metropolitan authority is represented by a range of employees including facility managers. Senior sports development managers play an integral role as advocates for the citizens and agencies they serve whilst representing strategic interests of the partnership within their own organisations. Whilst a partner in WYS, each sports development manager is principally employed to work towards the best outcomes for her/his own organisation, so there is an inevitable competitive element as each constituent organisation considers how it can ensure that a substantial proportion of the limited resource pool can be secured to support its work.

This scenario hints at the need for certain skills and knowledge in order for individuals to be successful in partnership settings. Many of the generic skills for sports development can be transferred into the unique partnership environment but it is important to examine whether there is a set of 'partnering skills' that can be developed in isolation.

The National Occupational Standards for Sports Development

Many workers (paid and unpaid) in the sport and leisure sector are familiar with National Vocational Qualifications (NVQs) and the National Occupational Standards which underpin them. Standards exist across a range of professions, each set providing a benchmark of the competences required in a profession. They can be used for a variety of purposes such as defining job roles, planning staff training and development programmes and appraising staff (SkillsActive, 2007). Until recently sports development did not have its own identity within the Standards framework and consequently there was little consistency in continuing professional development (CPD).

In 2005 the first bespoke set of sports development standards was published. The significance of this was the recognition of sports development as a graduate profession, something which is reflected in the mix of skills and knowledge identified in the standards (SkillsActive, 2005). Acknowledging that sports development has less to do with the delivery of activities and far more with negotiating with and influencing decision makers and other stakeholders, the Level 3 standards include units entitled *Contributing to change through implementing and reviewing strategy and policy, Support the efficient use of resources* and *Apply for external funding for sport and physical activity*. More recently, in 2006, a set of Standards in Managing Sport and Active Leisure was approved at Level 4 (senior management), with senior sports development managers' roles given prominence. Embracing the strategic nature of roles at this level, some of the units include *Manage an effective workforce for sport and leisure* and *Initiate and manage change to improve sport and active leisure structures and services* (SkillsActive, 2006).

Partnership skills for sports development

The standards at Levels 3 and 4 also capture what is required for successful partnership working in settings such as WYS. In Unit A324, *Develop productive working relationships with colleagues*, for instance, emphasis is placed on the notion that 'colleagues' is an all-embracing term which includes anyone, at any level, paid or unpaid, inside or outside the organisation, with whom the sports professional has a working relationship (Management Standards Centre, 2004a). This offers a new dimension to outcomes and behaviours specified in the unit, such as 'Provide feedback to colleagues on their performance and seek feedback from colleagues on your own performance' and 'Clearly agreeing what is expected of others and holding them to account' (Management Standards Centre, 2004a: 2). Clearly the expectation is that, subject to a sports development manager having no direct authority over partners, they should otherwise behave no differently whether in intra- or inter-organisational situations.

Unit A328, *Develop your personal networks* (Management Standards Centre, 2004b), appears in the Level 4 standards and is even more explicitly biased towards partnership working. The unit embraces the idea of reciprocity, which underpins the theoretical discussions presented earlier on the theme of resource dependence. Expected behaviours include 'Identifying and working with people and organisations and people that can provide support for your work' and 'Clarifying your own and others' expectations of relationships' (Management Standards Centre, 2004b: 2). The knowledge and understanding aspects of the unit include 'How to make use of the information and resources gained through personal networks' and 'The range of information and resources people may need' (2004b: 3). The accent here is on taking a broader strategic view of benefits which may accrue from interpersonal and interprofessional relationships.

These are just two examples from an array of educational outcomes, behaviours and knowledge embedded in the standards at Levels 3 and 4, and the reader is encouraged to engage fully with them in order to appreciate their scope and function. The units focused upon here are especially pertinent as they underscore the transferability of most skills and competences from the organisational setting into the sports development partnership.

Partnership skills in WYS

Returning to the three main functions of CSPs (strategy, performance management and marketing) it is self-evident that these are activities which sports development professionals would undertake within their own organisations. A professional would need a conceptual understanding of how these functions would apply to WYS's sphere of influence but the principles would be otherwise the same. For example, a sports development manager would be expected to manage the performance of any paid employees, looking at issues such as value for money and attainment of goals. Acting as a member of WYS, s/he would need to be able to consider how effectively the wider (paid and unpaid) work force (county governing bodies, clubs, etc.) was performing in pursuit of a different set of goals. Other functions would map across just as readily into the larger setting.

Perhaps we can conclude that rather than specific partnership *skills* being required for success in this arena, an intellectual *understanding* of the nature and value of partnership working and its accompanying political machinations are keys to securing benefits set out earlier in the chapter.

CONCLUSION

The foregoing discussion has demonstrated that partnership working continues to occupy a critical role in the strategic development of sporting opportunities. Partnership working is predicated upon intelligent, respectful but challenging interactions between professionals from a range of disciplines. Sports development professionals often demonstrate an extra-ordinary flair for shifting seamlessly between the parochial setting of the organisation and the vibrant and diverse partnership environment. This commitment to the spirit of collective effort characterises modern sports development as outward-looking and orientated towards wider goals that benefit a broader cross-section of society.

REFERENCES

Active York (2005) *The Development Plan for the North Zone in York, 2005–2008*, York: Active York.

Audit Commission (2006) *Briefing on the Audit Commission's Comprehensive Performance Assessment Frameworks*, London: Audit Commission.

Caradon District Council (2006) *Caradon Sports Development Strategy*, Liskeard: Caradon District Council.

Carter, P. (2005) *Review of National Sport Effort and Resources*, London: Sport England.

Cherrington, D. (1989) *Organizational Behavior: The Management of Individual and Organizational Performance*, Boston MA: Allyn & Bacon.

Child, J., and Faulkner, D. (1998) *Strategies of Cooperation: Managing Alliances, Networks and Joint Ventures*, Oxford: Oxford University Press.

Cousens, L., Barnes, M., Stevens, J., Mallen, C. and Bradish, C. (2006) 'Who's your partner? Who's your ally?' Exploring the characteristics of public, private and voluntary recreation linkages, *Journal of Park and Recreation*, 24(1): 32–55.

Crowther, D. and Green, M. (2004) *Organisational Theory*, London: Chartered Institute of Personnel Development.

Department for Culture Media and Sport and Cabinet Office Strategy Unit (2002) *Game Plan: A Strategy for delivering Government's Sport and Physical Activity Objectives*, London: HMSO.

Drucker, P. (1990) *Managing the Non-profit Organization*, Oxford: Butterworth Heinemann.

Dussauge, P. and Garrette, B. (1999) *Co-operative Strategy: Competing Successfully through Strategic Alliances*, Chichester: John Wiley & Sons.

Ellis, S. and Dick, P. (2003) *Introduction to Organisational Behaviour*, 2nd edn, Maidenhead: McGraw-Hill.

Green, P. (1999) *Managing Time*, London: Chartered Institute of Marketing.

Hatch, M.J. (1997) *Organization Theory: Modern, Symbolic and Postmodern Perspective*, Oxford: Oxford University Press.

Henry, I.P. (2001) *The Politics of Leisure Policy*, London: Macmillan.

Hogan, R. and Kaiser, R. (2005) What we know about leadership, *Review of General Psychology*, 9: 169–80.

Houlihan, B. (1997) *Sport, Policy and Politics: A Comparative Analysis*, London: Routledge.

Huntingdonshire District Council (2003) *Comprehensive Performance Assessment: Corporate Self-assessment*, Huntingdon: Huntingdonshire District Council.

Huntingdonshire District Council (2007) *Summer Holiday Activities*. Available at: http://www.huntsdc.gov.uk/Leisure+and+Culture/Leisure+Development/Holiday+Activities.

Kingdom, J. (2003) *Government and Politics in Britain: An Introduction*, 3rd edn, London: Polity Press.

Leeds City Council (2007) *PFI New Leaf Leisure Centres*. Available at: http://www.leeds.gov.uk/page.aspx?pageID=6ba36d43-4d98-492e-ab3f-41da994283d9.

Management Standards Centre (2004a) *Unit A324: Develop Productive Working Relationships with Colleagues*, London: Management Standards Centre.

Management Standards Centre (2004b) *A328: Develop your Personal Networks*, London: Management Standards Centre.

Office of the Deputy Prime Minister (2004) *Research Report 9: Joint Working in Sport and Neighbourhood Renewal*, London: ODPM, www.//neighbourhood.gov.uk.

Oxford English Dictionary (2006) 6th edn, Oxford: Oxford University Press.

Pettinger, R. (2000) *Mastering Organisational Behaviour*, Basingstoke: Palgrave.

Pugh, D. and Hickson, D. (1996) *Writers on Organizations*, 5th edn, London: Penguin.

Reid, G. (2003) Charitable trusts: municipal leisure's 'third way'? *Managing Leisure*, 8(4): 171–83.

RoFTRA (2007) *RoFTRA: Formation*. Available at: http://www.roftratenants.net/formation.htm.

SkillsActive (2005) *NVQ/SVQ Level 3 in Sports Development: Qualification Structure*, London: SkillsActive.

SkillsActive (2006) *Managing Sport and Active Leisure NVQ/SVQ Level 4: Qualification Structure*, London: SkillsActive.

SkillsActive (2007) *National Occupational Standards (NOS)*. Available at: http://www.skillsactive.com/training/standards.

Slack, T. (1997) *Understanding Sports Organizations: The Application of Organization Theory*, Champaign, IL: Human Kinetics.

Slack, T. and Hinings, C. (1994) Institutional pressures and isomorphic change: an empirical test, *Organization Studies*, 15(6): 803–27. Reprinted in T. Slack (ed.) *Understanding Sport Organizations: The Application of Organization Theory* (1997), Leeds: Human Kinetics.

Sport England (2004) *The Framework for Sport in England*, London: Sport England.

Sport England (2005) *Whole Sport Plan: Communications update, 27 January 2005*, London: Sport England.

Sport England (2006) *The Delivery System for Sport*, London: Sport England.

Sport England (2007a) *National Governing Bodies and Whole Sport Plans*. Available at: http://www.sportengland.org/index/get_resources/ngbs.htm.

Sport England (2007b) *The Community Investment Fund: Priorities for Yorkshire*, Leeds: Sport England Yorkshire Region.

Sport England (2007c) *The Core Functions of a CSP*. Available at: http://www.sportengland.org/index/get_resources/county_sports_partnerships/what_is_a_csp/csp_core_functions.htm.

Sport Leeds (2006) *Taking the Lead: A Strategy for Sport and Active Recreation in Leeds, 2006–2012*, Leeds: Sport Leeds.

The FA (2003) The FA and McDonald's Community Coaching Programme. Available at: http://www.thefa.com/GrassrootsNew/Coach/Postings/2003/07/58471.

Thibault, L., Kikulis, L. and Frisby, W. (2002) Partnerships between local government sport and leisure departments and the commercial sector: changes, complexities and consequences. In T. Slack (ed.) *The Commercialisation of Sport*, Harlow: Frank Cass.

West Yorkshire Sport (2006) *West Yorkshire Sports Partnership Strategy, 2006–2009*, Huddersfield: West Yorkshire Sport.

Yoshino, M. and Rangan, U. (1995) *Strategic Alliances: An Entrepreneurial Approach to Globalization*, Boston MA: Harvard Business School Press.

CHAPTER 7

PHYSICAL EDUCATION AND SCHOOL SPORT

Anne Flintoff

Over the past decade, young people have increasingly become a focus of UK sport policy (Houlihan and Green, 2006). Fuelled in part by concerns such as increasing levels of childhood inactivity and obesity and lack of international success in sport, a plethora of policy initiatives have been developed aimed at young people. This chapter will consider some of these initiatives in the context of school Physical Education (PE).

Any discussion about PE and school sport generates many questions of definition. What is PE? How does it differ from school sport? How different is school sport from sport in the community? One straightforward view of PE focuses on *where* physical activities take place and *who* is responsible for them. In this view, PE would refer to all activities that go on within school curriculum time whereas school sport relates to all those physical activities that take place outside of curriculum time but are organized and run by the school. Arguably, these are traditional and somewhat limited working definitions and tell us little about the aim of physical activities. The first National Curriculum in PE (NCPE) was clear that PE and sport were not synonymous:

> PE . . . is a process of learning, the context being mainly physical. The purpose of this process is to develop specific knowledge, skills and understanding and to promote physical competence. Different sporting activities can and do contribute to the learning process, and the learning enables participation in sport. The focus however, is on the child and his or her development of physical competence, rather than on the activity.
>
> (DES, 1991: 7)

Some authors have suggested that, whilst learning should remain central, it is not helpful to define PE as limited to formal and informal activities which happen in particular places such as schools or other educational institutions. Evans and Davies (2006) have suggested that PE needs to be conceived of as a complex social process that occurs in a wide variety of settings. This involves families, peer groups and the media and is not just limited to schools. As Macdonald (2002) maintains, whilst schools remain 'modernist' institutions, structured by timetables, subjects and so on, postmodern perspectives show us that young people learn about 'physical culture' (see Kirk, 1993, 1999) from a much wider range of sources and across a range of contexts. Certainly, one feature of the recent national strategy in PE – the PE and School Sport Club Links (PESSCL) (DfES/DCMS, 2003) – is that it recognises the importance of building links between opportunities in curriculum PE and those physical activity contexts outside school. Young people's learning does not stop at the school door. So, although this chapter focuses on the particular context of curriculum PE and the formalised school sport opportunities, it is cognisant of these wider conceptions and the implications they raise for teachers and coaches.

Those who support PE as an important aspect of schooling argue its importance for introducing young people to different kinds of physical activity and for developing basic skills required to take part (DfEE, 1999). In addition, young people learn about the relationship between physical activity and health so that they are able to make informed choices and adopt an active lifestyle later in life. Others stress that school PE – in partnership with other agencies – plays an important role in the identification and development of future champions (DCMS/DfEE, 2001; DCMS/Delivery Unit, 2002). At different times, these and other rationales for PE, have gained recognition and acceptance. Struggles over 'what counts as PE' have been reflected in contradictory and competing initiatives and policies.

This chapter traces the key policy changes and initiatives in relation to young people's opportunities to be physically active in school and beyond over the past two decades. In particular, the chapter explores ways in which particular conceptions of PE and school sport opportunities benefit some groups and marginalise others. It examines the challenges facing different agencies working in partnership to implement change. Key policy initiatives considered include the National Curriculum in PE (NCPE), Specialist Sports Colleges (SSCs) and the School Sport Partnership Programme (SSPP), all central elements of the PESSCL strategy (DfES/DCMS, 2003). Drawing on national evaluations of these policy initiatives and other smaller scale qualitative case study research, the chapter highlights key questions and issues for those involved in working with young people.

THE SOCIAL CONSTRUCTION OF PE

Whilst few might take issue with the aim of PE as stated in the NCPE above, what it should look like in practice – for example, which activities should be included; who should teach PE and how should it be taught – have all been subject to much scrutiny and debate. Although there is insufficient space here for detailed historical analysis, Fletcher (1984) has documented how girls' PE began in the late nineteenth century with the training of specialised women PE teachers in separate colleges, with a distinctive 'female tradition' and culture. Underpinned by a strong educational discourse, women's PE teacher training emphasised the importance of physical activity for women's health and well-being and incorporated a child-centred approach, drawing on a broad range of physical activities which included dance, gymnastics and some games (Hargreaves, 1979, 1994). It was only much later that the first training college for men PE teachers opened at Carnegie in Leeds in 1933, where the tradition of men's PE was influenced by militarism and competitive team games (Kirk, 1992). Although the single-sex training colleges are now long gone, tensions between sporting and educational discourses within PE nevertheless continue to impact on contemporary practice. Gender remains an important factor in young people's experiences of PE.

How PE is structured is not just a matter of academic debate for those of us working in universities or in sports development units. It matters for young people's everyday experiences in the gymnasium or on the playing field. Not all young people have a positive experience of PE. In 1986 Evans and Williams wrote:

> The most that many pupils may have learnt in . . . the Physical Education curriculum is that they have neither ability, status nor value and that the most judicious course of action to be taken in protection of their fragile educational and physical identities is to adopt a plague-like avoidance of its damaging activities.
> (Evans and Davies, 1986: 16)

After twenty years of change and innovation, one would be justified in thinking that this scenario no longer exists. However, there remain huge disparities between young people's experiences of PE and school sport. PE is *socially constructed* – that is, particular kinds of knowledge, pedagogies and assessment strategies are selected, others omitted or marginalised – and these constructions serve particular group interests better than others (Evans and Davies, 2006).

UNDERSTANDING YOUNG PEOPLE'S PARTICIPATION IN AND EXPERIENCES OF PE

The first point is that we know much more about *levels of participation* than young people's *experiences* of PE and school sport (Wright et al., 2003; Dyson, 2006). This may be for two reasons: first, methodologically it is easier and cheaper to conduct large-scale surveys that measure rates of participation than to embark on time-consuming qualitative methodologies to understand and explore experiences. For the past ten years Sport England has conducted surveys of young people and sport, with the latest report analysing trends over time (Sport England, 1995; Rowe and Champion, 2000; Sport England, 2003). Second, it is only recently that teachers and researchers have acknowledged that young people have something valuable and important to offer to our understanding of PE. Even with this acknowledgement, it is still the case that we know little about particular groups of young people, such as ethnic minority or disabled young people (Fitzgerald, 2006; Kay, 2005).

By its very nature, 'participation levels' research is limited in what it can tell us about young people, PE and school sport. Although useful for mapping broad trends, it cannot, as Wright et al. (2003: 18) argue, tell us much about the significance or place of physical activities in young people's lives or how this might change or how they might 'draw on discursive and material resources associated with broader aspects of physical culture to construct their identities in relation to physical activity'. Coakley and White (1992) highlighted this some time ago, when they argued that young people should not be seen as 'dropping out' of physical activity or sport but instead as actively negotiating when and where they will be active, depending upon changing circumstances in their lives. Another limitation of 'participation levels' research is that particular groups of young people become highlighted as the 'problem' when compared with a 'norm' (usually the participation of young white middle-class males), so that the policy response to such 'deficit' is to provide more of the same opportunities. The participation rates of girls have been identified as lower than boys in several surveys, so one policy response has been to provide more opportunities for girls to participate, to 'target provision' and make a few changes to 'suit their differing needs'. The Nike/Youth Sport Trust (YST) sponsored project Girls into Sport (Nike/YST, 1999, 2000) serves as a good example. Although there were several worthwhile aspects of the project, such as engaging teachers in reflection and discussion about their own practice, it remained orientated towards making PE more 'girl-friendly' rather than challenging the nature and structure of dominant practices within PE (see also Penney, 2002a).

Despite their limitations, participation figures form the central basis for government evaluation of many of the current policies and practices in PE. The impact of PESSCL is evaluated primarily through participation figures against targets set as part of a Public Service Agreement (PSA), shared by the two government departments involved in the initiative – Education and Sport.[1] The PSA set ambitious targets:

> The aim is to increase the percentage of school children in England who spend a minimum of two hours per week on high quality PE and school sport within and beyond the curriculum to 75 per cent by 2006.
>
> (DfES/DCMS, 2003:1)

This target has been extended to 85 per cent by 2008, with the long-term ambition by 2010 to offer all children at least four hours of sport every week, with the *expectation* that at least two hours of this will be within the curriculum and the rest delivered beyond the school day by a range of school, community and club providers (DfES, 2006).[2]

The most recent survey of school sport shows that participation levels are improving (DfES/DCMS, 2005a). According to the report, 69 per cent of pupils in partnership schools[3] participate in at least two hours of PE and sport in a typical week, with the figure rising to 71 per cent of pupils in the older more established partnerships. The greatest improvement has been made by the primary sector, with the levels of participation rising from 52 per cent in 2003/04 to 64 per cent in 2004/05. Other notable successes include:

- 35 per cent of pupils in partnership schools were involved in some form of inter-school competition, with 25 per cent of pupils involved in intra-school competition.
- Each partnership school has school links on average with five different sports, and

22 per cent of pupils participated in at least one club with links with the school (including dance).

- ▪ In years 10–13 (age fourteen to eighteen), 11 per cent of pupils have been actively involved in sports volunteering and leadership during 2004/05.
- ▪ Schools have targeted out-of-school provision, with the most common criteria used being age, gender, special educational needs, and gifted and talented. Few schools targeted on the basis of ethnicity or religion.

There was little change between 2003/04 and 2004/05 in the time devoted to *curriculum* PE – that has remained at, on average, 107 minutes. The pattern varies between year groups and between schools; for example, primary-age pupils in years 1 and 2 receive on average ninety-six minutes of curricular PE, whereas year 7 pupils receive on average the most time of all school ages, 124 minutes. Averages do hide differences. A closer analysis of the report data shows that there are still 18 per cent of year 1 pupils and 36 per cent of year 11 pupils that receive just seventy-four minutes of curriculum PE or less. Although the report shows that schools are likely to target their out-of-school provision to particular groups of young people, it is not possible to know from this kind of research whether this strategy is successful. Other research suggests teachers have struggled with the concept of targeting, and that it has not been particularly successful in attracting pupils who have not traditionally been involved in extra-curricular sport, such as ethnic minority pupils (Flintoff and Cooke, 2005; Big Lottery Fund Research Issue 15, 2005; Shah, 2003, 2005).

Research that considers young people's *experiences* of PE is still a developing field, and there are significant gaps in our knowledge base. Such research highlights that the ethos and atmosphere in the PE classroom and the teacher's role are crucial. Young people view some of their PE teachers as unfair and elitist, as they spend more time with able pupils at the expense of the less able and with boys rather than with girls. Young people are critical of teachers who deploy pedagogical practices which centre on competition and winning for the elite minority at the expense of learning and enjoyment for all (see Dyson (2006) for an overview). Innovative PE programmes such as Sport Education or Co-operative Learning, which shift the locus of power and control away from the teacher to young people – where young people are given more responsibility for their own learning, through working in teams, adopting and learning different roles and working co-operatively – have been well received as alternative models (Penney *et al.*, 2005). The chapter will return to the importance of high-quality pedagogy in PE.

Other research has explored the way in which young people's PE lessons are structured by relations of gender, class, ability, sexuality and 'race'. There is now a large body of literature that has explored girls' experiences of PE and school sport (see Flintoff and Scraton (2006) for an overview). Flintoff and Scraton (2001) show how young women are active decision makers in the intensity and extent of their involvement in PE, and that these decisions are often made within the wider context of economic and gender relations that have to be negotiated and managed. There is, however, little research that explores boys' experiences of PE (see Parker, 1996; Bramham 2003; Gard, 2006) and even less that centralises the experiences of ethnic minority or disabled young people (Kay, 2005; Fitzgerald, 2006) or the important impacts of social class (Evans and Davies, 2006) or sexuality (Clarke, 2006). Whilst this work is developing slowly, too much of it has tended to be what Penney (2002a) has called 'single issue' research – focusing on either gender or ethnicity or sexuality and so on – without recognition of the complexities of young people's 'multiple identities' (Azzarito and Solomon, 2005). Understanding the place of PE and school sport in young people's lives needs to go beyond participation figures to appreciate the complex, changing ways in which young people make sense of physical cultures in and out of school as they actively construct their own physical identities. Research such as Wright et al.'s (2003) longitudinal study in Australia provides one such example.

ANALYSING POLICY

This section turns to a consideration of three aspects of contemporary PE policy and assesses their impact in meeting the needs of young people. In exploring the impact of any new policy initiative, the importance of *how* policy and practice are conceived is significant. In PE, Penney and Evans's research on the introduction and implementation of NCPE over the past decade and a half has been influential in contributing to this body of work (e.g. Penney and Evans, 1999, 2005).[4] Penney and Evans (1999:19) reject 'a traditional, hierarchical view of policy in which policy is reified as an artefact, commodity or "thing" made by certain individuals . . . to be implemented by others in levels or sites "below", thereby giving rise to "practice"'. Instead they argue for a more sophisticated understanding of policy, whereby neither making nor implementing policy is restricted to one single site or an individual or to a point in time. They argue that policy should best be seen as a *process*. This conception accommodates the different numbers of sites in which policy gets transformed or reinterpreted by different individuals – where 'slippage' occurs between the original and reinterpreted policy. The whole process of policy making and implementation is one in which there is the transmission of 'not one but rather a series of different policy texts', so transforming policy into a 'new' or 'hybrid text' (Penney and Evans, 1999). In arguing for a more 'fluid' conception of policy based on interactions between 'content and context' Penney and Evans stress inequities that exist in any policy process. They draw on the concept of *discourse* as a key tool to help explain how different values and interests get promoted and expressed through policy texts, and how others get marginalised or overlooked. Discourses are not simply sets of 'ideas' that can be accepted or dismissed but, as Penney and Evans (1999: 24) note, they are about language and meanings, about knowledge and power and their interrelationship, and about what can be said and by whom. They are about 'expressions of particular interests and values, they create and promote particular meanings and values'. Policy texts are necessarily political, serving and promoting particular interests whilst ignoring and subordinating other interests. Whilst their work has shown clearly the importance of attending to the capacity of individual actors, such as PE teachers, within specific contexts to *reinterpret* and implement the NCPE, it has also shown the *determining* influence of central government throughout the process, seeking to control the degree to which 'slippage' occurs. The extent to which others can exploit and use marginalised discourses depends not only on discursive power but also on institutional, positional and material power.

The National Curriculum in Physical Education

Drawing on such a conception of policy, it is clear that the NCPE should best be seen as a policy that is 'unfinished', 'always in the making'; 'in the process of (de- and re-) construction and contested and contestable' (Penney, 2006: 567). Teachers are now implementing the third revision of the NCPE. The first was introduced in 1992 as part of the Education Reform Act in 1988. Penney and Evans (1999) have detailed the complex ways in which the process of defining the first NCPE unfolded, showing the influence of dominant discourses and contexts outside education, most notably of sport, on the finalised school version (Evans and Penney, 1995). The NCPE became (and remains even after two revisions) a curriculum constructed around discrete activity areas – games, gymnastics, dance and so on – with an emphasis on skill acquisition and performing, whilst privileging games over other activity areas (Penney, 2001). However, it is important to note that there are significant continuities between PE prior to the introduction of the NCPE and current practice. Whilst, on one hand, the last decade and a half in PE could be described as one in which there has been much curricular change, on the other there are also clear interests (at school, local government as well as at national level) in the maintenance of the *status quo* (Penney, 2006). The flexibility inherent in the NCPE official curriculum texts means that there is plenty of room for teachers to accommodate new requirements in what is essentially unchanged pedagogical and curricular practice. Curtner-Smith (1999: 57) has described this as 'the more things change, the more things stay the same'. Historical research has shown how the multi-activity curriculum model, privileging and reproducing the dominance of discourses of sport performance, has remained *the* dominant model in PE (Penney, 2006). This model has been reinforced and reproduced in the extra-curricular or out-of-school hours learning opportunities provided in PESS. Office for Standards in Education (Ofsted) reports (2005a, b) have confirmed that this picture remained stubbornly resilient to change. The primary and secondary curricula were reported as too games-dominated, with teachers insufficiently skilled at differentiating their lessons to cater for pupils of different abilities. They concluded that there was much underachievement among different ability groups in PE, leaving individual needs often ignored. So, whilst the NCPE may have provided a new discourse of PE, there remains more focus on the *what* should be taught than on the *how* it should be taught and the types of pedagogies that might bring about real change at the level of young people's everyday experience (Evans *et al.*, 1996).

Another aspect that appears resistant to change is the gendered nature of the NCPE. Penney (2002b) argues that through the privileging of games, the flexibility in the policy, and the silences and omissions around issues of equity, the NCPE is an implicitly gendered text. Although the current version of the NCPE does make mention of teachers paying 'due regard' in their teaching to three principles of inclusion (Penney, 2002b), they are given no guidance about how they might work to these principles, and, to date, inclusion has tended to be interpreted in terms of ability, with a focus on the inclusion of children with special educational needs or with exceptional talent (Bailey and Morley, 2003; Vickerman, 2003). In addition, male and female teachers continue to deliver different aspects of the curriculum (Waddington et al., 1998); teachers use their gender as a key pedagogical resource (Evans et al., 1996; Brown and Rich, 2002), and even areas of the curriculum that have a less gendered history, such as Health Related Fitness, are delivered in very different ways to boys compared with girls (Harris and Penney, 2002).

Whilst flexibilities in policy texts allow for teachers to continue existing practice, it is also important to acknowledge that these are also spaces for others to develop new practice. As mentioned earlier, the introduction of sport education as a new pedagogical model is beginning to provide some young people with different experiences of sport (Kirk, 2006; Penney et al., 2005). Sport Education is a pedagogical model in PE that aims to offer young people a more 'authentic' experience of sport through different kinds of learning and sport engagement in PE lessons (Seidentop, 2004). Typically, young people work in 'teams' over a significant period of time or 'season' of sport, and get to experience a number of different roles within that team (coach, scorer, referee, player). The focus is on a more holistic approach to learning; on sport *education*, rather than simply sport activity, and engages young people in taking responsibility for their own and others' learning (Penney et al., 2005). Another example is the Step into Sport programme, one of the key strands of PESSCL, where sport and physical activity are used as vehicles to develop leadership skills with young people.

In reviewing the impact of the NCPE on young people's experience of PE, we need to go beyond a taken-for-granted view that it has necessarily been beneficial. By adopting a more critical perspective, we need to ask what has actually changed as a result of its introduction and who has benefited from the changes? A curriculum dominated by games, with a sport-performance pedagogy, fosters *particular* conceptions of ability in PE. In so doing, some young people will succeed and enjoy PE but others will lose out, and will be constructed as 'lacking in ability' (Evans, 2004; Fitzgerald, 2005; Wright and Burrows, 2006). Perhaps one final point to be made about the NCPE is that it is not a national curriculum at all, since private schools are not required to adhere to it!

Specialist Sports Colleges

The second policy initiative considered here is Specialist Sports Colleges. These were first introduced in 1997 by the Labour government, although the broader specialist schools initiative originated from the previous Conservative government.[5] SSCs are secondary schools that receive extra funding from government to develop and raise standards in the specialist subject area but also to use the specialism to raise school standards and to support

150

the work of families of neighbouring schools. The DfES (2006) outlines the vision of sports colleges below:

> to raise standards of achievement in physical education and sport for all their students across the ability range leading to whole school improvement. They are regional focal points for promoting excellence in physical education and community sport, extending links between families of schools, sports bodies and communities, sharing resources, developing and spreading good practice and helping to provide a structure through which young people can progress to careers in sport and physical education. Sports Colleges are expected to develop a visible sports ethos throughout the school and within their local community which inspires their students.
>
> (DfES, 2006)

A key feature of the introduction of SSCs has been their phased implementation, with a total of 400 schools planned for designation.[6] Most secondary schools will not specialise in sport, although by 2006 it is anticipated that all primary and secondary schools will benefit from a school sport partnership that has a sports college at its hub (see below). By phasing implementation, the body responsible for supporting and developing the programme, the Youth Sport Trust,[7] has exercised some control over how policy has become embedded within school practice (through, for example, its application, evaluation and redesignation procedures; its annual conference, and other continuing professional development opportunities for those teachers working in the colleges). As a result, this has produced a much differentiated PESS context, with many schools and teachers only marginally involved in innovations emanating from the programme as it has progressively developed over the past nine years. Whilst Houlihan (2000) has suggested that the policy field of youth sport is 'crowded', such is the number of new policies introduced, not all teachers (and therefore young people) have been beneficiaries of their impact.

A second point worth noting about SSCs in comparison with other specialist schools is how the particular subject area of PE, with its link to school sport, creates a complex policy space for teachers to occupy. As Houlihan (2000) and Houlihan and Wong (2005a, b) have argued, since it is difficult to delineate the policy boundaries of school sport, one result is that different interest groups struggle for influence and control over the kinds of activities privileged and introduced (see Figure 7.1), leaving PE teachers with little power to establish and assert policy leadership. Sports colleges have to meet the demands not just of wider educational and school agendas but also of those challenges from elite sport, sports development and health and fitness communities. So, for example, in order to get sports college redesignation for an additional four years, schools have to show increased performance in their school-wide General Certificate in Secondary Education (GCSE) results, year on year. They are also expected to support the development of talented youngsters in sport, as well as be key players in the development of community sports participation programmes.

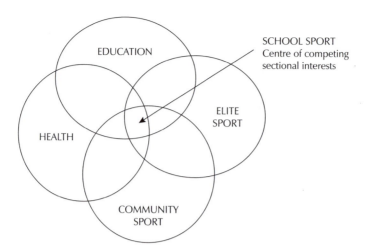

Figure 7.1 School sport: at the centre of competing sectoral interests

Source Adapted from Houlihan (2000).

The phased implementation of the programme, and the methodological challenges of measuring the specific impact of the specialism, together with what Houlihan and Wong (2005a) call a general paucity of research in this area, caution against presenting simplistic 'headline' achievements here.[8] Keeping these caveats in mind, emerging evidence suggests that SSCs are changing PE practice in a number of ways in relation to curricular activities and attainment, collaboration and development activities (Houlihan and Wong, 2005a, b). One important difference in SSCs relates to the amount of *curricular* time allocated to PE. In order to gain SSC accreditation, all young people must have access to two hours of PE on the curriculum – which, as highlighted above, is not the case with many other schools. Other notable achievements include:

- Young people's attainment levels in PE at Key Stage 3 (years 11–14) appear to be steadily increasing, particularly for boys.
- SSCs appear to have helped to raise the levels of achievement of the lower end of the ability range in PE rather than stretching those at the higher levels.
- There is no evidence that SSCs do better or worse than other specialisms in helping raise general attainment levels as measured by GCSE A*–C grades.
- However, it is clear that the provision of non-traditional awards in leadership and NGBs courses (e.g. Junior or Community Sports Leaderships Award) is one of the strengths of the SSCs.
- Progress in developing collaborative activities, particularly with the family of primary schools, has been good. Primary teachers, who are not specialists in PE, have been responsive to help and support.
- Collaborative activities between secondary schools have been less well developed and mainly in the areas of Continuing Professional Development (CPD) and in the development of sports leadership awards.

- Becoming a SSC has been beneficial in many cases in helping to win additional capital funding from key agencies and NGBs: for example, the Big Lottery Fund, the Football Foundation or the Lawn Tennis Association.

At the heart of the success of the SSCs is the ability to work in partnership – with other schools, sports and community clubs, other teachers and so on. The final initiative discussed here, the School Sport Partnership Programme (SSPP), aims to build these links between the SSCs, their neighbouring family of schools and sports and other community organisations.

School Sport Partnership Programme

The School Sport Partnership Programme[9] involves a number of different schools working together in a partnership, with (usually) a SSC acting as the lead or hub school. Partnerships aim to increase sporting opportunities for young people by developing and enhancing links between school PE and sporting opportunities in the wider community. Although each partnership develops its own development plan, there is a partnership model, as shown in Figure 7.2.

Primary and secondary teachers work within each partnership to plan, deliver and evaluate the strategic work of the partnership. There are three different roles in each partnership:

- The Partnership Development Manager (PDM), an experienced teacher, normally based at the Specialist Sports College, who generally works full time to lead its development.
- School Sport Co-ordinator (SSCo), an experienced teacher from each of the partnership secondary schools who is released from a teaching timetable for two or three days a week to work with an identified primary teacher in each of their feeder primary schools.
- Primary Link Teacher (PLT), a primary teacher responsible for PE in their school who is released from the teaching timetable for approximately twelve days per year.

In addition, to fill the gaps created by releasing teachers as SSCos, every two secondary schools in a partnership are able to appoint a Specialist Link Teacher – an additional qualified PE teacher.

Like the Specialist Sports College, the SSPP has been implemented in phases but, by the end of 2006, all schools should be part of a school sport partnership.

Funding from the government pays for the above posts and teachers' release, with additional funding from the Big Lottery Fund – on average £75,000 over three years – to 'kick-start' additional out-of-hours sports activities designed to widen participation. In addition, competition managers have been introduced into some sports partnerships in order to develop and enhance competitive sport opportunities for pupils.

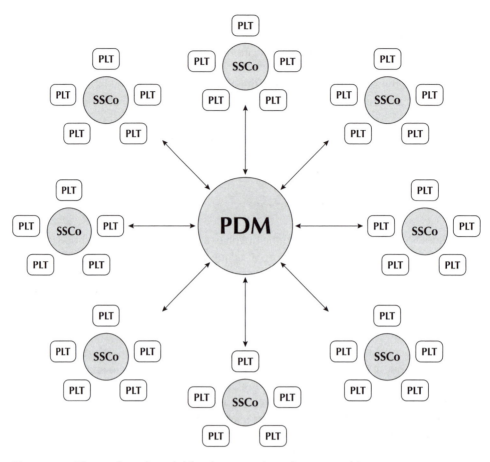

Figure 7.2 The preferred model for the operation of a partnership

In evaluating the success of the SSPP, it is important to stress the 'roll-out' strategy for the programme. Some schools have been working together within a partnership for over six years, whilst others have only just been incorporated into a partnership. Hence any evaluation data need to be viewed with this in mind. Each partnership develops its own unique practices, with distinctive strengths and weaknesses, although some clear trends are emerging. Like the Specialist Sports Colleges, one of the key evaluations is being conducted by researchers at the Institute of Youth Sport at Loughborough University (Loughborough Partnership, 2005). There are also other, earlier evaluations of the programme available (Quick and Goddard, 2004; Ofsted, 2002, 2003, 2004). The Loughborough partnership evaluation offers a six-year study that includes the collection of annual quantitative data from all partnerships nationally, with more qualitative in-depth studies of a sample of individual partnerships. To date, few studies have attempted any longitudinal study of the development of a partnership (see Flintoff, 2003; Flintoff and Cooke, 2002, 2005).

The SSPP raises important questions about the nature of young people's school sport opportunities and who are best placed to manage and develop them. Organising and running extra-curricular sport teams and clubs have historically always been part of the secondary PE teachers' role, and seen by many as one of the most positive aspects of the job (Armour and Jones, 1998). As a result, PE teachers have been somewhat cautious about policy initiatives that have attempted to encroach on what they regard as an integral and important part of their professional role. For example, the Champion Coaching Scheme – in many ways a forerunner of the SSPP – was not well received by many PE teachers, who felt threatened by the establishment of out-of-school centres where young people could receive quality sports coaching (Collins and Buller, 2000). In similar vein, the development of the SSPP has not always been straightforward. The new roles of SSCo and PDM present PE teachers with very different challenges and require different skills to delivery curricular PE within one school. Moving outside the 'safety net' of one single school environment into strategic development work, and working across a number of different schools and contexts, have been challenging for some PE teachers (Flintoff, 2003). One of the key challenges for the implementation of the programme has been staffing. Not all head teachers have been happy to see one of their experienced teachers lost to teaching for two days a week. There have also been ongoing problems with the provision of 'back-fill' posts to cover the time lost to a school by the SSCo role. The appointment of specialist link tutors to replace the gaps left by teachers adopting SSCo roles has not yet materialised in many partnerships. However, there are several positive aspects of the programme worth identifying here:

- The programme allows for the building of local networks and opportunities, around families of schools as the 'hub'.
- The fact that PE teachers are central to the decision making in each of the partnerships should ensure that the activities that are developed are educationally sound and appropriate.
- The links between curricular PE and the programme are enabled by the dual positioning of SSCos as both teacher (three days a week) and co-ordinator (two days a week).
- Teachers' continuing professional development is an underlying element of the programme so that sustainable practice is inbuilt.
- The programme includes a focus on primary as well as secondary-age children; arguably, this group has not always been well served by previous policies.

It is clear that the programme is producing some important gains for young people, particularly by increasing the range and quality of opportunities to be physically active (Loughborough Partnership, 2005). Big Lottery Funding has enabled partnerships to buy in additional coaches to deliver programmes. The number of young people now taking part in two hours of high-quality PESS within and beyond the curriculum is impressive. The impact of the programme on primary PE has been particularly substantial – a welcome but perhaps not surprising result, given that the generally poor state of primary PE has been a concern for the profession for some time (Evans *et al.*, 1996; Williams, 2000). There are also indications that many more pupils are taking part in inter-school competitive sport, and that participation in district- and county-level competition is increasing, particularly for boys.

However, the impact of the programme on raising the status and position of PESS generally is less clear. Although the picture is improving somewhat, the time allocated to *curricular* PE remains very variable, both between schools and between year groups within schools. Whilst 76 per cent of schools in the national evaluation of the programme of 2004/05 provide two hours of curricular PE for year 7 pupils (aged eleven to twelve) this drops to only 32 per cent for girls (36 per cent for boys) at year 10 (Loughborough Partnership, 2005). So, although there have been many gains, there is still much variety, with no formal entitlement to two hours of curriculum PE for *all* young people. Inevitably, increased opportunities to participate in after-school activities will be taken up by some young people and not by others. We need to ask which young people are benefiting from the particular activities provided. Simply offering more opportunities for competitive sport is unlikely to attract those young people who have been marginalised in the past from positive physical activity experiences. It is interesting to note that the previous focus of the programme – to address specifically the participation levels of particular groups of young people – ethnic minorities, girls, disabled youngsters and those from socio-economically deprived backgrounds – has been downplayed in recent policy documents. Instead the focus has shifted away from groups of young people to different types of activity experience. The new handbook for SSCos stresses the importance of providing high-quality opportunities in curriculum PE, in out-of-school hours learning, informal physical activity opportunities, as well as in competitive sport (Youth Sport Trust, 2005). In addition, recent publications, such as *Dance Links* (DfES, 2005), specifically address the need to widen the conception of being physically active to be more inclusive of the different needs of young people. Nevertheless, with the introduction of new competition managers, with a sport-based NCPE at the centre of the partnerships and with the successful bid to host the Olympic Games in 2012, it is difficult to see how a sport-dominated PESS can be shifted from centre stage.

HIGH-QUALITY PESS FOR ALL?

It is clear that there has been much change within the policy context of PESS over the past decade or so. Building on the NCPE, the SSC and the SSP programmes represents a significant restructuring of the policy field, bringing with it new opportunities for young people to be physically active. In addition, it opens up possibilities of new roles and responsibilities for PE teachers and sports development workers interested in working with young people. As with any new policy, the success of programmes relies heavily on the ability and enthusiasm of the people involved in its day-to-day implementation. However, increasing the range and amount of opportunities should not take second place to the quality of that provision. Although Ofsted (2005c) noted a slight improvement from its report in 2004, it also voiced concern over the quality of some teaching and assessment, as well as a lack of evaluation of the impact of programmes on the quality of provision overall. As Ofsted has noted elsewhere, underachievement is more likely to be seen in PE lessons when the emphasis is on activity rather than learning (Ofsted, 2005a). The publication of two documents about high-quality PE and sport (DfES/DCMS, 2004, 2005b) and the redrafting of SSPP outcomes, to stress 'high-quality' participation in different types of physical activity, is a step in the right direction in helping teachers recognise the need to go beyond simply providing 'more opportunity'. These documents focus on the pupil outcomes of high-quality PE and school sport (PESS) or what teachers might expect to see children doing when they are involved in high-quality PESS. However, there is a danger that in focusing on pupil outcomes the actions of the teachers or coaches are marginalised or that different lifestyles and cultures of individual pupils that shape their responses to PE are simply ignored. If PESSCL and associated programmes are to have a sustained impact and change the nature of young people's participation in physical activity and sport, it will be the pedagogy underpinning new provision that remains the key. Teachers, sports development officers and others working within the remit of PESSCL will require support to engage in critical reflection about the nature of their pedagogy if they are to provide programmes capable of engaging the very different needs of today's young people.

NOTES

1   The School Sport Partnership programme is evaluated annually through the collection of quantitative participation data and is also part of a wider evaluation conducted by the Institute of Youth Sport at Loughborough University. This evaluation includes more detailed evaluations of a sample of school sport partnerships which includes observation of SSPP activities, interviews with key staff as well as detailed questionnaire. Similarly, sports colleges are evaluated through a comprehensive questionnaire which considers the broad range of activities within their remit. It remains the case that it is participation statistics (SSPP) and GCSE A–C rates (SSCs) that are used by government to mark the success or otherwise of these initiatives.
2   The wording is interesting here. There has not yet been a definitive commitment to two hours of PE within curriculum time and the wording 'expected' rather than 'will' allows schools to deliver much less than this if they so wish.
3   It is important to note that both the School Sport Partnership programme and Specialist Sports Colleges are initiatives that are being rolled out in phases. This means that although they started some time ago (Specialist Sports Colleges in 1997; School Sport Partnerships in 2000), it took until 2006 for all schools to be involved in a sports partnership. At the time of the 2004/05 report only 50 per cent of schools in England were in a sports partnership.
4   This is explored in Flintoff (2003).
5   Specialist Sports Colleges are maintained secondary schools in England that receive additional funding from the DfES to raise standards in PE and sport within its own

school, in a local family of schools and in the community. To apply, schools are required to raise £50,000 from private sector sponsorship and submit a four-year development plan.

6   There were just eleven colleges designated in 1997, with the total of 400 expected to be in place by 2006.

7   The Youth Sport Trust is a registered charity, launched in 1994. Since then it has grown in size, status and influence, with a particular focus on the promotion of sport in schools. Until recently its Chief Executive was Sue Campbell, a government adviser on PE and sport. It has a major remit in supporting and developing the government's Specialist Sports Colleges, secondary schools which are seen as the 'lead' schools in the PESSCL strategy, including the SSPP programme.

8   There have been three annual evaluation reports published on the Institute of Youth Sport, Loughborough University, web site, www.lboro.ac.uk/departments/sses/IYS/.

9   The programme was previously known as the School Sport Co-ordinator Programme.

REFERENCES

Armour, K. M. and Jones, R.L. (1998) *Physical Education: Teachers' Lives and Careers*. London: Falmer Press.

Azzarito, L. and Solomon, M. (2005) A reconceptualisation of physical education: the intersection of gender/race/social class. *Sport, Education and Society*, 10, 25–47.

Bailey, R. and Morley, D. (2003) Towards a Model of Talent Development in PE, presented at the annual conference of the British Educational Research Association, Edinburgh, September.

Big Lottery Fund Research Issue 15 (2005) New Opportunities in PE and Sport Evaluation Update [Internet]. London: Big Lottery Fund Research, www.nof.gov.uk (accessed 22 November 2005).

Bramham, P. (2003) Boys, masculinity and PE. *Sport, Education and Society*, 8, 57–71.

Brown, D. and Rich, E. (2002) Gender positioning as pedagogical practice in physical education. In D. Penney (ed.) *Gender and Physical Education: Contemporary Issues and Future Directions* (pp. 80–100). London: Falmer Press.

Clarke, G. (2006) Sexuality and physical education. In D. Kirk, D. Macdonald and M. O' Sullivan (eds) *The Handbook of Physical Education* (pp. 723–39). London: Sage.

Coakley, J. and White, A. (1992) Making decisions: gender and sport participation among British adolescents. *Sociology of Sport Journal*, 9, 20–35.

Collins, M.F. and Buller, J.R. (2000) Bridging the post-school institutional gap in sport: evaluating champion coaching in Nottinghamshire. *Managing Leisure*, 5, 200–21.

Curtner-Smith, M.D. (1999) The more things change the more they stay the same: factors influencing teachers' interpretations and delivery of National Curriculum Physical Education. *Sport Education and Society*, 4, 75–97.

Department for Culture Media and Sport and Department for Education and Employment

(2001) *A Sporting Future for All: The Government's Plan for Sport*. London: Department for Culture, Media and Sport.

Department for Culture Media and Sport and Strategy Unit (2002) *Game Plan: A Strategy for Delivering the Government's Sport and Physical Activity Objectives*. London: Crown Publications.

Department for Education and Employment (1999) *Physical Education: The National Curriculum in England*. London: Department for Education and Employment/ Qualifications and Curriculum Authority.

Department for Education and Skills (2005) *Do you Have High Quality Physical Education and School Sport in Your School*? London: Crown Publications.

Department for Education and Skills (2006) *Physical Education and School Sport Club Links*. Available from: http:www.teachernet.gov.uk/teachingandlearning/subjects/pe (accessed 23 October 2006).

Department for Education and Skills and Department for Culture Media and Sport (2003) *Learning through PE and Sport: A Guide to the Physical Education, School Sport and Club Links Strategy*. Nottingham: DfES.

Department for Education and Skills and Department for Culture Media and Sport (2004) *High Quality PE and Sport for Young People*. Nottingham: DfES.

Department for Education and Skills and Department for Culture Media and Sport (2005a) *The Results of the 2004/05 School Sport Survey*. Nottingham: DfES.

Department for Education and Skills and Department for Culture Media and Sport (2005b) *Dance Links: A Guide to delivering High-quality Dance to Children and Young People* [Internet]. London: Crown (accessed 5 December 2005).

Department of Education and Science (1991) *Physical Education for Ages 5–16 Years: Proposals to the Secretary of State for Education and Science*. London: HMSO.

Dyson, B. (2006) Students' perspectives of physical education. In D. Kirk, D. Macdonald and M. O'Sullivan (eds) *The Handbook of Physical Education* (pp. 326–436). London: Sage.

Evans, J. (2004) Making a difference? Education and 'ability' in physical education. *European Journal of Physical Education*, 10, 95–108.

Evans, J. and Davies, B. (1986) Sociology, schooling and physical education. In J. Evans (ed.) *Physical Education, Sport and Schooling: Studies in the Sociology of Physical Education* (pp. 11–37). London: Falmer Press.

—— (2006) Social class and physical education. In D. Kirk, D. Macdonald and M. O'Sullivan (eds) *The Handbook of Physical Education* (pp. 796–808). London: Sage.

Evans, J. and Penney, D. (1995) The politics of pedagogy: making a National Curriculum Physical Education. *Journal of Education Policy*, 10, 27–44.

Evans, J., Davies, B. and Penney, D. (1996a) Teachers, teaching and the social construction of gender relations. *Sport, Education and Society*, 1, 165–83.

Evans, J., Penney, D., Bryant, A. and Hennink, M. (1996b) All things bright and beautiful? PE in primary schools post the 1988 Education Reform Act. *Educational Review*, 48, 29–40.

Fitzgerald, H. (2005) Still feeling like a spare piece of luggage? Embodied experiences of (dis)ability in physical education and school sport. *Physical Education and Sport Pedagogy*, 10, 41–59.

—— (2006) Disability and physical education. In D. Kirk, D. Macdonald and M. O'Sullivan (eds) *The Handbook of Physical Education* (pp. 752–66). London: Sage.

Fletcher, S. (1984) *Women First: The Female Tradition in English Physical Education, 1880–1980*. London: Athlone Press.

Flintoff, A. (2003) The School Sport Co-ordinator Programme: changing the role of the Physical Education teacher? *Sport, Education and Society*, 8, 231–50.

Flintoff, A. and Cooke, B. (2002) An evaluation of an out of school hours learning in PE and sport programme: interim report February 2002. *Bulletin of Physical Education*, 38, 99–110.

—— (2005) Playing to learn: out of school hours learning in PE and sport. *British Journal of Teaching Physical Education*, 36, 43–7.

Flintoff, A. and Scraton, S. (2001) Stepping into Active Leisure? Young women's perceptions of active lifestyles and their experiences of school Physical Education. *Sport, Education and Society*, 6, 5–22.

—— (2006) Girls and PE. In D. Kirk, D. Macdonald and M. O'Sullivan (eds) *The Handbook of Physical Education* (pp. 767–83). London: Sage.

Gard, M. (2006) More art than science? Boys, masculinity and physical education. In D. Kirk, D. Macdonald and M. O'Sullivan (eds) *The Handbook of Physical Education*. London: Sage.

Hargreaves, J. (1979) Playing like Gentlemen while behaving like Ladies. Unpublished MA, University of London.

—— (1994) *Sporting Females: Critical Issues in the History and Sociology of Women's Sports*. London: Routledge.

Harris, J. and Penney, D. (2002) Gender, health and physical education. In D. Penney (ed.) *Gender and Physical Education: Contemporary Issues and Future Directions* (pp. 123–45). London: Routledge.

Houlihan, B. (2000) Sporting excellence, schools and sports development: the politics of crowded policy spaces. *European Physical Education Review*, 6, 17–93.

Houlihan, B. and Green, M. (2006) The changing status of school sport and Physical Education: explaining policy change. *Sport, Education and Society*, 11, 73–92.

Houlihan, B. and Wong, C. (2005a) The Operation and Impact of Specialist Sports Colleges, British Educational Research Conference. University of Glamorgan, 14–17 September.

—— (2005b) *Report on the 2004 National Survey of Specialist Sports Colleges*. Loughborough: Institute of Youth Sport, Loughborough University.

Institute of Youth Sport (2005) *School Sport Partnerships: Annual Monitoring and Evaluation Report*. Loughborough: Institute of Youth Sport. Available from http://www.lboro.ac.uk/iys (accessed 25 November 2005).

Kay, T. (2005) The voice of the family: influences on Muslim girls' responses to sport. In A. Flintoff, J. Long and K. Hylton (eds) *Youth Sport and Active Leisure: Theory, Policy and Practice* (pp. 91–114). Brighton: Leisure Studies Association.

Kirk, D. (1992) *Defining Physical Education: The Social Construction of a Subject in Postwar Britain*. London: Falmer Press.

—— (1993) *The Body, Schooling and Culture*. Geelong: Deakin University Press.

—— (1999) Physical culture, physical education and relational analysis. *Sport, Education and Society*, 4, 63–74.

—— (2006) Sport education, critical pedagogy and learning theory: toward an intrinsic justification for Physical Education and youth sport. *Quest*, 58, 225–64.

Loughborough Partnership (2005) *School Sport Partnerships: Monitoring and Evaluation Report 2004*. Loughborough: Institute of Youth Sport, Loughborough University.

MacDonald, D. (2002) Extending agendas: physical culture research for the twenty-first century. In D. Penney (ed.) *Gender and Physical Education: Contemporary Issues and Future Directions* (pp. 208–22). London: Routledge.

Nike and Youth Sport Trust (1999) *The Girls in Sport Partnership Project: Interim Report*. Loughborough: Institute of Youth Sport, Loughborough University.

—— (2000) *Girls into Sport: Towards Girl-friendly Physical Education*. Loughborough: Institute of Youth Sport, Loughborough University.

Office for Standards in Education (2002) *The School Sport Co-ordinator Programme: Evaluation of Phases 1 and 2, 2001–2003*. London: HMSO.

—— (2003) *The School Sport Co-ordinator Programme: Evaluation of Phases 1 and 2, 2001–2003*. London: Crown Publications.

—— (2004) *The School Sport Partnership Programme: Evaluation of Phases 3 and 4, 2003*. London: Office for Standards in Education.

—— (2005a) *Ofsted Subject Reports 2003/04: Physical Education in Secondary Schools*. London: Crown Publications.

—— (2005b) *Physical Education in Primary Schools*. London: Ofsted.

—— (2005c) *The Physical Education, School Sport and Club Links Strategy: The School Sport Partnerships Programme. Support for Gifted and Talented Pupils in Physical Education*. London: Crown Publications.

Parker, A. (1996) The construction of masculinity in boys' PE. *Gender and Education*, 8, 141–57.

Penney, D. (2001) The revision and initial implementation of the National Curriculum for Physical Education in England. *Bulletin of Physical Education*, 37, 93–135.

—— (2002a) Equality, equity and inclusion in PE and school sport. In A. Laker (ed.) *The Sociology of Sport and Physical Education* (pp. 110–28). London: Routledge.

—— (2002b) Equality, equity and inclusion in Physical Education. In A. Laker (ed.) *The Sociology of Sport and Physical Education*. London: Routledge.

—— (2002c) Gendered policies. In D. Penney (ed.) *Gender and Physical Education: Contemporary Issues and Future Directions*. London: Routledge.

—— (2006) Curriculum construction and change. In D. Kirk, D. Macdonald and M. O'Sullivan (eds) *The Handbook of Physical Education* (pp. 565–79). London: Sage.

Penney, D. and Evans, J. (1999) *Politics, Policy and Practice in Physical Education*. London: E. & F. N. Spon.

—— (2005) Policy, power and politics in physical education. In K. Green and K. Hardman (eds) *Physical Education: Essential Issues*. London: Sage.

Penney, D. and Harris, J. (1997) Extra-curricular Physical Education: more of the same for the more able. *Sport, Education and Society*, 2, 41–54.

Penney, D., Clarke, G., Quill, M. and Kitchin, D. (2005) *Sport Education in Physical Education*. London: Routledge.

Quick, S. and Goddard, S. (2004) *Schools in the School Sport Partnership Programme: PE, School Sports and Club Links Survey 2003–2004*. London: Department for Education and Skills.

Rowe, N. and Champion, R. (2000) *Young People and Sport: National Survey 1999*. London: Sport England.

Seidentop, D. (1994) *Sport Education: Quality PE through Positive Sport Experiences*. Leeds: Human Kinetics.

Shah, A. (2003) Out of School Hours Learning: The Views and Opinions of the New Opportunities Fund Staff. London: New Opportunities Fund. Available from http://www.nof.gov.uk (accessed 22 November 2005).

—— (2005) *Achievements and Challenges in Delivering Out of School Hours Learning: Final Report*. London: New Opportunities Fund. Available from http:/www.nof.gov.uk (accessed 22 November 2005).

Sport England (1995) *Young People and Sport Survey*. London: Sport England.

—— (2003) *Young People and Sport in England: Trends in Participation, 1994–2002*. London: Sport England.

Vickerman, P. (2003) Inclusion Confusion? Official line Perspectives on including Children with Special Educational Needs in Physical Education, paper presented at the annual conference of the British Educational Research Association, Edinburgh, September.

Waddington, I., Malcolm, D. and Cobb, J. (1998) Gender stereotyping and Physical Education. *European Journal of Physical Education*, 4, 34–46.

Williams, A. (2000) Research and the primary school teacher. In A. Williams (ed.) *Primary School PE: Research into Practice*. London: RoutledgeFalmer.

Williams, A. and Bedward, J. (2001) Gender culture and the generation gap: student and teacher perceptions of aspects of National Curriculum Physical Education. *Sport, Education and Society*, 6, 53–66.

Williams, A. and Woodhouse, J. (1996) Delivering the discourse: urban adolescents' perceptions of Physical Education. *Sport, Education and Society*, 1, 210–13.

Wright, J. and Burrows, L. (2006) Re-conceiving ability in physical education: a social analysis. *Sport, Education and Society*, 11, 275–91.

Wright, J., Macdonald, D. and Groom, L. (2003) Physical activity and young people: beyond participation. *Sport, Education and Society*, 8, 17–34.

Youth Sport Trust (2005) *Welcome Pack for School Sport Coordinators*. Loughborough: Youth Sport Trust. Available from: http://www:yst.org.uk/ssco/documents (accessed 22 November 2005).

ABBREVIATIONS

DfES	Department for Education and Skills
DCMS	Department for Media, Culture and Sport
GCSE	General Certificate of Secondary Education
IYS	Institute of Youth Sport
NCPE	National Curriculum in Physical Education
Ofsted	Office for Standards in Education
PDM	Partnership Development Manager
PE	Physical Education
PESS	Physical Education and School Sport
PESSCL	Physical Education and School Sport Club Links
PSA	Public Service Agreement
SSC	Specialist Sports College
SSCo	School Sport Co-ordinator
SSPP	School Sport Partnership Programme
PLT	Primary Link Teacher
SLT	Specialist Link Teacher
YST	Youth Sport Trust

CHAPTER 8

SPORT AND HEALTH

Stephen Robson and Jim McKenna

In recent years sport's role as a key form of physical activity in the battle against obesity and other forms of ill health has become more widely acknowledged by all policy sectors, including central government. Due to the mutual recognition of competence between sports development professionals and health care providers the current environment has demonstrated that their initial bureaucratic suspicions have abated. This chapter introduces key concepts in relation to sport, physical activity and exercise as well as updating the reader on political developments in sport and health discourses. Finally, the chapter maps out key stages in a transtheoretical model of behaviour change in relation to health promotion.

KEY TERMS: HEALTH AND FITNESS

In many settings, terms such as 'health' and 'fitness' are often used interchangeably, although they carry distinct meanings. Consequently, it is helpful to establish working definitions to help understand this growing aspect of sports development. The distinction between fitness and health is an important one. It is most useful to think of fitness as a component of health, with 'health' as an all-embracing term used to describe the individual's overall well-being. Various established definitions of health, including that of the World Health Organisation, emphasise a holistic approach. Health is not merely the absence of disease but complete and optimal physical, mental, social and spiritual functioning. To quote Bouchard *et al.* (1990: 6–7), health is a:

> human condition with physical, social and psychological dimensions, each characterized on a continuum with positive and negative poles; positive health is associated with a capacity to enjoy life and withstand challenges, it is not merely the absence of disease; negative health is associated with morbidity and, in the extreme, with mortality.

Experts consider health as an all-embracing concept, which cannot be measured simply by objective physical criteria but also must take into account an individual's subjective perception of his or her status. The concept of fitness is therefore but one important dimension of health. It deals specifically with the capacity to perform given tasks such as work satisfactorily.[1] Whilst fitness is conventionally thought of in terms of capacity to achieve physical goals, most definitions acknowledge ideas of mental fitness. 'Mental toughness' and other psychological factors (such as commitment, motivation, coping with stress, resilience, hardiness, anxiety and so on) occupy a vital role in the preparation and performance of aspiring and elite athletes.

Physical aspects of fitness status (e.g. speed, power, strength, endurance and flexibility) can be developed – fitness as behaviour – in elite performers to a high degree and are specific to the particular demands of sport. Fitness can also be achieved by recreational sport participants to secure benefits for individual health; for example, an older person taking up cycling may experience gains in endurance and leg strength, and subsequently be able to undertake daily tasks with increased ease and vigour. However, public health professionals are sensitive to the lack of interest, shared throughout the UK population, in activities which demand intense physical exercise that sporting forms often take for granted. Adherence figures bear this out. Relatively few adults will regularly engage in anything called 'sport' but people are content to walk with their dogs, swim at lunchtime or cycle in pleasant surroundings. Two national reports, both released in the same week in December 2006, highlight these issues. The Active People Survey found that only one in five adults was involved in sport or active recreation on three days per week (Sport England, 2006). If one subtracts 'walking', a category that Sport England researchers have defined as 'sport', these figures deteriorate. In contrast, Local Exercise Action Pilots (LEAP) evaluated interventions that encouraged public health recommendations for active living (at least thirty minutes of at least 'moderate'-intensity activity on five or more days per week). Results show that, of sedentary recruits to such interventions, three in five people changed to meet official health standards.

Fitness is clearly relative, problematic and ambiguous as a status. It is shaped both by individual needs and wants but also by political, economic, social and cultural contexts. For example, compare a young Premiership football player with a slight injury, unable to play on in a crucial Saturday fixture and described by his coach or physiotherapist as 'unfit', with the condition of a middle-aged smoker with obesity, discharged from hospital and described by doctors as 'fit' to return to work. The footballer is significantly fitter in general terms but, weighed against his individual and team needs, has been declared unfit.

Such distinctions lead to concepts of health-related fitness:

> an ability to perform daily activities with vigor . . . and demonstration of traits and capacities that are associated with a low risk of [movement-restricting] diseases and conditions.
>
> (Bouchard and Shephard, 1994: 81)

and performance-related fitness:

> Fitness necessary for optimal work or sport performance . . . [that] depends heavily upon motor skills, cardio-respiratory power and capacity, body size, motivation, etc.
>
> (Bouchard and Shephard, 1994: 81)

Individual fitness needs are personal and unique, and, other than in the case of the competitive performer, need not be measured or compared with other individuals. Consequently, sports development professionals should enable people at different life stages and with diverse physical capacities to access the benefits of sports participation. To accrue benefits of an active, sport-based lifestyle, some individuals will be encouraged into activities that minimise competitiveness and opportunities for destructive comparison with others.

So health is defined as an all-embracing indicator or expression of a person's state of being whilst fitness focuses on one aspect of health which deals with the capacity to perform tasks. Neither is solely confined to physical condition; a crucial contemporary issue is to understand the importance of physical activity behaviour over any state or outcome that it might produce.

Another confused area of terminology involves the behaviours and activities that develop aspects of health and fitness. In particular, the terms 'sport' and 'exercise' are frequently interchanged, yet they carry very different meanings, both in the behavioural sciences and in everyday life. The following section explores this important concept of physical activity. One recurrent practical theme of this chapter is the numerous ways in which sports development professionals can work to change many people's negative perceptions of involvement in sport through careful packaging, promotion and delivery.

KEY TERMS: SPORT, EXERCISE AND PHYSICAL ACTIVITY

> I get my exercise acting as a pallbearer to my friends who exercise.
>
> (Chauncey Depew, cited in Geddes and Grosset, 1997: 113)

This homage to idleness is an acerbic reminder that for many people the notion of indulging in any activity offers nothing but negative connotations. Those with the responsibility of encouraging and enabling sport participation should therefore be familiar with the language or discourse of activity and be able to articulate different positive elements of sport and exercise to those in need of persuasion to take part. It is also important to understand that deploying strong counter-arguments to such pro-sedentary maxims is important in creating a culture where active rather than inactive living is the norm.

At this stage it is useful to remind ourselves of definitions of sport, so that distinctions from other aspects of physical activity can be made. Notions of sport generally focus upon competitiveness and the presence of structured rules. Writing in the United States,

Bouchard and Shephard (1994: 79) link sport with wider concepts of activity: 'a form of physical activity that includes competition.' However, it is important to recall that some activities considered by participants and administrators as sports do not sit comfortably within such a conception. 'New' games, co-operative sports and 'lifestyle' or 'alternative' sports (see Wheaton, 2004) have significant roles to play, and are often more welcoming to the reluctant or anxious participant. Cognisant of this, writers also acknowledge that the broadness of the term may also embrace recreation and exercise.

Exercise is something that can be gained as a consequence of participating in certain sports or it can be practised outside of a sporting context for its own sake. Exercise is usually seen to be a structured form of activity, undertaken with particular (usually fitness-related) instrumental objectives in mind:

> A form of leisure time physical activity . . . with a specific external objective, such as the improvement of fitness, physical performance or health (in which the participant is advised to a recommended mode, intensity, frequency or duration of such activity).
>
> (Bouchard and Shephard, 1994: 78)

It follows logically that physical activity is an overarching, generic concept, of which sport and exercise are two significant and meaningful forms. The idea of physical activity encapsulates the full range of major movements undertaken by a person, including those subject neither to structure nor form. Consequently, to paraphrase Bouchard and Shephard (1994: 77), physical activity comprises any body movement produced by skeletal muscles which results in energy expenditure above the resting state.

Clearly, this working definition accommodates a wide range of actions unrelated to sport or formal exercise but which offer people pleasure and fitness gains, e.g. gardening, walking, dancing or yoga. With care, sport development staff can promote the benefits of physical activity to further the cause of sport. In 2005 Sport England acknowledged this link by launching a campaign entitled 'Everyday Sport' which encouraged work-based physical activity. We await the outcomes of this intervention. These issues will be explored in detail later in the chapter; a summary of the benefits of physical activity, and sport in particular, identified in research will help set the scene for this discussion and so provide a compelling discourse or rationale to motivate reluctant participants. In the UK at least one local authority – Derby – has changed the name of its sports development service in order to integrate sport, exercise and physical activity; from 2006 the new name is 'Get Derby Active' (Derby City Council, 2007).

THE BENEFITS OF PHYSICAL ACTIVITY

Governmental initiatives in the area of health have placed increasing emphasis upon positive aspects of physically active lifestyles. Reports from the Chief Medical Officer

(Department of Health, 2004a) have been prepared for health professionals although there is as yet no policy exegesis for sport. However, policy shifts throughout the 1990s and early in the new millennium have reflected growing evidence that individual activity-related gains have also generated collective health benefits. Primary and preventative health care policies were encouraged for economic, political, social as well as medical reasons. Reductions in the incidence of coronary heart disease, stroke victims and a wide range of other sedentary-related illnesses would reduce demands placed upon pressurised health care budgets and growing waiting lists, whilst enabling individuals to play a more productive role in everyday life (Booth *et al.*, 2000). Indeed, within the world of work, estimates are that achieving the UK government target of 70 per cent of the population being regularly active would cut annual sick leave among the 29 million employees by almost 3 million days, reduce NHS attendance to save about £80 million and boost the economy by £487 million (Deloitte and Touche, 2006).

The Chief Medical Officer's report (DoH, 2004a) identifies an impressive range of benefits from participating in physical activity, but it is useful to remember key health gains. Regular participation in moderate levels of physical activity has a wide range of physical health benefits, including:

- Reducing the risk of coronary heart disease by up to 50 per cent.
- Helping to control blood pressure.
- Helping to maintain strong muscles and healthy joints.
- Enhancing sleep quality and quantity.
- Controlling weight.

In each case, it can clearly be seen how the quality of a person's life can be positively affected. To this list can be added a series of less visible but equally potent psychological and social benefits. These include stress reduction, work productivity, subjective well-being and increased opportunities to develop social capital through socialising, personal and community development.

As may be expected with such a diversity of positive outcomes, nine out of ten adults believe that it is 'very' or 'fairly' important to exercise regularly (Health Education Authority, 1995), yet in the most recent survey only 50.6 per cent of adults in England had participated in thirty minutes' moderate intensity physical activity in the preceding four weeks (Sport England, 2006). The Active People Survey (2006) also highlighted that people aged sixteen years or over engage more regularly in non-competitive activities like walking, swimming and recreational cycling.

A major challenge for providers of physical activities is to develop local awareness and to provide means for people to access activities suited to their needs and tastes. This is true for sports development professionals, fitness and leisure centre managers and walks co-ordinators. The precise role of sport as a form of physical activity, with all the attendant benefits, has not always been clearly defined. The next section concentrates on sport as a force for health gain and offers practical ideas as to how sports development professionals can exploit contemporary research.

THE HEALTH BENEFITS OF SPORT

For many non-participants, sport is less a source of health gain than an activity ripe with the potential for physical injury and social embarrassment. Those with responsibility for the provision and promotion of sporting opportunities need to be aware of common misconceptions regarding sport, and to be in a position to work towards challenging them. Changing the rules, and officiating practice, of sports may reduce rates of injury but there is also a need to address how different sports are portrayed. In some sports, or at least local expressions of sports, active exclusion of minority groups is a subcultural norm and cannot be condoned or supported through the public purse with its policy commitment to equity and access.

Numerous sports are intensely physical and carry inherent risks of injury. To participants, the extreme physicality of such sports is attractive; to the majority of the population, it is inhibiting. Indeed, it has been shown that joint injury sustained at age sixteen years manifests as osteo-arthritis on average twenty-two years later (Gelber et al., 2000). It is important to differentiate such notions of risk and personal injury in order to distinguish more 'gentle' sporting forms that might encourage even the most timid.

Many sports, though, do provide the full gamut of health benefits linked with physical activity. Even weekend warriors can accrue many of the health-related benefits of involvement in sport (Min-Lee et al., 2004) despite not always meeting the behavioural targets or standards associated with public health campaigns. Taking part also brings a wide range of social and psychological benefits. Many volunteers, paid officials and administrators consider themselves to be more rounded, accomplished individuals as a consequence of their roles in sport. Further, these individuals help to create groups, traditions, customs and an 'atmosphere' that may attract and welcome newcomers or returnees.

Naturally, each person's current health status and their disposition towards given activities will be highly influential in decisions whether to take up any particular opportunity. The sports development professional, or other promoter of an activity, must identify sections of the community to which the activity may be particularly suited or attractive. However, whatever the sport and the situation, the scope for health gains is vast. There are population groups where attention may not be focused but where important physical activity benefits can be achieved. For example, the number of adults receiving hip or knee replacements is rising annually and there are considerable post-operative benefits for regular involvement in physical activity. Up to 50 per cent of patients can go on to take up new sports and activities after their surgery (Orbell et al., 1998), suggesting a growing market for effective programmes.

Improvements in speed, power, strength, endurance and flexibility are intended or unintended outcomes of doing most sports. As has been stated, health gains do not have to be sought solely to improve athletic performance in a particular sports discipline. Physical fitness improvements can also enhance lost or diminished function to those with any of the plethora of medical conditions affecting mobility and daily living. Many conditions, such as diabetes or osteoporosis, may be prevented by physical activity programmes that address biological needs throughout the life course. For example, in the context of epidemiology, osteoporosis may be understood as a disease of youth that becomes manifest only in later life. This underlines the need for sport promoters to engage with developments in epidemiology and medicine, to understand disease processes better and to understand how physical activity can play a central role in primary prevention and in secondary prevention (once initial signs of problems occur).

The unequivocal message resonating throughout this research work is that the UK, as a nation, is not physically active enough. Yet there is a general and ubiquitous, if under-informed, awareness that physical activity is good for you. It is as if the individual acknowledges activity is good for others but not for oneself. There are always mitigating circumstances which excuse the majority of the UK population from routine physical exercise – tiredness, work, expense, lack of time, lack of facilities, family, life circumstances, and not least alternative passive leisure opportunities.

The social and psychological gains to be found in sporting lifestyles should not be underestimated. Sport provides an ideal vehicle for individuals to express themselves in a variety of ways. Playing sport and affiliation to a club or team offer tremendous opportunities for improved self-esteem, socialising and community identity. However, sport can provide the means for social and psychological health gain in other ways.

High numbers of people fulfil vital administrative and leadership roles at all levels of sport, with no financial or other tangible reward. The estimated 1.9 million volunteers who give at least one hour a week to English sport (Sport England, 2006) have a multitude of motivations for engagement with their chosen sport. Reasons for giving up free time to perform bureaucratic and coaching functions are often expressed as 'helping with the kids', 'giving something back', etc. Volunteers acknowledge the importance of their role – the majority of sports opportunities are founded upon goodwill – and volunteers experience enhancement of self-esteem and community solidarity. They may also enhance their level of social capital (Putnam, 2000) and their social connectedness (Eng et al., 2002), which provides another – perhaps unvoiced and undervalued – health benefit of involvement with sport. Indeed, as mentioned elsewhere, Bishop and Hoggett (1986) argue that the voluntary sector is where local democratic involvement is uniquely possible. Sports and leisure organisations can sometimes include those excluded from the serious worlds of work, religion and politics. In other instances, people experiencing social isolation can tap into a vibrant network of friends by becoming involved in volunteering in sport.

In summary, the case for the health benefits of sport is a compelling one, and researchers will doubtless continue to add to the growing body of impressive evidence. The propensity for sports development and health care professionals to work together to encourage and enable sedentary and largely inactive people to take up sporting activity is great. The following section will examine how such initiatives can be realised.

PROMOTING THE PHYSICAL BENEFITS OF SPORT

There has been an emerging trend of 'healthy alliances' or health partnerships between sports development professionals and health practitioners to promote physical activity. In many instances past mutual suspicion has been supplanted by strategic partnerships, and debates about joint working have largely been won.

There are many examples of the value of sport as an instrument for medical rehabilitation, often (but by no means exclusively) where older patients are concerned. For instance, heart patients may access swimming through an organised club setting. Those recovering from a stroke may be provided with a pathway into the local croquet club, where walking is combined with co-ordination skills.

In terms of the integration of sport into wider physical activity programmes one major policy development, with health benefits a consequence for many, has been the implementation of the national Physical Education, School Sport and Club Links Strategy (PESCCL) (Department for Education and Skills/Department for Culture, Media and Sport, 2002). This is discussed in full in Chapter 7 of this book, but at the time of writing the 2006 target of 75 per cent of young people participating in a minimum of two hours a week on high-quality PE and school sport within and beyond the curriculum had been exceeded by 5 per cent (DfES/TNS, 2006). This illustrates powerfully that financial resources (in total over £1.5 billion invested in physical education and school sport, 2003–08 (Teachernet, 2007)) supported by professional development and strategic restructuring (e.g. the onset of School Sport Partnerships) can lead to enormous gains.

PESSCL places huge importance on schools' linkages with local communities and, in particular, sports clubs. Teachers will need extra help to make community collaborations work effectively since they can be dominated by school-centred attitudes and behaviours. This is where sports development's existing links and expertise can be exploited. Sports development professionals are accustomed to the notion of permeable boundaries rather than barriers and here they can be instrumental in ensuring that sport's potential as a tool for wider health benefits can gain acceptance and bear fruit. Within schools – as for any potentially health-promoting environment – there is a need to encourage employees (in this case, teachers) to become more healthy (Fox et al., 2004), since work with doctors and nurses has shown that they are more active promoters of active living if they themselves are active (McKenna et al., 1998). Taylor (2005) has written about the paradox of reducing activity among staff employed to promote health-related behaviours. The significance of increasing sedentarism among sports development (or education or health) employees should not be underestimated.

PHYSICAL ACTIVITY ON THE UK POLITICAL AGENDA

Throughout Tony Blair's tenure as Prime Minister the government's interest in sport and physical activity was apparent. The most public affirmation of this commitment was political support for the bid to bring the 2012 Olympic and Paralympic Games to London. New Labour and Lord Coe's bid presentation celebrated mass participation and a sporting legacy or heritage to be enjoyed throughout the nation. There were numerous other political drivers for the bid but the attention given to the Games' ability to inspire citizens to be more active was perhaps unprecedented in Olympic history. The Blair government also presided over increased investment, e.g. the £250 million per annum injection into physical education and school sport, as it was finally acknowledged that solutions to an impending obesity 'crisis' did not lie solely with provision of medical care for those already ill.

This political attention to physical activity is in sharp contrast to the situation only two to three decades ago when the position was one of relative indifference. For example, close links between 'exercise' promotion and sport were not developed until the early 1990s. The benefits of 'active living' and the opportunities for a syndicate approach to health promotion were recognised in Conservative government policies at the time. The Allied Dunbar National Fitness Survey (Health Education Authority, 1992), conducted around the turn of the decade and published in 1992, had highlighted the need for greater co-operation between agencies in the war against inactivity and ill health. Experts defined national 'standards' as appropriate weekly levels of 'vigorous', 'moderate' and 'low' levels of physical activity. It became increasingly clear that the majority of people could articulate the developing discourse stressing health benefits of physical activity but were reluctant to embrace exercise regimes in their everyday lives.

In 1992 the Conservatives' major health policy statement, *The Health of the Nation* (Department of Health, 1992), set out to tackle the risk factors associated with five major disease groups, including coronary heart disease/stroke. The status of physical activity within the initiative on coronary heart disease and stroke was not as high as may have been desired. Poor diet, smoking and other risk factors were given greater prominence. However, physical activity, individual lifestyle and preventative health were now on the New Right agenda for a variety of economic, political and ideological reasons. Perspicacious sports development professionals, health promoters and medical practitioners were able to envisage a range of joint undertakings which could flourish from post-Thatcherite endorsements of active living.

In 1993 a Physical Activity task force was created. This quango consisted of delegates from the Health Education Authority (HEA), the medical profession and higher education. Under its auspices the traditional health prescription, twenty minutes' *vigorous* aerobic exercise *three* times a week, was 'realistically' downgraded to a *moderate* level of physical activity *five* days a week. Everyday activity – including, for example, gardening and walking – was acknowledged to provide health gains and, most important, the concept of 'moderate' exercise was relative to the individual.

John Major's (Prime Minister 1990–97) decisive break with the 1980s New Right legacy came with the success of the National Lottery and his distinctive personal interest in sport. *Sport: Raising the Game* highlighted that sport in schools enabled young people to 'appreciate the long-term benefits of regular exercise and [be] able to make informed decisions about adopting a healthy and active lifestyle in future years' (Department of National Heritage, 1995). The National Curriculum at Key Stage 4 encouraged PE teachers to develop health-related exercise and empower pupils to adopt active lifestyles on leaving school and embarking on adult life. Significantly, however, there was no additional investment identified in support of this move.

The Active for Life campaign

The Health of the Nation and the work of the task force initiated the HEA's Active for Life campaign in 1995. Active for Life heralded an overarching crusade both to elevate awareness and to encourage the population to acquire the benefits of physical activity. The campaign took the form of comprehensive media promotion, allied with efforts to develop the HEA's level of contact with practitioners 'on the ground' to an unprecedented level over the three-year 'live' period of the project (April 1996–March 1999).

Active for Life took a target group approach to physical activity. In each of its three years the bulk of its output was aimed at one segment of the population, with another group selected for 'special targeted initiatives' where communication and access needs were of high importance.[2] This approach may be criticised for politically correct tokenism, i.e. 'name-checking' as many special interest groups as possible in the three-year project. Straddling the demise of the Conservatives' eighteen-year reign and the onset of the New Labour regime, however, Active for Life was an important stepping stone towards the greater prevalence of physical activity on the contemporary agenda.

Physical activity into the new millennium

As New Labour took up office it became apparent that new public health priorities would overwhelm the *Health of the Nation* message. New Labour's health action plan *Saving Lives: Our Healthier Nation* (Department of Health, 1999) heralded a shift away from New Right policy priorities, and offered a social reformist commitment to tackle health problems associated with social, economic and environmental inequalities. The paper made little reference to physical activity *per se*, and distanced itself from setting performance indicators, icons of early 1990s health policy. Emphasis shifted away from specific risk factors liable to bring about the onset of disease to the broader determinants of health. A dominant aim of this political era was the eradication of social exclusion or conversely the promotion of social inclusion. Health was no longer seen as a private domain where individuals were free to make lifestyle choices, but rather as a collective issue where citizens had rights to health care, guaranteed by strong government action and funding.

The diminution of physical activity on the health agenda was offset against a more prominent role for sport elsewhere, not least in the establishment of the Department for Culture, Media and Sport (DCMS) in 1997. Government proclamations on sport in the late 1990s frequently centred upon the need to increase participation in sport among the whole population, often alluding to the health benefits as the drive towards mass participation in sport and active recreation gained momentum.

The year 2002 saw the publication of *Game Plan: A Strategy for Delivering the Government's Sport and Physical Activity Objectives* (DCMS/Cabinet Office, 2002), in which new participation data were presented, indicating that only one-third of the population was engaged in thirty minutes of moderate-intensity physical activity five times a week. The scale of the challenge to sports development and other interested professions was as great as ever. *Game Plan* attracted criticism and even ridicule due to its headline target that by 2020 no less than 70 per cent of the population should be active according to the above prescription. It remains, however, the only comprehensive, evidence-based government statement on sport and physical activity and should be viewed by professionals as a useful resource.

The 70 per cent target was pragmatically revised by the DCMS to a desired increase of 1 per cent per year. Even this presented a substantial challenge to professionals; for example, in a region the size of Yorkshire and the Humber it would entail persuading enough people to fill Leeds United's Elland Road Stadium to take up physical activity *every year*, whilst simultaneously maintaining the participation of those who had become active in earlier years. Just how difficult this is will be emphasised in the final section of this chapter when the 'Transtheoretical Model' of behaviour change is considered.

To achieve this annual increase Sport England refocused its work and in so doing recast itself as the *de facto* national physical activity agency. Campaigns such as Everyday Sport, whilst seen by some as potentially diluting core messages around sports participation, attempted to persuade the inactive that they could obtain health benefits of physical activity by making small changes to their everyday lives, a theme reminiscent of the Active for Life campaign of the previous decade. However, there is a potential counter-effect of this new focus and agency. For many inactive individuals any association with sport is negative, so they are unable to see beyond the semantics. Interestingly, Canada's physical activity promotion has always been under the banner of 'Participation' (strongly avoiding links with sport). Canada is one of the few developed nations reporting year-on-year increases in physical activity among adults.

In 2004 the government published the White Paper *Choosing Health: Making Healthier Choices Easier* (Department of Health, 2004b), complemented by the Chief Medical Offer's report *At Least Five a Week: Evidence on the Impact of Physical Activity and its Relationship to Health* (Department of Health, 2004a). The emphasis here is strongly upon enabling all citizens to make the 'right' lifestyle choices. This preventative rather than curative tone is reflected in the many references to physical activity to be found within *Choosing Health*. It had taken until some way into the new millennium for the 'penny to drop' but finally the government publicly acknowledged the links between physical activity, sport and health that others had espoused for so long.

Strategic shift

Central government policy changes can be detected in strategic developments at regional, sub-regional and local levels. In many areas the traditional sports development plan has been supplanted or augmented by a holistic physical activity strategy. The Redcar and Cleveland Physical Activity Strategy for the period 2005–10 (Redcar and Cleveland Borough Council/Langbaurgh PCT, 2005), for example, was compiled on behalf of a multi-agency steering group by a health professional, a situation which would have been virtually unthinkable only a few years previously. Whilst there is undeniably still great potential for partnership problems to be encountered in such circumstances (see Chapter 6), and whilst it might be argued that the physical activity experts in sports development could become strategically marginalised, in general this represents a very positive development for the promotion of physical activity.

The enhanced status of physical activity is confirmed by policy documents such as *Active Living: A Physical Activity Framework for Yorkshire and the Humber* (Government Office for Yorkshire and the Humber/Sport England Yorkshire, 2006). This outlines a clear direction for agencies at all levels, providing service deliverers with a useful tool to pursue political and financial support within their organisations.

Local initiatives in practice

Many sports development professionals have responded to the emerging physical activity agenda with typical flexibility and creativity. The following section provides some interesting local examples of grounded practice. The following case studies provide an indication of benefits secured in targeted policy initiatives.

CASE STUDY 8.1

MIDDLESBROUGH LIFESTYLE CO-ORDINATOR

The existence of a Middlesbrough Lifestyle Co-ordinator exemplifies many of the issues discussed earlier in the chapter, i.e. that relations between sports development and health care have often matured into more strategically astute arrangements, and that former bureaucratic mistrust has been replaced by a shared understanding of what can be achieved collectively. The Lifestyle Co-ordinator position is hosted by the Middlesbrough Sports Development Team but funded by Middlesbrough

Primary Care Trust (PCT), securing a link between sport and health that had many of its origins in the GAP exercise referral scheme, established over a decade earlier and covered in the first edition of this book (Robson, 2001).

The success or otherwise of the Lifestyle Co-ordinator is measured solely by the PCT in terms of quantitative weight reduction statistics; the role is by no means solely confined to physical activity promotion, with nutritional and other lifestyle targets having equal status as tactics in the 'war on obesity'. However, in supporting the Lifestyle Co-ordinator financially but in not being part of the decision making and day-to-day management, the PCT is acknowledging the experience and expertise of the sports development team in terms of engaging the community in healthier behaviours. The Lifestyle Co-ordinator is well placed to exploit the network of the sports development team and attempt to persuade those unconvinced of the merits of sport that there are other, equally if not more beneficial, lifestyle changes they could take up; at the same time the use of sport as a way of reaching the previously difficult to reach within the PCT system becomes a distinct possibility.

The counterpoint to this optimistic stance on the role is that the development of sport and the development of communities through sport are not a priority for the post holder, and sports development managers may find themselves at odds with PCT managers as they strive to protect their service from dilution and diminution. It is also common in sports development to seek holistic, qualitative measures when evaluating programmes and this cultural difference in approaches has the potential to add tension to the relationship. Overwhelmingly, this type of arrangement will give heart to those who advocate an inextricable link between sport and the wider physical activity/health agenda, and for whom this kind of alliance represents an avenue for sports development to access a greater share of the comparatively massive resources of the National Health Service.

Note. The PCT also committed £75,000 in 2005–06 to support a free swimming programme across four venues (Middlesbrough Council/Middlesbrough PCT, 2006). With sport development activity in place to enable those interested to make permanent their association with swimming the notion of a permeable boundary between physical activity and 'traditional' sport was realised.

MERTON SPORT, HEALTH AND PHYSICAL ACTIVITY STRATEGY

Similar to the Redcar and Cleveland Physical Activity Strategy discussed earlier, the Merton strategy for the period 2006–09 (London Borough of Merton, 2006) embraces the blurring of boundaries between sports development and wider physical activity. For the most part the strategy makes no distinction between sport and physical activity, which can be perceived as a lack of rigour on one hand or a demonstration of political astuteness on the other.

The strategy sets out to explicitly address Merton's wider corporate aims, reinforcing the need for sport and physical activity providers to be ever more flexible in pursuing their goals. Merton also seeks to demonstrate its links with external policy and strategy. For instance, linked with the Merton corporate aims of developing 'Sustainable Communities' and 'Healthier Communities' (London Borough of Merton, 2006: 23) is the sport, health and physical activity priority:

> Implement national and local initiatives to engage more of Merton's community in more physical activity and sport more often, thus improving their health.
>
> (London Borough of Merton, 2006: 23)

This is to be addressed via the 'opportunities' provided by the 2012 Olympic and Paralympic Games and in particular the desired community sport legacy (Sport England, 2006). Among other things Merton intends to drive up participation across the borough by using the Games as an 'inspiration and catalyst' (London Borough of Merton, 2006: 23). It is difficult to discern from the specific plans designed to achieve this precisely what will be done differently and how established good sports development practice will be modified in the light of the 2012 Games.

It should be noted at this stage that 2012 is by no means universally viewed as a panacea for the disappointing levels of sport and physical activity participation currently encountered in the UK. For some, the notion of a universal remedy in the form of the Games is a triumph of hope over experience. Merton and many others will understandably seek to encourage the serially inactive to use the essentially sedentary pursuit of watching the 2012 Games as a springboard for a sustained, active lifestyle thereafter. This is in spite of the overwhelming evidence, to be considered in full in the next section, that the process of adopting and maintaining a physical activity habit is a complex psychological process which often requires bespoke support for the inactive individual.

TRANSTHEORETICAL MODEL OF BEHAVIOUR CHANGE

Studying models of practice developed by academic researchers can often present a bewildering and intimidating prospect. The Transtheoretical Model provides an interesting perspective on how individuals achieve self-change. The model was developed by Prochaska and DiClemente (1982) and is based on psychological studies of human behaviour, and can be of great relevance to those without a specialisation in this area. In studying a group of people attempting to quit smoking without professional intervention, they cultivated the notion that these individuals were at differing *stages of change*, and that identifying the stage a person was at would enable suitable 'treatment' to be offered to future clients. They and others have since applied the notion of stages of change to the scrutiny of other health behaviours.

Physical activity is one such area of study. As opposed to the majority of health-promoting interventions where people are encouraged to cease a negative behaviour (smoking, alcohol and drug abuse, etc.), the message of physical activity and sport focuses upon adopting a positive lifestyle choice. This is hopefully a 'friendlier' theme than simply regulating or overcoming undesirable physical addictions and dependencies. Various authors have linked the model with physical activity participation. It can be usefully applied to refining how sport is promoted, not least because it supports a range of intervention approaches that span one-to-one counselling (motivational interviewing) through to group recruitment and retention strategies.

The six stages of change

The researchers propose that six stages of change exist on a continuum. It begins with people who have no intention to change and ends with those individuals who have suc-cessfully and (almost) permanently modified their behaviour. The six stages provide the main spine of the model and have been labelled thus:

- *Pre-contemplation*. The individual has no intention to change (i.e. take up sport) in the foreseeable future. The person may be ignorant of their need for change or have deep doubts about their capacity for change. Where the individual has considered, but rejected, the need for change the existing benefits of sedentary behaviour outweigh the prospective costs of becoming active.
- *Contemplation*. There is a serious intent to change soon. (The standard for this varies in different studies – from within thirty days to within the next six months.) The key word here is *serious*. Change, however, is often put off ('I'll come to the badminton club next week . . .'). Chronic or long-term contemplators substitute thinking for acting (McKenna and Francis, 2003). They have identified that the pros of sedentary exis-tence roughly match the cons of changing, so taking up sport seems like a good thing but is not defined as an urgent priority.

- *Preparation*. The individual is involved but only on an irregular basis. They may have a plan for more involvement, but have yet to stabilise and consolidate their behavioural pattern (e.g. s/he may have attended an organised sports session irregularly). This person has evaluated that the pros of changing outweigh the cons of remaining sedentary, and change of some form is therefore likely.
- *Action*. Significant changes have occurred in the last six months, and the desired criterion or level has been attained (e.g. s/he regularly attended the swimming club twice weekly). Individuals in this stage face the greatest risk of relapsing into less active behaviour. Note that, whatever criterion has been reached in terms of active participation, this must have been previously determined in one of the earlier stages. Frustratingly, a proportion of people who appear to be in the Action stage are better described as *coerced Contemplators*, indicating that their mental condition is inadequate to support regular involvement even though their behavioural pattern does.
- *Maintenance*. Individuals in this stage have been regularly and frequently active for six months. However, although their behaviour has stabilised, they are still at risk of returning to their old behaviour (e.g. return to watching soap operas instead of being an active and permanent member of the cycling club). Maintenance represents a period of sustained, effortful change – smoking research suggests that five years of Maintenance leads to the final termination phase and is distinct from 'habit', which assumes effortless involvement.
- *Termination*. There is no temptation to return to the old behaviour. The person has attained 100 per cent self-efficacy (in other words, their participation in health-enhancing sport is completely self-managed). It is questionable whether it is realistic for a person to progress from a sedentary lifestyle to termination; they may always remain at risk of relapse. For active living, it is unlikely that 'termination' is realistic, especially given the temptations for inactivity that continually surround us.

Research has recently identified that self-efficacy is the crucial element that predicts forward stage progressions (Plotinikoff *et al.*, 2001). This describes situation-specific confidence to continue behaviour. An example of how confidence can shift might be seen by comparing your own confidence in actively and regularly involving yourself within a golf club and comparing that confidence with your involvement in, say, a boxing or martial arts gym. Along the continuum from Pre-contemplation to Maintenance, individuals are considered to experience a linear increase in self-efficacy, whilst temptation declines at a similar rate, as shown in Figure 8.1.

Note that the *preparation* and *action* stages are where a 'precarious balance' between the two factors occurs. For example, an individual, having joined a netball club and participated actively in sport for the first time since school, may be experiencing doubts despite gaining enjoyment from the activity. S/he will still require appropriate support from fellow club members, coaches, family, peer group, etc. to make the change more permanent. It is important to keep in mind that, at every stage of *change*, relapse is always a possibility. The challenge for sports development professionals is to offer support that

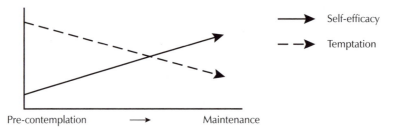

Figure 8.1 Changes in self-efficacy and temptation

engages inactive people but that also supports people with extensive experience of adherence. Both represent important features of the skill-set of modern sport development employees.

Individuals with a more practical orientation towards the delivery of sports services may still require some convincing as to the usefulness of this theoretical model. Not only does the model distinguish different levels of readiness for change, but Prochaska and Marcus also forward a series of 'intervention issues' which link stages of change with provision of opportunities aimed at encouraging participation. Sports development professionals may choose to bear these in mind when designing programmes of health-enhancing sport.

The Five Rs of intervention

- *Recruitment*. Promoting opportunities requires great care and skill in order to ensure that the right messages reach the right people. People in Pre-contemplation and Contemplation typically respond poorly to 'action-orientated' recruitment strategies, where too much emphasis is placed on the individual to access the activity on offer. Indeed, even though some Contemplators can be coerced into Action this can be premature; these individuals rarely have the right mind-set to support regular and frequent involvement and so they drop out. Proactive recruitment techniques should be used when targeting sedentary people. A simple example is that of the sports development professional choosing to visit groups or individuals in person to promote programmes rather than relying upon advertising alone to generate a response.
- *Retention*. Sports development professionals will appreciate that working with sedentary people is commonly linked with high drop-out rates. The client's stage is a predictor of the likelihood of drop-out. Consequently, close support and counselling should be provided to match stage needs and to identify and then tackle risks of relapse.
- *Resistance*. Increased 'prodding' by service providers can lead to increased resistance to messages encouraging positive behaviour change. Participants should be counselled to target small manageable changes to their lifestyles. Being told or scolded to 'be more active' is typically counterproductive for Pre-contemplators who become

actively resistant to subsequent strident messages. A more positive approach to overcoming possible individual resistance may be to negotiate within levels of behaviour change that are possible or to help individuals to develop a discrepancy between their current behaviour and their personal aspirations. For example, a person who has recently taken up swimming may choose to set goals related to the distance swum, or, equally, may focus on basic attendances at the club as an initial measurable target.

- *Relapse*. Clearly, the risk of relapse is a major issue, predominantly for individuals at the Action stage. The better prepared a participant is in the earlier stages, the greater the chance of successful progression towards Maintenance. However, researchers are convinced that, regardless of the nature and quality of the intervention, 'the majority of people will relapse after any single attempt to overcome most chronic behaviour problems' (Prochaska and Marcus, 1994: 168). This highlights a continued need for vigilance and support. Sports development professionals should endeavour to 'recycle' relapsed participants and to enhance the potential of subsequent involvement for creating greater adherence. Further, given that many people find sustained commitment recurrently problematic, inventive promoters will respond to support these clients – possibly by offering programmes where the content changes regularly.
- *Recovery*. This is 'a process rather than an immediate outcome' (Prochaska and Marcus, 1994: 162). In sports development terms, the 'recovery' taking place is from a sedentary existence: practising professionals will be all too aware of the pitfalls which can prevent this from being successfully accomplished. Typically the process describes 'climbing back on the pony' after a major setback. Individuals already in Preparation at the time of the intervention are more likely to 'recover'. Within a club setting recovery may involve a series of meetings – or casual engagements – within the practice area or club. This may refamiliarise those who feel that their social connections have been severed through absence.

A key principle to adhere to is appropriate 'treatment matching' to ensure that intervention by the sports development professional is in line with the individual's current stage of change. If time and resources permit, one potentially useful strategy is to help clients to progress by one stage per month. While this may risk presenting change at a pace faster than individuals might choose for themselves – and therefore present new obstacles to successful progression – instituting progression within delivery can only be considered good practice. Evidence from family doctors in Wiltshire showed how this stage-based delivery can be developed – in this case for the promotion of physical activity – even without formal training (McKenna and Vernon, 2004). Clearly, however, there will be a need to individualise the pace of this progression.

There is the implicit assumption that an individual's current stage of change is known, but, clearly, there must be some means of obtaining this information from the client. One such method is adopted in Project PACE (Physician-based Assessment and Counselling for Exercise) and its derivative PACE+, an American initiative designed to enable general practitioners to counsel patients into becoming more active (Patrick *et al.*, 1994; Calfas *et al.*, 2002). As part of an initial consultation, PACE uses a short questionnaire. The patient is asked to indicate which of eleven statements most accurately reflects his or her current physical activity status (e.g. Pre-contemplator: 'I do not exercise or walk regularly, and I do not intend to start in the near future'; Contemplator: 'I am trying to start to exercise or walk'). This idea could readily be adapted by sports development professionals to contextualise a set of questions to local activity opportunities on offer.

Much of the foregoing, in terms of matching interventions to individuals' stages of change, etc. is already performed by sports development staff, often on a 'commonsense' basis. Generating a deeper and more systematic understanding of the change process by means of a modified PACE questionnaire can help provide an enhanced and more refined service.

CONCLUSION

The overriding message of this chapter is that sport has a vital role to play in health enhancement. An understanding of the health benefits of specific sports enables the sports development professional to negotiate partnerships with health care practitioners and to access a vast potential clientele. Sport can provide the impetus for sedentary people, often not disposed to structured exercise, to become active. However, existing practice is unlikely to be any more effective in recruiting inactive people than it has been so far. At a time when the UK is preparing to host the 2012 Olympic and Paralympic Games there can scarcely have been a more opportune moment to bite this particular bullet. New approaches are needed that more obviously endorse and integrate an appreciation of the challenges that even involvement in modest levels of physical activity might represent to so many people.

Recent governmental policies have opened the door wider to progress work in this area, although greater explicit political endorsement is desired. Strategic recognition of the health-enhancing properties of sport is a useful bargaining tool within and outside of key organisations.

Many highly innovative and successful initiatives already take advantage of the opportunities provided by the link between sport and better health. An appreciation of academic research material, such as the Transtheoretical Model of behaviour change, can assist with critical appraisal of initiatives, and can help practitioners to offer more relevant sports opportunities.

NOTES

1 See definition from the World Health Organisation, 1968.
2 For example, in 1997–98: the lead target group was young women aged sixteen to twenty-four, with 'special targeted initiatives' aimed at disabled people.

REFERENCES

Bishop, J. and Hoggett, P. (1986) *Organising around Enthusiasms*, London: Comedia Press.

Booth, F., Gordon, S., Carlson, C. and Hamilton, M. (2000) Waging war on modern chronic diseases: primary prevention through exercise biology, *Journal of Applied Physiology*, 88, 774–87.

Bouchard, C. and Shephard, R. (1994) Physical activity, exercise and health: the model and key concepts, in C. Bouchard *et al.* (eds) *Physical Activity, Fitness and Health: International Proceedings and Consensus Statement*, Champaign IL: Human Kinetics.

Bouchard, C. *et al.* (eds) (1990) *Exercise, Fitness and Health: A Consensus of Current Knowledge*, Champaign IL: Human Kinetics.

Calfas, K.J., Sallis, J.F., Zabinski, M.F. *et al.* (2002) Preliminary evaluation of a multi-component program for nutrition and physical activity change in primary care: PACE+ for adults, *Preventive Medicine*, 34, 153–61.

Deloitte & Touche (2006) *Health of the Nation: An In-depth Report into UK Consumer Attitudes to Physical Exercise*, London: Deloitte & Touche.

Department for Culture Media and Sport and Cabinet Office (2002) *Game Plan: A Strategy for delivering Government's Sport and Physical Activity Objectives*, London: HMSO.

Department for Education and Skills and Department for Culture Media and Sport (2002) *The National Physical Education, School Sport and Club Links Strategy*, London: DfES/DCMS.

Department for Education and Skills and TNS (2006) *2005/6 School Sport Survey*, London: DfES.

Department of Health (1992) *The Health of the Nation*, London: HMSO.

Department of Health (1998) *The Health of the Nation: A Policy Assessed*, London: HMSO.

Department of Health (1999) Executive Summary, *Saving Lives: Our Healthier Nation*, London: HMSO.

Department of Health (2004a) *At least Five a Week: Evidence on the Impact of Physical Activity and its Relationship to Health: A Report from the Chief Medical Officer*, London: HMSO.

Department of Health (2004b) *Choosing Health: Making Healthier Choices Easier*, London: HMSO.

Department of National Heritage (1995) *Sport: Raising the Game*, London: HMSO.

Derby City Council (2007) Getting Derby Active Sport Development Team, www.derby.gov.uk/LeisureCulture/Sports/SportsDevelopment/.

Eng, P.M., Rimm, E.B., Fitzmaurice, G. and Kawachi, I. (2002) Social ties and changes in social ties in relation to subsequent total and cause-specific mortality and coronary heart disease in men, *American Journal of Epidemiology*, 155, 700–9.

Fox, K.R., Cooper, A.C. and McKenna, J. (2004) The school and the promotion of children's health-enhancing physical activity: perspectives, from the UK, *Journal of Teaching Physical Education*, 23, 336–55.

Geddes & Grosset (1997) *Dictionary of Quotations*, New Lanark: Geddes & Grosset.

Gelber, A.C., Hochberg, M.C., Mead, L.O.A. *et al.* (2000) Joint injury in young adults and risk for knee and hip osteoarthritis, *Annals of Internal Medicine*, 133, 321–8.

Government Office for Yorkshire and the Humber and Sport England Yorkshire (2006) *Active Living: A Physical Activity Framework for Yorkshire and the Humber.*

Hansbro, J. *et al.* (1997) *Health in England, 1996: What People Know, What People Think, What People Do*, London: Stationery Office.

Health Education Authority (1992) *Allied Dunbar National Fitness Survey*, London: HEA.

Health Education Authority (1995) *Young People and Health: The Health Behaviour of School-aged Children*, London: HEA.

London Borough of Merton (2006) *Merton Sport, Physical Activity and Health Strategy, 2006–2009*, London: London Borough of Merton.

McKenna, J. and Francis, C. (2003) Exercise contemplators: unravelling the processes of change, *Health Education*, 103, 41–53.

McKenna, J. and Vernon, M. (2004) How GPs promote lifestyle activity, *Patient Education and Counseling*, 54, 101–6.

McKenna, J., Naylor, P-J. and McDowell, N. (1998) Barriers to physical activity promotion by general practitioners and practice nurses, *British Journal of Sports Medicine*, 32, 242–7.

Middlesbrough Council/Middlesbrough PCT (2006) *Public Health Strategy for Middlesbrough Primary Care Trust and Middlesbrough Council.*

Min-Lee, I., Sesso, H.D., Oguma, Y. and Paffenbarger, R.S. (2004) The 'weekend warrior' and risk of mortality, *American Journal of Epidemiology*, 160, 636–41.

Naidoo, J. and Wills, J. (1994) *Health Promotion: Foundations for Practice*, London: Baillière Tindall.

Orbell, S., Espley, A., Johnston, M. and Rowley, D. (1998) Health benefits of joint replacement surgery for patients with osteoarthritis: prospective evaluation using independent assessments in Scotland, *J. Epidemiol, Community Health*, 52, 564–70.

Patrick, K. *et al.* (1994) A new tool for encouraging activity: project PACE', *Physician and Sportsmedicine*, 22, 45–55.

Plotnikoff, R.C., Hotz, S.B., Birkett, N.J. and Courneya, K.S. (2001) Exercise and the transtheoretical model: a longitudinal test of a population sample, *Preventive Medicine*, 33, 441–52.

Prochaska, J.O. and DiClemente, C.C. (1982) Transtheoretical therapy: toward a more integrative model of change, *Psychotherapy: Therapy, Research and Practice*, 19, 276–88.

Prochaska, J.O. and Marcus, B. (1994) The transtheoretical model: applications to exercise, in R.K. Dishman (ed.) *Advances in Exercise Adherence*, Champaign IL: Human Kinetics.

Putnam, R.D. (2000) *Bowling Alone*, New York: Simon & Schuster.

Redcar and Cleveland Borough Council and Langbaurgh PCT (2005) *Redcar and Cleveland Physical Activity Strategy, 2005–2010.*

Roberts, K. (1996) Schoolchildren and sport, *Sport, Education and Society*, 1, 47–57.

Robson, S. (2001) Sport and health, in K. Hylton and P. Bramham (eds) *Sports Development: Policy, Process and Practice*, 1st edn, London: Routledge.

Rowland, T.W. (1990) *Exercise and Children's Health*, Champaign IL: Human Kinetics.

Sport England (2006) Active People Survey: headline results, www.sportengland.org/index/ get_resources/research/active_people/active_people_survey_headline_results.htm.

Taylor, W.C. (2005) Transforming work breaks to promote health, *American Journal of Preventive Medicine*, 29, 461–5.

Teachernet (2007) National Physical Education, School Sport and Club Links Strategy, www.teachernet.gov.uk/teachingandlearning/subjects/pe/nationalstrategy/.

Wheaton, B. (2004) (ed.) *Understanding Lifestyle Sport: Consumption, Identity and Difference*, London and New York: Routledge.

CHAPTER 9

RESOURCES FOR DEVELOPING SPORT

David Jackson and Peter Bramham

This chapter provides an overview of some of the major resourcing issues in relation to the development of sport in recent times. It outlines key concepts to help understand the commercial, public and voluntary sectors of the UK economy. Particular attention is paid to the economic impact of volunteering as well as to the impact of National Lottery funding on sports development and sports facilities. It is no easy task to measure and assess the value of sports resources as they include tangential material resources such as capital and revenue, as well as less tangential human resources such as time, expertise and physical effort. The dominant paradigm for such measurement has its roots deeply embedded in the discipline of economics which has over time developed theories to explain changes in the supply and demand for goods and services and so understand the crucial role of the equilibrium price mechanism and primarily price elasticity in directing and monitoring production and consumption. As classical liberal economics has it, the individual behaves as a rational consumer. He or she makes choices in the market place to maximise satisfaction when consuming goods and services whilst firms seek to maximise profits. In a capitalist economy sport is no exception.

Economic textbooks on sport and leisure have long been established originally by key authors such as Chris Gratton and Peter Taylor (1988) and Andrew Cooke (1994). Such books examine the growth of sport and leisure markets which depend upon time, disposable income and technology. Some sports are 'goods-intensive' such as squash, whereas others are 'time-intensive' such as cricket or rambling. It is also important to acknowledge the recent growth of more individual 'lifestyle sports' (see Wheaton, 2004) and the move away from traditional team-based or more collective or community sports.

Macro-economics explores sport and leisure expenditure, employment, international trade as well as market failure, state regulation, subsidies and business sponsorship. Micro-economics examines what factors influence supply and demand for a particular sports product or service. It studies the structure of the market, acknowledging that perfectly competitive markets, the ideal of nineteenth-century liberal economics, also generate more restrictive market forms where a few firms (oligopoly) or even one single firm (monopoly) dominate production. Market structures such as oligopoly provide the business context for the operating policies of global companies such as Nike, Adidas and Reebok. But they too are interested not only in global marketing which involves sponsoring sports teams, sports celebrities, mega-sports events and sports stadia but also in local initiatives such as talent development training/coaching programmes and community-based junior sports initiatives.

Micro-economics focuses on the behaviour of individuals, households and firms, and has become increasingly interested in the field of marketing, with its key concepts such as branding, market strategies, capacity building, 'value for money' and consumer choice. Standard macro-economics can measure the economic contribution of sport and leisure towards the gross domestic product (GDP), i.e. the total value of goods and services measured by expenditure. Gratton and Henry (2001: 1) suggest that sport contributes 3 per cent to GDP in OECD countries. In the distant past the Sports Council attempted to estimate the real costs of sports voluntary labour, monetary inputs into voluntary organisations as well as expenditure by voluntary clubs. In 1985 Richard Emes, Chair of the CCPR, argued that revenue expenditure by the voluntary sector was twice the size of local authority spending. To pay for volunteering hours at average national wage rates in 2002 would have amounted to a sum of approximately £15 billion.

Irvine and Taylor (2001: 19) have suggested that commercial leisure has become big business and in 1998 contributed 17.5 per cent to the economy. They acknowledged that there are real conceptual problems around the way leisure and sport are defined. They defined commercial sports and leisure organisations as those concerned with generating profit. So the sports market includes all those resources for participation, equipment, clothing and footwear, and involves spectating. They choose to exclude costs of travel to sports venues, sports tourism and sports media which they locate in other areas of leisure. But even with a focus on just one sector of the sports industry, conceptual and ensuing problems of measurement abound. Indeed, one would imagine that resources designated to commercial sport would be the easiest to assess and evaluate in economic and financial figures, whereas the voluntary and public sectors generate more complex social problems for analysis.

It is precisely this conceptual conundrum that Nichols (2001) seeks to address when he draws a distinction between 'economic' approaches to measuring the voluntary sector in sport as against the 'socio-cultural' approach adopted by Bishop and Hoggett (1986). The first approach seeks to place an economic value on the output of volunteering work in sport and the publication *Valuing Volunteers in UK Sport* (Gratton et al., 1997) suggested that there were 1.5 million volunteers, who on average devoted two and a half hours a week to volunteering in sport. A follow-up survey completed in 2002 by the Leisure Industries Research Centre (LIRC) at Sheffield sought to improve the methodology of the original survey in order to avoid 'double counting' sports volunteers and to generate more accurate estimates of volunteers from key national governing bodies (see James, Nichols et al., 2003).

In their ground-breaking analysis of mutual aid in sport and leisure, Bishop and Hoggett (1986) acknowledge that the voluntary sector in leisure, the bulk of which constitute multi-functional sports clubs, is the unique home of enthusiasts who are prepared to volunteer time, energy and money towards their chosen leisure and sporting interests. The voluntary sector secures outcomes that commercial and public sectors fail to produce because it creates goods and services that are not economically profitable for the commercial sector or because there is a lack of political consensus to drive public policy to provide such goods and services collectively. In keeping with the nineteenth-century version of amateurism in sport, these sports enthusiasts constitute a vibrant residue that is, by definition, intrinsically motivated to participate in and administer its own sport and commit to its future development. Economic perspectives which stress professionalism, salaries and wages, capital investment, profits and business partnerships, targets and outputs may drive elite performance sport and policy discourses but, for enthusiasts, market processes and rational decision making are of much less significance. Indeed, one central argument of Bishop and Hoggett's (1986) research designates the voluntary sector as the cradle of democratic processes in local communities and the lifeblood of active citizenship.

The power of the market and that of the state are held at bay or at least negotiated by the local club itself through its officials and members. Sports and sports clubs mediate different local subcultures which may embrace commercialisation, new technologies, sport medicine and performance competition. The clubs may be inclusive of all members, disregarding differences in class, ethnicity, gender, age, sexuality and disability, or they may use sport as a site to maintain exclusivity and difference. For Bishop and Hoggett and more recently Putnam (2000) joining a sports club is not simply a rational choice by the individual as a consumer, rather it not only involves membership, a sense of belonging to a key institution in a local community, but it also opens up a 'community of interest' which may well extend beyond the local neighbourhood, thereby functioning to sustain trust and to build up social capital. One has only to contact the internet and sample, via search engines, the cornucopia of sporting web sites. Each boasts its own pages and archives as well as links to related sites, other forums, chat rooms and personal blogs.

At this stage it is useful to introduce a key distinction made by economists between private goods and services, public goods and merit goods. For the economist, the distinguishing characteristics revolve around who pays the costs associated with the production and distribution of goods and services. In the case of *private goods*, the individual consumer meets the full cost at the equilibrium market price at which firms are prepared to sell commodities and to make a profit, with adequate returns on capital and labour costs. However, some goods are designated as *public goods* whereby the government intervenes in the market either by taxation, subsidy, direct provision or regulation such as planning strategies to guarantee unpolluted air, clean rivers, forests, quiet green spaces, urban parks and playing fields. These are provided by the state cost-free either as citizen rights or because of the difficulty of charging individual users or consumers of the resource. They are non-excludable, provide benefits for all citizens and are non-rival, i.e. one person's consumption does not necessarily impinge on others, e.g. law and order, clean air, public lighting, neighbourhood parks (see Veal, 1994). The third and final category of goods and services is *merit goods* whereby the individual consumer meets only part of the cost, the remainder covered by subsidy either from central or local state budgets or from business sponsorship. Local authorities building and managing swimming baths are good examples of delivering merit goods because conventional pricing policies result in swimmers paying up to half the price of the actual cost of the swim. In a capitalist economy, merit goods may be seen as 'inferior goods' as wealthier consumers move out of public sector provision, shifting their consumption to more exclusive and expensive facilities provided at full cost in the commercial sector. As we shall see later, local authorities that directly provide leisure gyms and swimming baths find it hard to compete with the private sector, dominated by chains such as David Lloyd and Virgin Active.

Governments may intervene in sport for reasons of market imperfections, in search of externalities, in order to provide free public goods or because of public policy needs for equity. Market imperfections usually stem from monopolies or from unequal income distribution and inadequate purchasing power within sections of the population. Externalities focus on the psychological and physiological health benefits of sports participation or on diverting youth from crime, vandalism or drug abuse. As we have seen in Chapters 4 and 5, demands for equality in provision, and more recently for equity with respect to sporting outcomes, have become import icons of sports policy. This should cause little surprise, as sport is ideologically defined as an area of life deemed free from class, gender, 'race' and disability discrimination.

It is important to retain a firm grasp on the differences between the three sectors involved in sport, as well as the economists' distinction between private, public and merit goods and services. Roberts (2004) argues that each sector possesses different capacities; they are driven by different motivations and in policy terms offer different discourses and rationales:

> these sectors are not just alternative ways of providing much the same range of leisure goods and services. Each sector has its own 'engine', and the provisions that result are distinctively commercial, voluntary or public sector products.
>
> (Roberts, 2004: 8)

When writing about sport he argues that sport in the UK has historically been provided by the voluntary sector. Few sports are commercial and only some elite sports have been recently transformed by commercialisation, although some writers would stress sport's mediatisation, with the influx of finance from satellite television broadcasting rights (see Rowe, 1999; Whannel, 1999, 2002; Horne, 2006).

THE POLICY BACKGROUND

This wider consideration of the nature of economic resources suggests that one simply cannot ignore the scope of public sector involvement in sports development during a climate of greater economic accountability. Whilst New Labour's *Game Plan* (pp. 32–3)

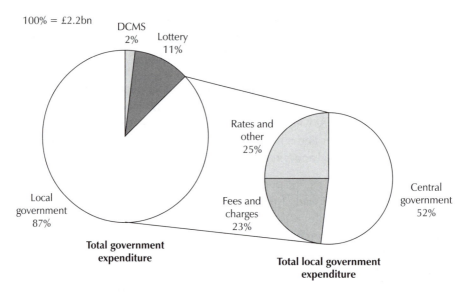

100% = £2.2bn

DCMS
2%   Lottery
       11%

Rates and
other
25%

Central
government
52%

Local
government
87%

Fees and
charges
23%

**Total government
expenditure**

**Total local government
expenditure**

Figure 9.1 Estimated government and Lottery expenditure on sport and physical activity, 2000

Total expenditure on sport estimated on the basis of Lottery grants, Sports Council allocations, local government expenditure on leisure and recreation, education, sundry policing and grants to local clubs, sundry central government expenditure through departments such as MoD, Royal Parks and the prison service.

Source DCMS, Leisure Industries Research Centre, cited in *Game Plan* (2002: 32), reproduced by courtesy of the Department of Culture, Media and Sport and of Sport England.

in Figure 9.1 suggests an overall public investment in 2000 of £2.2 billion, the validity of any figures is questionable, due to complex accounting procedures and to the different funding streams involved. Figure 9.1 shows overall percentage breakdowns of public sector investment in sport as described in *Game Plan*: central government 2 per cent, local government 87 per cent and the National Lottery 11 per cent.

Flexibility in the estimation of sport expenditure is confirmed by figures published in the Carter Report (2005), which suggested that for England 'investment by central government = 11%; by local government = 67%; and by the national Lottery = 22%' (2005: 17). Such discrepancies may be accounted for by government funding for school sport sourced through the Exchequer and the New Opportunities Fund. As Carter (2005: 17) points out, it is difficult to compare UK levels of investment with other countries as nation states support sporting endeavours in very different ways. There is insufficient space here for detailed cross-national analysis; what follows is an historical perspective which maps UK changes in sporting aspirations and resource support.

Whilst local authorities face specific local challenges in terms of resource provision, these have been largely shaped in the context of major national policy developments, particularly Compulsory Competitive Tendering (CCT) during the early 1990s and the Best Value regimen introduced in 1997. Subsequently, New Labour sought to build on positive aspects of CCT through Best Value. This policy initiative aimed to provide a framework where a sensitive balance could be struck between universal high-quality provision for all citizens within the confines of a constrained public sector budget.

Since 1994 one other major feature of the sports policy universe has been the introduction of the National Lottery, which was to 'transform forever the prospects for British sport' (*Sport: Raising the Game*, 1995). Introduced in the dying years of John Major's Conservative government, the National Lottery represented one policy initiative where cross-party support was clearly evident. Any thoughts that New Labour would abandon the Lottery were quickly dispelled. The newly formed Department of Culture, Media and Sport published its first strategy document, *A Sporting Future for All* (DCMS, 2000). This emphasised that the success of sports development at all levels was closely connected with the effective use of National Lottery capital and revenue monies.

The importance of sport and sport development resources can simply be measured by £20 billion of consumer spending. This equates to 2.2 per cent of GDP (more than twice that of agriculture) and the employment of some 400,000 full-time equivalent jobs (Carter Report, 2005: 11). Interest in the economic value of sport with its putative 'multiplier effect' has extended to consider sport business in relation to its economic impact on tourism, urban regeneration, heritage and media. Gratton *et al*. (2001) have confirmed that major international events tend to be of a 'one-off' nature, whereas major national spectator events, such as the FA Cup Final, test match cricket, open golf and so on generate the largest economic benefits for host cities. Such financial attractions and high-profile media coverage highlight resource implications embedded within top-level performance sport. Elite sport is identified by government as a major platform in *Game Plan* (2002), which highlighted the importance of achievements on the international stage and also the need to attract major international events. Subsequent support for the successful bid to bring the Olympic Games to London in 2012 is demonstrable proof of government belief in the economic benefits of hosting the largest sports event in the world.

In response to *Game Plan* (2002), Sport England has set out its own distinctive strategy to develop sport, *The Framework for Sport in England* (Sport England, 2004) (see Figure 9.2). The document restates increasing sports participation as its principal aim but its overarching ambition is to co-ordinate all sectors to achieve targets set out for 2020 and beyond.

The policy intention is to encourage a sustainable system that can provide sporting opportunities for all across all levels of achievement. In a sense this could be seen as one final attempt to resolve the contradiction apparent in the drive for Sport for All and more recent interest in elite sport at performance and excellence levels. Indeed, academic commentaries have noted this fundamental conflict within the sports policy universe which in turn has generated different interests groups, each advocating different policy agendas and outcomes (see Houlihan and White, 2002; Green and Houlihan, 2005). Whether such policy tensions can be resolved depends ultimately upon sustained commitment from disparate partner organisations such as national governing bodies, sports clubs and local

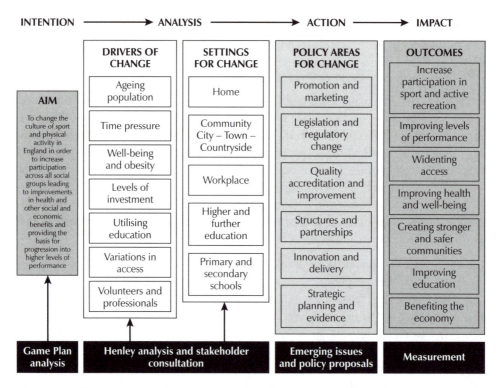

Figure 9.2 The framework for sport in England

Source Sport England (2004: 9).

authorities. Whilst traditional funding, facility provision and coaching development are essential components, the role of sports development has received a level of recognition not previously acknowledged. Indeed, Sport England has emphasised that it is determined to improve sport as an experience for participants, spectators and volunteers. This clearly echoes government ideology and public policy in terms of social inclusion. If genuinely achievable, the Framework for Sport in England (2004) will challenge those critical voices (e.g. Lentell, 1994; McDonald, 1995) who argued that Sport for All was abandoned in practice and concept.

SPORTS PARTICIPATION

Whilst leading the way in trying to increase sports participation to levels prescribed in *Game Plan* (2002) one corollary must be to attract sections of local communities that are or that have not been active in the past to take part in sport and physical activity. Indeed, broadening access is a key target of the National Framework for Sport. According to research in the Yorkshire Region (Yorkshire Plan for Sport, 2005) there is a large percentage

**Increase participation in sport and
active recreation**

Segmentation of participation, Yorkshire

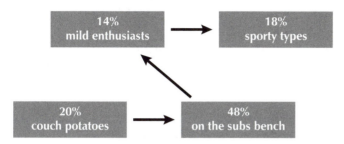

Figure 9.3 Yorkshire Plan for Sport, 2004–08

Source Unpublished presentation, 2004, reproduced by courtesy of Sport England.

of the population who are marginal participants. These must be the main target for action if an increase of 1 per cent per annum to 2020 is to be realised.

Policy issues of social inclusion, community development and equity are considered directly in Chapters 4 and 5 as well as motivation to engage in sport and physical activity (Chapter 8). For those actively involved in realising the ambitions set out by the government and Sport England, the main barrier to increased participation is often perceived to be more fundamental: more investment! This may be imagined in a number of forms, e.g. improved facilities, subsidised access, transport, improved leadership and coaching and myriad more ways of investing in infrastructure. But ultimately many see the only way to achieve more is to plough in more resources whilst making more efficient use of those already employed.

Many see Lottery funding as enabling local authorities to catch up with the lack of investment caused by financial retrenchment during the Thatcher era. Rather than 'additionality' funding, the Lottery has functioned as another competitive funding stream for constrained local authority budgets. It could be argued not only that the very significant increase in funding provided by the National Lottery has assisted agencies in meeting the sporting needs of more people, but that, of equal importance, it will continue to highlight where the challenges and difficulties are not primarily about finance. The next five to ten years will provide much information about how realistic and achievable current targets are and bring a sharper edge to discussions around sporting opportunities, collective needs and individual motivations.

Sport England's call for what realistically is a sea change in participation rates up to 2020 may intensify current academic debate between sociologists who emphasise controlling structures and society and psychologists such as Chelladurai (1985) who focus on individual agency, motivations and intentions. Again, the renewed welfarist drive to attain genuine Sport for All may well flounder during what some commentators describe as a pluralist postmodern era.

In Western culture at least, postmodernity has been linked with the apparent rise in individual freedoms, as seen in lifestyle choices and the rapid disintegration of nation states in the face of global materialism. In terms of sport development during the past two to three decades, a much professed respect for individual choice and motivation has been accompanied by increasing efforts to induce all groups in society to participate in sport. This tension between providing opportunities for all, whilst recognising that not all individuals will want to become involved, is well understood by many at the sharp end of sports delivery. The conundrum has also been clearly articulated by academics such as Coalter (1998). Interestingly, whilst it has been generally accepted that the financial cost usually represents the major barrier to greater participation, especially from the low participant groups, other research by Coalter for the Sports Council, as long ago as 1991, suggested that such is not always the case. Coalter and Allison (1996) began to include a sharper focus on lifestyle and individual choice in terms of identifying reasons for low or non-participation. Nevertheless, Sport England's determination to involve the entire community in sport may turn out to be largely unattainable where individuals within groups and society itself exercise choice to be indifferent or reject sport. The sometimes missionary and evangelical zeal of those agencies and organisations committed to sport must be understood in the context of an increasingly open and flexible culture, where sports discourse is reminiscent of Victorian ideals of muscular Christianity, character building and moral development through sport (McIntosh, 1987). Policy documents that have emerged from New Labour administrations since 1997 reveal the Cabinet Office's enthusiastic embrace of traditional conservative concerns such as respect for the rule of law, sound public finance and self-sufficiency. However, policy statements and strategies cannot effect change without concerted efforts from those closest to delivery. Not everyone is convinced of the potency of government exhortations to play sport, volunteer, adopt healthy lifestyles and become good citizens.

The extent of the task of achieving the shifts in the participation habits of the nation are highlighted in Sport England's Active People Survey (2006). Only 21 per cent of the population over sixteen years old were found to take part regularly in sport and active recreation. Some of the other headline findings of the survey are shown in Table 9.1.

The wider focus of encouraging more people into sport is in another sense much broader than Sport for All. Effort is to be targeted at increasing volunteering and spectating as well as participation. Whilst spectators are vital in terms of generating revenue through sponsorship opportunities and advertising, and in helping to generate atmosphere at events, the main concern is with volunteers and participants.

RESOURCES FOR DEVELOPING SPORT: VOLUNTEERING

The role of the volunteer in sport has received much greater attention and scrutiny. There are several important reasons for this. However, arguably the most significant relates to the special place occupied by volunteers in the formation and development of sport in

Table 9.1 Sport England Active People Survey

Participation

- 21% of the adult population aged sixteen and over (8.5 million people) take part regularly in sport and active recreation.
- 28.4% of adults (11.5 million) have built some exercise into their lives.
- 50.6% of adults (20.6 million) have not taken part in any moderate intensity sport and active recreation of thirty minutes' duration in the past four weeks. Many of these will be switched off from sport but many more are likely to want to participate but face barriers that make it difficult for them to be active.
- Regular participation (this is defined as taking part on at least three days a week in moderate intensity sport and active recreation for at least thirty minutes continuously in any one session) in sport and active recreation varies across different socio-demographic groups:
    - Males 23.7% (4.7 million); females 18.3% (3.8 million).
    - 32.7% sixteen to twenty-four years; 24.7% thirty-five to forty-four; 16.0% fifty-five to sixty-four; and 6.0% seventy-five to eighty-four years.
    - People with a limiting long-standing illness or disability 8.8%; those without 23.3%.
    - Black and other ethnic minority groups 18.6%; adults of white origin 21.2%.
    - 17.5% of black Caribbeans regularly participate and 17% of Asians.
    - Lowest socio-economic groups 16.3%.
    - Highest socio-economic group 25.1%.

Source Sport England (2006: 1),
www.sportengland.org./061206_national_factsheet_embargo_7_dec_final.pdf.

the UK. As outlined by Roberts (2004) the state and the government historically have left the provision of sport and physical recreation to unpaid, dedicated and enthusiastic amateurs. It can be argued that sport in the community, beyond that offered by schools or in a small number of professional sports, was designed, delivered and developed by a disparate group of people who often shared a common love of sport in general and of their sport in particular. Communities both large and small, and from the very affluent to the poor, worked to lay the foundations of what was probably the most extensive and diverse sporting provision in the world. That it was owned, shaped and developed at almost no cost to the government was quite remarkable; that individuals, companies and local communities nourished and sustained these opportunities without any significant outside help seems difficult to believe in a more individualised and fragmented culture.

During the rapid expansion in local authority-funded sports provision in the 1970s and early 1980s the contribution of the voluntary sector remained important despite its lower profile. Whilst local politicians invested huge sums of money in building and staffing flagship sport and leisure centres in their areas, the volunteer work force continued to supply the coaches, administrators, treasurers and club secretaries without which most formal competitive sport provision would have disappeared. Increasingly, local authorities began to seek closer ties and develop partnerships with the voluntary sector, most notably clubs and community groups. Sports development workers, with the remit to take sport to people through outreach working, and those required to help young performers fulfil their sporting

Table 9.2 The value of volunteering

Type of sports volunteer	Volunteer hours (million) per year	Value of volunteer hours at £8.31 per hour (£million)
Governing bodies and sports clubs in 94 sports	165.5	1,375
International events hosted in the UK	0.3	2
Disabled sport	3.2	26
Schools	2.6	21
Youth organisations	11.6	96
Total	183.2	1,522

Source Leisure Industries Research (1996) in *Game Plan* (DCMS/Cabinet Office, 2002: 36), reproduced by courtesy of the Department of Culture, Media and Sport.

potential both worked ever more closely with the voluntary sector to achieve these aims together. During the late 1980s initiatives such as Champion Coaching were launched by the National Coaching Foundation (now Sport Coach UK) and the Sports Council to help improve performance levels in children and to develop a network of coaches. Although often led by local authorities and sports development staff, these projects relied heavily on partnership with the voluntary sector in the form of coaches, leaders, parents and clubs and national governing bodies (NGBs).

The UK has a network of 110,000 community amateur sports clubs run by 1.5 million volunteers (CCPR, 2002: 3). The value, in monetary terms, associated with the extensive use of these volunteers in English sport has been estimated at over £15 billion (Sport England, 2002: 4) (see Table 9.2).

Although local authorities and governing bodies were enthusiastic recipients of volunteering work, little formal planning was undertaken to attract, retain or reward sports volunteers. Champion Coaching represented the first nation-wide initiative where volunteers were provided with vouchers to assist them to acquire further and more advanced coaching qualifications. These subsidies were offered to coaches in return for their work in helping to deliver quality youth sports programmes for those aspiring to improve their performance levels. The success of many of these programmes around the country led to a number of positive developments which did much to strengthen existing links between clubs and coaches, NGBs and local authorities. Facility managers and sports development officers played a significant role in facilitating these ties and sought additional opportunities to establish initiatives aimed at other levels of the sport development continuum, through closer co-operation with the voluntary sector.

Interestingly, the 1990s witnessed a growth in a new type of volunteer in sport, according to Shibli *et al.* (1999). Initiatives such as Champion Coaching at a national level and a number of similarly organised local schemes helped contribute to raise expectations among some volunteers in terms of greater and more tangible recognition of their role. In common with other areas of voluntary work, distinctions between the volunteer and the hourly-paid casual staff sports worker have become increasingly blurred. Many volunteers, especially those involved in coaching and coach education, have become accustomed to receiving payment for their services, although often the rates offered amount to little more than expenses and are used to convey token recognition for the work provided. Nevertheless, governing bodies of sport, local authorities, Sport England and Sportscoach UK have continued to press for a greater recognition of the work of the voluntary sector and have recommended that coaching in particular should be rewarded financially where possible. This has led to an increased profile for coaches and coach education. However, some sports either because of tradition or lack of funding are reluctant to offer remuneration. For example, some Rugby Union Development Officers have anecdotally pointed out that leaders and coaches working within their sport have no desire to be paid for a service which they are willing to offer to clubs and others in their free time. In contrast, many coaches in football development do expect some form of payment and not least because of the significant number of schemes at all levels of the continuum where participants are charged for taking part.

Beyond this a greater recognition of the key role of the voluntary sector in sports development work has emerged as a result of a number of changes. One such change has been the transition by many local authorities from service providers to that of enablers. The notion behind this shift in focus and policy was that local authorities needed to share their traditional role more fully with their local communities. The intention was to move from what Henry (2001) had called a paternalistic form of provision to a more equal and active partnership with the local community. It was hoped that needs rather than demand would be identified and addressed. During the 1990s pressures on capital expenditure, a declining revenue base and increasing expectations made the new enabling role a necessity for local authorities rather than an option. More positively, local authorities' sports providers were forced to reassess the vital role played by the voluntary sector and to involve them more in planning and work across the sports development continuum.

This approach was reinforced into the early years of the twenty-first century through the move to Best Value. Local authorities had by necessity to embed the role of the voluntary sector into a local and regional strategy for the comprehensive delivery of sporting opportunities. The need to consider all aspects and sectors was now politically essential rather than just desirable.

At a national level the Sports Council responded to this new environment with more support for voluntary groups, including devising training and education initiatives such as the Running Sport programme. The aim of this programme is to improve the quality of sport management, sports development and the delivery of sporting experiences for everyone involved in sport in England. Recently redesigned to meet the changing needs of sports development professionals and schoolteachers, the workshops and home study materials were primarily aimed at the voluntary sector in the sports clubs and governing bodies. A further development along similar lines is Sport England's Volunteer Investment Programme (VIP). This aims to increase recognition of the important role of volunteers in sport, encourage good practice in recruitment and retention and to help volunteers develop leadership and managerial skills.

One major problem, according to Shibli *et al.* (1999), is that with more expected of the voluntary sector in sport any substantial decline in numbers could be very harmful. Unfortunately, there are signs that this may be happening as leisure time declines and the number in full-time work continues to rise. Increasingly, it is not a matter of whether people possess the skills and motivation to become involved in local clubs or in sport development initiatives but the problem stems from lack of time. The demographic increase in people aged over fifty appears to be a welcome development because traditionally this group has been heavily involved as sport volunteers, often as club administrators and advisers. However, it may be that fewer seem able or prepared to devote themselves to voluntary roles in sport and are attracted by myriad competing interests and leisure pursuits.

RESOURCES FOR DEVELOPING SPORT: THE PROFESSIONALISATION OF SPORTS DEVELOPMENT

During the past three decades there have been periods of substantial growth in full-time paid employment within sports development. Those working in the public sector have diverse roles to play in developing sporting opportunities. Growth in the commercial and voluntary sectors has been difficult to chart, given that much has occurred when growing existing business. For example, increases in health, fitness and sport provision in the tourism and hospitality industry, or the emergence of leisure theme parks, illustrate how difficult it is to quantify this dimension of the sports development industry. What is clear is that the human resource involved in all these forms of sports development is a key factor in improving sport participation.

Within local authority settings staff have experienced important changes, with a strong emphasis on accountability, planning and cost effectiveness. Different elements of everyday operation, dictated by the culture of CCT, performance indicators and further sustained by Best Value regimes, have contributed to a continual squeeze on both capital and revenue budgets. Effective sports development workers have had to develop skills and competences to work in partnership with a range of others, both inside and outside sport. This has led to growing concern with training, education and qualifications. National governing bodies of sport, local authorities, public non-government agencies and higher education institutions all offer a plethora of courses and training opportunities, ranging from one-day seminars to postgraduate qualifications.

Although not everyone would agree, the drive towards professional status in sports development is set to raise standards of operation and improve service delivery. The emergence of the National Association of Sports Development (NASD) and the Institute for Sport Parks and Leisure (ISPAL) is an example of the continued movement towards professional status. Hutton (1995) and Sennett (2006) have emphasised the modern state's project to modernise public sector values by questioning their organisational efficiency and effectiveness. As a result social workers, teachers and health professionals have all been exhorted to join professional associations and embark on continuous professional development programmes (CPDs).

At NASD's inception there were members of the profession who felt that their voice and needs were not met sufficiently well by traditional bodies, the Institute of Amenity and Leisure Management (ILAM) and the Institute of Sport and Recreation Management (ISRM). With encouragement from Richard Caborn, the Sports Minister, to speak with one voice, a new professional body representing the wider sport and leisure profession has emerged. The Institute of Sport, Parks and Leisure (ISPAL) is a new body formed from the merger of NASD and ILAM but it may still not represent a unified industry, as the Institute of Sport and Recreation Management (ISRM) could not agree to join forces. Fragmentation of purpose and effort is unlikely to help with future status.

MATERIAL RESOURCES FOR DEVELOPING SPORT

When reviewing factors that impact on levels of sport resources, central government funds will be of major significance. Relative disinterest in sport by the modern state will not only be confirmed in government plans for public spending but will also shape attitudes towards financial investments by other stakeholders. A positive lead may provoke a different response. Changing public sector finances have had a profound impact on those working in sport development. Since local government reorganisation in 1974 there have been periods of plenty and periods of famine. The two most significant changes have been the National Lottery (1994) and New Labour's *Game Plan* (2002). Recent financial support for sport that government policy has secured through direct Exchequer funding stands in marked contrast to previous history. There has been a transformation of how we view sporting expectations. Since the early 1970s there have been enormous changes in the financial landscape in sport. In the commercial sector there has been the impact of the media and sponsorship on professional football, rugby, golf and other mainstream sports. This has taken place on both a national and transnational scale and sport is usually cited as a key indicator of the processes of globalisation (see Horne, 2006). The emergence of a health and fitness industry, based on private clubs, has not only seen a shift in large-scale business away from public sports centres to commercial brands such as David Lloyd and Virgin Active, but also witnessed a substantial growth in total turnover, based on increasing awareness of the benefits of an active and healthy lifestyle.

One key period of change centred on local government reorganisation in 1974. In the run-up to 1 April 1974 many small authorities saw the opportunities for sports facility building on a comparatively grand scale which was fuelled by a number of influences. First, councils that were about to be absorbed into much larger bodies grasped the opportunity to make political capital by spending on modern leisure facilities that had come into vogue. There was clearly a huge latent demand in local communities to be satisfied. This pragmatism coincided with a period of relative prosperity in local government which meant that budgetary provision on leisure as welfare was sustained to satiate contemporary aspirations. The Sports Council also supported capital investment with a modest but crucial budget that was deployed to great effect as a 'pump primer' for projects. Consequently, there was a massive capital resource input concentrated in a comparatively short period of time. The corollary of such expenditure on facilities was a concomitant increase in revenue budgets to run these new sport and leisure centres. Providing more comprehensive public services meant that the majority of ongoing expenditure was allocated to staffing. Sport and leisure are often described as 'a people business' and this emerging industry was generating job opportunities at all levels: from cleaners and catering staff to centre managers and directors of burgeoning new leisure services departments in town halls across the country.

The emphasis during the 1970s and early 1980s was spending on facilities. Policy drivers took the view that if good facilities were provided then local communities would take full advantage of them and so develop individual and collective sporting aspirations. The focus on local community facilities resulted in compromises in funding and provision of specialist facilities for elite athletes. For example, whilst many large urban conurbations had ambitions for major swimming and athletics facilities, local authority budgets were concentrated on the lower levels of the continuum. Sport for All was the dominant policy discourse and the focus was clearly on participation.

As noted by Hylton and Totten in Chapter 5 this strategy of 'bringing people to sport' proved to have serious limitations. Subsequent attempts to change direction during the mid-1980s by 'bringing sport to people' were the epiphany of good practice in sports development as many understand it today. In local authorities it was the first time that budgets were dedicated to direct community sport interventions. This meant that leisure departments began to expand their remit beyond the operational functions of facility management into realms of both generic and sport-specific development. Resources for this expansion came partly from within local authority budgets but also from central government funding through the Sports Council. This was substantially initiated by the promotion of Action Sport in response to urban unrest in the early part of the decade but there was also a clear determination on the part of many authorities to establish strong leadership in sport development. At its inception there was still a climate of relative affluence, and making budgetary provision was not too onerous. But the growth of both facility building and what was in effect an exercise in sports marketing, delivered by a growing band of teams and detached officers, began to falter as the pressure exerted by central government started to take its toll on local government finances.

In the early 1990s the subsequent introduction of Compulsory Competitive Tendering, with its concentration on the management of sports facilities, also had an impact on public sector practice. As a result of serious managerial analysis, and as the fear of commercial competition increased, pressure was placed on covering the real costs of providing sport. The potential for savings in expenditure and growth in income produced a managerialist practice that focused on an improvement in the financial 'bottom line'. There is considerable anecdotal evidence that facility managers prioritised revenue generation to the detriment of quality sports development in order to try and balance budgets in an increasingly straitened financial environment. Five-a-side football and mass aerobics became the order of the day, impairing the development of high-level performance programmes designed to produce future champions or to provide purposeful activity for local youth.

This retrenchment in public expenditure was exacerbated by a powerful mixture of high interest rates, economic recession and increased financial stringency. Further difficulties were encountered which included the rise of competing leisure interests as well as the emergence of a very competitive, high-quality health and fitness product from the commercial sector.

The arrival of new entrepreneurial developments in private health, fitness and leisure clubs is crucial. Much of the groundwork in developing awareness and opportunities in personal fitness training was pioneered (often with few resources) by local authorities. But as soon as the commercial possibilities of niche markets emerged the lack of ability to compete on an equal financial footing led to a haemorrhaging of business, paradoxically in an expanding market. Thatcherism proved to be hostile to local government finance and sought to introduce business entrepreneurialism in public sector service delivery. Any sport or leisure service that had a viable commercial future should quite naturally be supplied by private enterprise operating in a free market. Whilst private enterprise cherry-picks the best of commercially viable ideas, residual sport and leisure services remain non-profit-making and therefore in need of support if they are to continue. The necessary financial support may come in the form of public subsidy, 'below the line' resourcing through the voluntary sector or perhaps via commercial sponsorship.

Faced with real political and economic pressures, advances gained in less turbulent times in both facility and outreach sports development often froze or went into retreat in the early 1990s. The opportunities for access to sport were also under constraint from other elements of government policy, the Local Management of Schools and the National Curriculum, which were outlined in the Education Reform Act 1988, planning policy in relation to selling school playing fields and the teachers' industrial disputes of the late 1980s. Against this centralising policy background John Major as Prime Minister began to show interest in what was happening in sport and set out to provide guidance on how improvements could be achieved. After years of ambivalence to sport under Margaret Thatcher and a series of ineffectual Sports Ministers, government began to take a policy interest in the role sport played in society. *Sport: Raising the Game* (1995) was viewed by many in both the public and voluntary sectors as a flawed attempt to raise the profile of sport in the political agenda and to improve the competitiveness of national teams in international events after a series of uncomfortable defeats. Whilst there was much to consider in plans for raising the nation's sporting capabilities through the establishment of a UK Sports Institute there was also some salvation with the promise of resources from the National Lottery.

The emergence of sport as one of the National Lottery's five good causes and the subsequent election of New Labour in 1997 held the potential for a real change in the outlook for sport. Much of the future of the nation's plans for sport became inextricably linked with the emergent gambling habits of the population.

THE NATIONAL LOTTERY

The introduction of the Lotteries Act in 1993 and the implementation of the National Lottery in 1994 by the John Major government were viewed in a number of ways. To some, it was a sparkling new initiative designed to capture the imagination of the country with the added potential of providing real benefit for a range of causes close to the nation's heart. To others, it was state gambling which would function as indirect taxation, falling most heavily on disadvantaged income groups. Politicians had pragmatically succumbed to forces of darkness that would generate an undesirable dependence on gambling which would sap the poor and create unrealistic expectations of an escape from poverty. The reality that faced the government at the time was that a number of lottery games were emerging in many European countries. Preventing people in Britain from taking part was impossible, even if it had been desirable, and would have led to any monetary benefit, other than prizes, going elsewhere. The National Lottery has changed the complexion of financial support for UK sport. Though not perhaps in exactly the way he intended, the words of the former Prime Minister John Major do carry a ring of truth: 'The existence of the National Lottery has transformed forever the prospects for British sport' (*Sport: Raising the Game*, 1995). Indeed, some political commentators view the Lottery as John Major's one and only significant policy legacy.

The Lottery has generated enormous interest and significant amounts of revenue both as prizes for individuals and funds for good causes. It has also made a sizeable contribution to tax revenue as well as rapidly establishing itself as part of national popular culture. Figure 9.4 shows the breakdown of how each pound of Lottery income is used.

There has been little political debate about the Treasury receipt of a windfall of 12 per cent of total revenue generated. It is clear that more could have been made available for distribution to the original five good causes, nominated at the inception of the Lottery. These originally were: sport; the arts; charities; heritage and the Millennium Fund. Each received one-fifth of the designated 28 per cent of funds generated. The original financial estimates of what this would actually mean proved to be underestimates, such was the Lottery's success.

Rules for the distribution of proceeds from Lottery sales were delivered to the relevant body, which, in the case of sport, was a reprieved and revitalised Sports Council. Several important problems were encountered.

- None of the money designated for the Sports Lottery Fund was to be used for revenue purposes; the intention was to provide funding for a new wave of modern facilities and to refurbish older ones. The breadth was expected to stretch from major international venues to changing rooms for local clubs.

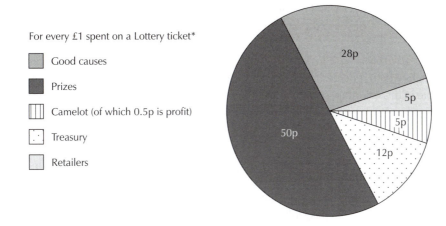

For every £1 spent on a Lottery ticket*

- Good causes
- Prizes
- Camelot (of which 0.5p is profit)
- Treasury
- Retailers

28p

5p

5p

50p

12p

Figure 9.4 The distribution of every £1 spent on a Lottery ticket

The breakdown is based on sales outlined in Camelot's bid for the licence.

Source National Lottery Funding Decision document, DCMS National Lottery Distribution and Communities Division (2003: 10), reproduced by courtesy of the Department of Culture, Media and of Sport England.

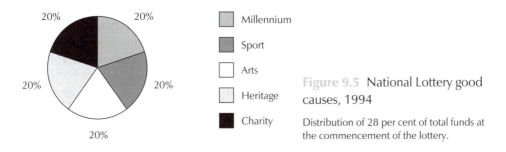

- Millennium
- Sport
- Arts
- Heritage
- Charity

Figure 9.5 National Lottery good causes, 1994

Distribution of 28 per cent of total funds at the commencement of the lottery.

- Partnership funding of a minimum of 35 per cent of the cost of the project was to be provided by the organisation applying.
- The Sports Council, as distributing body, was not allowed to solicit bids and was expected to remain neutral in the allocation process.
- Funds provided by the lottery were intended to be new 'additional' resources, with no reductions in existing budgets.
- Grants could not be made to commercial enterprises.

It soon became clear that the new stream of money was not necessarily reaching sectors of the community most in need. Many organisations were unable to comply with the strict requirements of bureaucratic process, as well as struggling to reach the minimum 35 per cent level of capital funding. In addition, even if they could overcome such obstacles there was still the need for the project to provide a realistic business plan that could robustly predict a sustainable income and expenditure stream. There were also issues around certain sectors of the community who were disenfranchised from the whole process. How realistic was it to expect small community groups in impoverished inner-city or rural locations to begin to develop the dream of Lottery-funded facilities?

> In the early days . . . a lot of the grants in London tended to go to suburban boroughs which reflected the fact that these places have lots of articulate wealthy people in the voluntary sector running sports clubs that already owned their own land and were able to make the most of the scheme.
>
> (Downes, 1996)

The role of local authorities in the early days of the Lottery was also interesting in that there was a need to fulfil a multiplicity of roles. They were part of the consultation process for applications but they were soon attracted to Lottery funding for sport projects in local communities because they felt a responsibility and desire to promote, co-ordinate and develop initiatives. There was also a clearly sharpening focus on the need to plan strategically to maximise local benefits.

Limitations of the distributive regulations constraining the Lottery Sports Fund were tackled incrementally by the Sports Council through introducing the Priority Areas Initiative and the Schools Community Sports Initiative scheme. The real opportunity for change came with the election of the New Labour government in 1997. The Department of Culture, Media and Sport instigated a thorough review of ways in which Lottery funds were allocated. After extensive consultation and deliberation of options the rebranded Sport England published a strategy document in May 1999, *Investing in our Sporting Future* (Sport England, 1999). The main thrust of this new plan was to split the estimated £200 million per year (projected over each of the following ten years) into a Community Projects Fund using three-quarters of the total, and a World Class Fund that would use the balance to support national and international sport. The total amount available to sport at the time had been reduced by falling revenue from Camelot, the Lottery organiser, and also by the introduction of the New Opportunities Fund (NOF), but this amount still remained above the original estimates made when the Lottery had first begun. The Community Projects Fund incorporated three elements to try and ensure a more comprehensive coverage of the population. These were Small Projects (capital and revenue schemes up to £5,000), Revenue Awards for schemes over £5,000 and Capital Awards for large-scale developments. It was anticipated that National Lottery funding would address the major shortfall in specialist sport facilities relative to other nations. There was considerable potential for aspirations, expressed in strategic plans for facility development, to be achieved. Figure 9.6 shows the overall strategy for the distribution of money from the Sports Lottery Fund.

There were significant differences between new and old Lottery strategies. The most important were proactive participation in the process by Sport England and the inclusion of support for a wide range of revenue activities previously excluded. There were clear links drawn between Lottery funding targets and the application of Sport England's overarching strategic plans. The supporting Active Programmes formed a fundamental element in developing sporting opportunities, particularly at participation levels. The objectives of

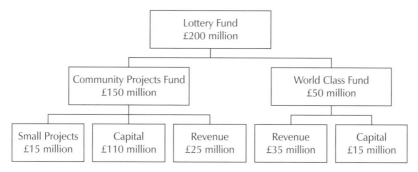

Figure 9.6 Distribution strategy, Sports Lottery Fund

the new Lottery strategy were devised to channel funding to those communities most in need in designated Sport Action Zones, the Priority Areas Initiative and the School Community Sports Initiative. The influence of current national policies continues in that sporting aspirations, supported by the Lottery Sports Fund, are significantly wedded to New Labour issues of social inclusion, community development and health as well as sustaining the other targets of Best Value services defined by both government and Sport England.

The introduction of the New Opportunities Fund led to a subsequent change in the distribution ratios from October 1999, as shown in Figure 9.7. The share of the Sports Lottery Fund pound was reduced from 5.6 per cent to 4.66 per cent but this still represents an estimated Lottery income of £200 million per annum on which the projections for the next ten years were made.

The proactive role of Sport England allows a strategy to achieve maximum benefit from Lottery money. There is also an enhanced role for local authorities to play in attracting Lottery funding into their geographical area and increasing evidence of the employment of Lottery specialists to generate funds from a range of partners. Without a co-ordinated strategy for sporting development in all-sector provision there will inevitably be concern

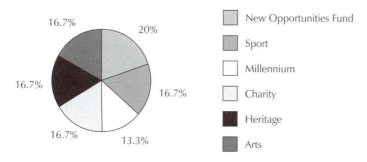

Figure 9.7 National Lottery good causes, 1999

Distribution of 28 per cent of total funds to good causes after October 1999. Sport, the arts, heritage and charity each received 4.66p from each £1 ticket sold.

that Lottery money may not reach where it may be needed most. This requires local authorities to work with many partners in the sporting environment in order to ensure that plans for provision are clearly defined and agreed as part of a comprehensive strategy. Similarly national governing bodies are required to ensure they have well-developed strategies for their own sports at all levels if they are to receive funding to support their activities on the national and international stage (see Houlihan and White, 2002). The World Class Fund is itself split between revenue and capital schemes and aims to support both facilities and events programmes and also a range of support services, targeted at producing future champions.

In the search for improved performance on the international stage, UK Sport is 'charged with leading sport in the UK to world-class success' (see the UK Sport web site) and it is financed by a mix of Exchequer and Lottery funding. In turn the four home countries' Institutes of Sport are primarily funded by Lottery money and work together with governing bodies to realise their shared aims. A major challenge facing national governing bodies in the past has been a lack of adequate funding to support those at the very highest level. Grant-aid awards from the Sports Council during the 1980s and early 1990s rarely satisfied the expectations of athletes or administrators and arguably undermined success on the international stage.

Whilst the Sports Council promoted the concept of performance and excellence among its partner agencies, political, financial and structural obstacles reduced this to an aspiration rather than a reality. However, the advent of the National Lottery provided a dramatic increase in capital and subsequently (and more important) revenue. The role of national governing bodies in planning, managing and supporting this area of work was given a major lift with this influx of substantially increased resources. This shift has put governing bodies centre stage in performance and excellence work and reduced the need for hard-pressed local authorities to take the lead in this and other conflicting demands and responsibilities.

Alongside continued Lottery support there is the essential corollary of the responsibility to deliver success. It will be interesting in the years ahead to chart how closely resources will follow achievement. A number of further changes in the way that funding from the Lottery is distributed have been made in recent years but they have not significantly changed the amount received by sport in total. However, there has been a change in the reach of funding.

In 2004 the Big Lottery Fund was created and this body now distributes half the Lottery money for good causes, incorporating the previous Community and New Opportunities Funds. The BLF gives Lottery grants to charities and the voluntary sector, as well as sup-porting projects concerned with health, education and the environment. Awards for All is a joint programme set up to support community groups to enable people to take part in sport, arts, heritage and community activities, as well as projects which promote education, the environment and health in the local community. Both of these programmes extend the reach of the Lottery into the wider sporting arena, including school sport and PE.

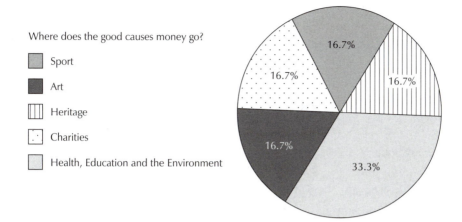

Where does the good causes money go?

- Sport
- Art
- Heritage
- Charities
- Health, Education and the Environment

Figure 9.8 National Lottery good causes, 2006. Distribution of 28 per cent of total funds at November 2006

Responsibility for distributing the proceeds from the Lottery rests not with the government or Camelot but with a number of independent distributing bodies.

Table 9.3 provides figures for the amount of funding that has been invested in sport since the inception of the National Lottery. Funding through the BLF and Awards for All has supplemented this overall amount but it is difficult to disaggregate owing to the nature of the grants made. Nevertheless an investment in sport since 1994 in excess of £3 billion (National Lottery web site, 2006) provides a significantly different picture from the programme of direct investment in sport experienced during the twenty years prior to the Lottery's arrival.

The London 2012 Olympic Games and Paralympic Games will be beneficiaries of up to £1.5 billion of Lottery funding which it is anticipated will be secured by additional Lottery games, thereby leaving the existing beneficiaries' shares intact. It will remain to be seen if the Lottery is capable of generating this level of additional interest to support London 2012 without impacting on other funding streams.

There is much optimism about the potential for success in developing sport at all levels of the continuum and for achieving strategic objectives set out for sport by government, Sport

Table 9.3 Distribution of funds by Sport England and UK Sport to November 2006

Sport England	
No. of projects funded	15,520
Total awarded	£2,188,057
UK Sport	
No. of projects funded	5,936
Total awarded	£231,520

England, NGBs, local authorities and other stakeholders. The significant input made by lottery funding has the potential to deliver considerable achievements but success is far from guaranteed. The ability of other countries to apply similar principles more effectively has to be considered in relation to international competitions and the emergence of complementary policies may play a role in determining the potential for success.

Future changes to the Lottery format may well have an important impact on resources for sport. An interesting exercise in relation to Lottery funding would be to ask the question 'What if?' and to reflect on the position of sports development had the National Lottery never come about.

The final thought in this chapter goes to the area of funding sports development in the public sector that is both the largest element under discussion and one under most pressure – local authority spending on sport. Having been through sustained budgetary constraints and having responded to a raft of policy developments that have impacted on the role of providers in local communities, there are new options appearing for hard-pressed service facilitators and front-line deliverers. *Game Plan* (2002: 13) acknowledged that, whilst there may be considerable resources available for school sport, there is pressure on local government leisure budgets. The Carter Report (2005: 20) paints a picture of tired and ageing facilities and variable management that are bound to impact on the ability of local authorities to deliver the *Game Plan* agenda, especially in relation to participation. In order to tackle some of these issues local authorities are now developing new strategies to ease the burden and deliver more high-quality services. These include investing in facilities through Private Finance Initiatives (PFIs) and moving delivery departments to 'arm's length' trust status.

PFI is simply described as long-term mortgaging of facilities by using funding from the private sector to build or refurbish facilities and manage them over a long-term contract, usually twenty-five years. Private finance initiatives are not new in the public sector and are common in both health and education policy as ways of delivering new facilities without the Chancellor having to raise public taxation to pay for them. It remains to be seen if taxation has to be raised in future to fund the ongoing costs associated with these schemes, as there is insufficient evidence to be able to deliver a clear verdict. Anecdotally there are problems already emerging in relation to inability to vary contracts, which often frustrates service departments in meeting strategic objectives. For example, the promotion of desirable after-school community sporting initiatives that require variations in financial arrangements may prove to be neither financially viable to a PFI school contractor nor affordable to a local authority department. The new facility therefore remains closed at a time when it is clearly in demand. These teething problems are beginning to work themselves through complex finance systems but there appears to be some way to go in resolving them. Issues may be even more complex on sites that are not linked into education venues. In schools the bulk of use is perhaps relatively straightforward to map out over a long-term contract. As new 'stand alone' sport and leisure facilities emerge it will be interesting to see how these arrangements cope with the volatile and dynamic sporting participation habits of local communities.

The move to arm's length trusts is another variation considered by hard-pressed local authority departments for their direct delivery operations. By moving out of direct control to charitable trust status, relief on both business council taxation and value added tax is viable and alone can transform the budgetary situation of a service. The challenge for politicians and senior managers in town halls is that, in order to achieve this new trust status, they must relinquish direct control of operations. The private sector has produced a number of contractors who, since the advent of CCT in the early 1990s, have provided very high-quality community-based services within strict financial regimes set out in contractual arrangements. There have been notable failures too. For many politicians this is a step too far in handing too much control to the private sector that needs to make a return on capital employed. By taking the step to charitable trust status there is perhaps a view that if trusts manage to perform financially well, then at least the fruits of those labours must be returned to the provision of services within the trust and not into shareholder dividends. A number of local authorities have already taken this step and more are considering the move. A membership body – SPORTA – provides umbrella support and advice for the growing number of trusts that have emerged. The future may see more local authority departments transformed into charitable trusts to act on behalf of their local communities.

CAVENDISH METROPOLITAN DISTRICT COUNCIL

Looking to the future of public sector sports development

The realisation of the implications of both Best Value and the National Lottery was that clear, strategic plans for the development of sporting opportunities across the council's area were no longer just desirable but essential. Sport was an integral component of council services and therefore had to have a strategy in its own right that incorporated public, voluntary and private sector contributions and aspirations. Not only that, but under the banner of Best Value the services provided by sport had to be clearly integrated into the overall council strategies to meet the cross-cutting agenda relating to health, social inclusion, economic and community development, and drugs and crime. Cavendish had brought together its facility operations and sports development arms some time ago and the delivery of sporting opportunities as defined by the five-year strategy was clearly an improvement on the somewhat disjointed provision previously on offer to the local population.

Whilst all this strategic planning was exercising the minds of senior politicians and managers in the town hall, an array of Lottery-funded schemes in schools, sports centres and voluntary clubs were appearing on the ground, making the dream of the Lottery a reality for some and holding out aspirations for others that their turn might come. However the council's own flagship scheme for a major new international multi-sports complex was floundering, as there were insufficient funds for such large-scale projects and there were question marks about long-term viability and strategic fit with other facilities across the country. Having taken the view early on that access to funding from the Lottery was more of a marathon than a sprint, there were some in the authority who wished they had been perhaps a little quicker off the starting block. Neighbouring Fairfax MDC had made the early decision to go for a grandiose international-standard athletics stadium as a priority ahead of a range of smaller community-based schemes and this project was completed before many others started to put their bids together.

The declining physical condition of Cavendish's ageing sports facilities was also a real concern, as falling visitor numbers began to prove what many elsewhere had predicted and were also beginning to experience. The public were voting with their feet. Many were failing to be tempted by lower quality facilities and were not taking part in the great move to increase participation rates. Others were taking their business to an expanding commercial sector. This was a double whammy for Cavendish MDC, as not only were they failing to achieve the strategic aims they had set in line with government policy, they were also faced with falling revenue, which threatened an ever faster financial downward spiral.

In an attempt to halt the decline, moves were under way to set up the Cavendish Sports Trust. This would allow more financial freedom and release funds for reinvestment in facilities but it would also mean that the council would have less direct control of operations. Having researched the options, the decision to go ahead had been taken and a target date set for hand-over to the new trust after a period during which a shadow body would act out the scenario that would operate in the future. The confidence engendered by the success experienced by others was tempered by uncertainty among elected members, senior managers and shop floor workers alike. Only time would tell if the new trust was able to deliver.

SUMMARY

In the years since 1997 and the election of a New Labour government much has changed in the world of sports development whilst continuities persist. The government has introduced a clear agenda for sport, as articulated through *Game Plan* (2002). This focus is in marked contrast to the ambivalence displayed by the previous New Right administration. Sport is clearly higher on the agenda both in its own right but more important as a medium for achieving a range of wider policy objectives. Considerable resources have been made available to enhance sporting opportunities in schools and the National Lottery continues to be a major factor in supporting sport at all stages of the continuum.

However, prudent fiscal management of the economy has determined that local government as one of the key providers is still working in a stringent budgetary environment that requires a continual search for innovative ways of delivering existing and new services. Whilst the focus of resource management may be on finance, the importance of human resources in the sector has never been more clearly highlighted. With the impending London Olympics of 2012 the need for a highly trained work force is a target that will stretch the abilities of professionals and volunteers to the full. The cost of putting on the biggest event in world sport is also a concern for many as the potential for the redirection of already scarce resources emerges.

REFERENCES

Bishop, J. and Hoggett, P. (1986) *Organizing around enthusiasms: Mutual Aid in Leisure*, London: Comedia.

Carter, P. (2005) *Review of National Sport Effort and Resources*, London: Sport England.

CCPR (2002) *Everybody Wins: Sport and social inclusion*, London: CCPR.

Chelladurai, P. (1985) *Sports Management: Macro Perspectives*, London, Ont.: Sports Dynamics.

Coalter, F. (1991) Sports participation: price or priorities? *Leisure Studies*, 12: 171–82.

Coalter, F. (1998) Leisure studies, leisure policy and social citizenship: the failure of welfare or the limits of welfare? *Leisure Studies*, 17: 21–36.

Coalter, F. and Allison, M. (1996) *Sport and Community Development*, Edinburgh: Scottish Sports Council.

Cooke, A. (1994). *The Economics of Leisure and Sport*, London and New York: Routledge.

Department for Culture Media and Sport (2000) *A Sporting Future for All*, London: DCMS.

Department for Culture Media and Sport (2001) *The Government's Plan for Sport: A Sporting Future for All*, London: DCMS.

Department for Culture Media and Sport and Cabinet Office Strategy Unit (2002) *Game Plan: A Strategy for Delivering Government's Sport and Physical Activity Objectives*, London: HMSO.

Department of National Heritage (1995) *Sport: Raising the Game*, London: HMSO.

Downes, G. (1996) Poor hope of rich pickings, *Guardian*, 13 September.

European Association for Sport Management (EASM) (1999) *Sport Management in the Next Millennium: Proceedings of the Seventh Congress of the EASM*, Thessalonica, September.

Gratton, C. and Henry, I. (2001) *Sport in the City: The Role of Sport in Economic and Social Regeneration*, London and New York: Routledge.

Gratton, C., Dobson, N. and Shibli, S. (2001) The role of major sports events in the economic regeneration of cities: lessons from six World or European Championships, in Gratton and I.P. Henry, *Sport in the City: The Role of Sport in Economic and Social Regeneration*, London and New York: Routledge.

Gratton, C. et al. (1997) *Valuing Volunteers in UK Sport*, London: Sports Council.

Green, M. and Houlihan, B. (2005) *Elite Sport Development, Policy Learning and Political Priorities*, London: Routledge.

Henry, I. (1993) *The Politics of Leisure Policy*, London: Macmillan.

Hogwood, B.W. and Gunn, L.A. (1984) *Policy Analysis for the Real World*, Oxford: Oxford University Press.

Horne, J. (2006) *Sport in Consumer Culture*, Basingstoke: Palgrave Macmillan.

Houlihan, B. and White, A. (2002) *The Politics of Sport Development*, London: Routledge.

Hutton, W. (1995) *The State We're In*, London: Jonathan Cape.

Hylton, K. (1998) Equal Opportunities and the Sport Policy Process, paper presented at 'Sport in the City' conference, Sheffield Hallam University.

Irvine, D. and Taylor, P. (2001) Commercial leisure: an international perspective, in C. Wolsey and J. Abrams (eds) *Understanding the Leisure and Sport Industry*, Harlow: Pearson.

James, M. and Nichols, G. *et al.* (2003) Volunteering in English sport: an interim discussion in relation to national governing bodies of sport, in G. Nichols, *Volunteers in Sport*, Eastbourne: Leisure Studies Association.

Kokolakakis, T. (1999) Leisure Volunteering: The Economic Significance of Volunteering in the UK, Seventh Congress of the European Association for Sport Management (EASM), Thessalonica, September.

Lentell, B. (1994) Sports development: goodbye to community recreation?, in C. Brackenridge (ed.) *Body Matters: Leisure Images and Lifestyles*, Brighton: Leisure Studies Association.

Lord Carter of Coles (2004) *Review of National Sport Effort and Resources*, London: DCMS.

McDonald, I. (1995) Sport for All: RIP?, in S. Fleming, M. Talbot and A. Tomlinson (eds) *Policy and Politics in Sport, Recreation and Leisure*, Brighton: Leisure Studies Association.

McIntosh, P. (1987) *Sport in Society*, London: West London Press.

Nichols, G. (2001) The UK voluntary sector: understanding the leisure and sport industry, in C. Wolsey and J. Abrams (eds) *Understanding the Leisure and Sport Industry*, Harlow: Pearson.

Putnam, R. (2000) *Bowling Alone: The Collapse and Revival of American Community*, New York: Simon & Schuster.

Roberts, K. (2004) *The Leisure Industries*, London: Palgrave Macmillan.

Rowe, D. (1999) *Sport, Culture and the Media: The Unruly Trinity*, Buckingham: Open University Press.

Sennett, R. (2006) *The Culture of the New Capitalism*, New Haven CT: Yale University Press.

Shibli, S., Taylor, P., Nicholls, G., Gratton, C. and Kokolakakis, T. (1999) The characteristics of volunteers in UK sports clubs, *European Journal for Sports Management*, 6: 10–27.

Sport England (1999) *Investing in our Sporting Future*, London: Sport England, www.english.sports.gov.uk.

Sport England (2002) *Volunteering in England in 2002*, London: Sport England.

Sport England (2004) *The Framework for Sport in England*, London: Sport England.

Sport England (2006) Active People Survey: Headline Results, http://www.sportengland.org/index/get_resources/research/active_people/active_people_survey_headline_results.htm.

Sport England (2007) More People, More Places, More Medals, www.sportengland.org/sport_england_annualreport_2000-2001_part_1.pdf.

Sport England and Local Government Association (1999) *The Value of Sport: Best Value through Sport*, London: Sport England, www.english.sports.gov.uk.

Sport England and Local Government Association (1999) Executive summary, *The Value of Sport: Best Value through Sport*, London: Sport England, www.english.sports.gov.uk.

Veal, A. (1994) *Leisure Policy and Planning*, Harlow: Longman/ILAM.

Whannel, G. (1999) Sport stars: narrativization and masculinities, *Leisure Studies*, 18: 249–65.

Whannel, G. (2002) *Media Sports Stars*, London: Routledge.

Wheaton, B. (ed) (2004) *Understanding Lifestyle Sports: Consumption, Identity and Difference*, London and New York: Routledge.

CHAPTER 10

SPORTS DEVELOPMENT AND SPORTS COACHING

John Lyle

Sports development is a term that has come to mean a public service, a measure of change in social policy, a professional rationale and a form of engagement in sport. The term is both ubiquitous and insubstantial. However, the very attempt at comprehensiveness creates a lack of focus and interpretation of purpose that render it almost worthless as a descriptor of function, and useful only as an occupational category. Nonetheless, the term has a common usage that embraces all levels of sport participation and, increasingly, physical activity. The use of the term conjures up a plethora of initiatives, personnel, social structures and shared meanings.

The most familiar of these are the structures and pathways within each sport that allow participants to perform and progress at all levels from initiation to excellence; the more casual forms of sport that, taken in aggregation, might be termed community or recreation sport; and initiative-led forms of participation with specific social or educational objectives. Sports development embraces these activities and the policies, procedures, processes and personnel that are required to both facilitate and deliver. This chapter adopts a critical and challenging approach to the assumption of a straightforward relationship between sports coaching and sports development.

Government proposals for the professionalisation of coaching have a clear developmental context (DCMS, 2002), and the discourse is directed to community sport and high-performance sport. It is further assumed that coaches play a significant role in the development of sporting talent (Martindale et al., 2005), and that there is a particular link between successful coaches and their developmental profile (Gilbert et al., 2006). This chapter goes beyond the initial question of a particular interrelationship between coaching and development to ask (1) does the social agenda of much of grass-roots sports development require a particular form of coaching; (2) is sports development adequately served by the 'quality' of coaching generally provided (Cassidy et al., 2004); (3) does coach education provide sufficient preparation for achieving social and other objectives (Cushion et al., 2003); and (4) is there a 'threshold' level of coaching activity, beyond which the term is most aptly applied, and does sports development activity generally reach this threshold, with implications for professionalisation?

Part of sport participation is dependent to a greater or lesser extent on sport leadership, teaching, instruction or coaching. In so far as sports development is a process that is intended to lead to increased sport participation, more sustained participation or improved standards of performance, sport coaching (as a collective term) becomes an extremely important element of provision. However, sports coaching is a contested term in the sense that there are quite distinct forms of coaching that can be associated with sport participation domains and contexts (Trudel and Gilbert, 2006). The initial part of this chapter examines the definitions, concepts and expectations of coaching in each of these principal contexts (e.g. recreational/community, club/performance, excellence), and proposes a simple model of the association between coaching practice and developmental aspirations (Lyle, 2002). Sports coaching is treated as a problematic element of sports development in so far as it can be argued that many of the typical objectives of sports development are dependent on appropriate forms of coaching leadership. Sports coaching must be interpreted not merely as delivery but as a process in which the coach increasingly adopts a strategic approach to the personal, organisational, environmental and technical factors that impact on performance. Thus sports development in performance or excellence sport involves the meta-strategic co-ordination of these factors (Jones and Wallace, 2006).

Following an examination of definitional terms and the relationship between the concepts, sports development is examined as a 'ladder of opportunity' in the second part of the chapter; that is, a staged, progressive pathway that young people have to travel to move from initiation into sport to sustained participation and skilled performance (Lyle, 2004). The chapter examines critically how the incorporation of Long Term Athlete Development (LTAD) principles into sports coaching and development may impact on a number of sports development imperatives (for example, competition between sports, early specialisation, team sports versus individual sports differences) and the implications for the balance between the technical development of sports and other sports development objectives. In the final part of the chapter the interdependence of coaching and environmental changes is demonstrated via a case study of a national representative team sport.

The UK government document *Game Plan* (DCMS/Strategy Unit, 2002) summarises the beneficial effects of sports participation. They range from social benefits such as social inclusion, community development, urban regeneration and improved health to more individual benefits such as a sense of social, psychological and physical well-being, and the impact of successfully pursuing international sporting achievement. In order to achieve this, there is a considerable infrastructure of organisations, agencies, practitioners and initiatives. Indeed, some of those deemed to be contributing may not think of themselves as sports developers (Hylton et al., 2001). The emergence of sports development as a national movement is chronicled by Coghlan (1990), Henry (1993), Pickup (1996), Hylton et al. (2001) and Houlihan and White (2002). As we move into the first part of the twenty-first century, sports development has become acknowledged as an occupational grouping; local and national governments are embarked on the delivery of a sports development policy framework (Sport England, 2004); the voluntary sector in sport is embroiled in initiatives designed to achieve the benefits described above and at the same time develop their sport; and a network of umbrella bodies (such as the Youth Sport Trust, Regional Sport Partnerships and County Sport Partnerships) has attempted to build partnerships between all concerned, including education and health agencies. Providing the glue for this entire enterprise are an enormous number of sports development strategic and planning documents.

There is a dearth of material on development principles applied to sport. Sport England[1] has produced policy papers on monitoring and evaluation, and on the (legislative) planning stages, but says little about the development process itself: 'Why have we been doing what we have been doing in the way that we have been doing it?' Most recently, large-scale national initiatives such as the School Sport Partnerships (see www.teachernet.gov.uk) and Active Schools (see www.sportscotland.org.uk) have adopted a more systematic approach to development. Nevertheless, these are facilitative interventions and do not prescribe local practice. There is undoubtedly a vast well of good practice, but much less evidence that this is being translated into education and training. There may be a perception that the chapter has a critical tone. This seems almost inevitable when considering the contribution of sports coaching in the context of an absence of consensual rationales for intervention, the acknowledged barriers to development, the social deficit model of provision and concern over existing participation rates.

The purpose of the chapter is to reinforce the danger of treating coaching as an unproblematic factor in the facilitation and delivery of sports development initiatives. At the same time, this requires an understanding about sports coaching concepts and the implementation of the coaching process. It would be simplistic but probably accurate to state that all sports coaching is a form of sports development. Key to the argument pervading the chapter is that all purposive sports development has not attended adequately to the role of the coach in achieving sports development outcomes.

SPORTS DEVELOPMENT AND SPORTS COACHING: TOWARDS A DEFINITION

Inevitably we have to deal with the task of defining what is meant by sports development and sports coaching and establish why and in which ways sports development differs from other processes. Is everything that involves sport participation to be considered sports development? In one sense the answer is 'yes'. In engaging in sport, the purpose of the coach, teacher or instructor and the motives of the participants will be to produce better quality/more skilled/ increasingly successful/better prepared/more enjoyable participation. Nevertheless, it is not a helpful attempt at a definition simply to say that everything is sports development. Definitional frameworks are intended to provide, and should be measured against their capacity to provide, discrimination, criticality, substance, applicability and competence. This is no easy task, since sports development is a policy space, an occupation, an intervention activity and a 'concept'. Sports development is about purposive engagement in changing sports participation, but it should not be thought of as solely the prerogative of the practitioner.

The approach adopted here is to say that sports development is purposeful intervention to bring about more extensive, better quality, more widely accessible sport participation and/or improved standards of performance. This can be sport-specific or multi-sport in focus. Intervention takes place at a number of levels – strategic facilitation, organisation and administration, and delivery – and is present at all levels and stages of participation, development and performance sport.

It would be a valuable first step to offer a catalogue of 'sports development categories' to bear in mind as an initial conceptualisation.

- *Sports development as the policy-led management of sport provision in the UK*. This involves the system-wide facilitation of improved provision, within a set of political and sporting goals. Agencies involved are Sport England,[2] UK Sport, local authorities, emerging regional governance, DfES and so on. Issues include the extremely wide set of stakeholders, huge variations in meaning and purpose, little consensus on the interpretation of sport, management by control of the political agenda and consequent funding. It is doubtful if this can be said to be a coherent system.
- *Sports development as the* de facto *maintenance or improvement in sport participation within established avenues of transmission*. This is generally to be found in sports clubs, representative sport and school sport. The continuing dynamics of sport (relative achievement, recruitment, growth, seeking competitive advantage) assume develop-mental characteristics. This category is divided into two sub-systems: developing and pursuing excellence in performance sport, and maintenance of activity in multi-level competition-led sport participation. In each case there is inherently a competition for limited resources, and the application, partial or otherwise, of strategic planning and development planning.
- *Sports development as initiative-led intervention activity*. Nationally directed – locally delivered intervention has characterised much of sports development in recent years (for example, Positive Futures, www.positivefuturesresearch.org.uk, or Active Schools, www.sportscotland.org.uk). Such initiatives are generally specifically targeted and directed at non-participants, casual participants or those (primarily schoolchildren) who are expected to become non-participants. Social deficit or ethnic disadvantage ideologies direct provision and resources. The preferred transmission medium is partnerships involving local authorities, national governing bodies (NGBs) and schools.
- *Sports development as facility-led local authority provision (leisure centres, swimming pools, education facilities, etc.)*. The activities promoted, facilitated and scheduled within these facilities are often overlooked as a form of sports development. It is impor-tant to look at the development messages about sport participation, often unintended, that can be transmitted by such use. There is significantly more casual and recreational use, and use by socially advantaged groups, despite inducements to other targeted groups. Sporting activities are generally dominated by a narrow range of popular sports.

- *Sports development as a form of sport participation.* Applied in a generic fashion, the term has come to be used for local authority, initiative and other grass-roots activities that are characterised by their induction and preparatory motives. It may variously be considered a stage or level in the participation continuum.
- *Sports development as the consequence of related physical activity.* The objectives of sports development (whatever we agree these to be!) are often contributed to by other self-contained and other-directed forms of sport-related activity. Into this category can be placed physical education, professional sport, commercial sector fitness clubs, and the play sector. Each of these – obviously some more than others – can be said to be contributing to the development of sport. Perhaps the most interesting characteristic is that none of these sectors is 'controlled' by those who devise mainstream sports development strategies.
- *Sports development as a descriptor of trends in the social sciences.* Sport sociologists largely focus on the emergence of historical patterns and trends in sport – issues such as gender, social class, 'race' and ethnicity, power relations, commercialisation and globalisation. Such analyses generally deal with the consequences of more significant factors such as education, the family, resource control, transmission of the culture and so on. In addition, their focus is most often the media-dominated commercialised forms of activity. Sports development practice plays but a small role in such analyses, and social scientists should be encouraged to be precise in their terms of reference.

The role of the coach is one that needs to be explored, particularly if the assumption that the coaching process and sports development are synonymous is to have any validity. To do this it is necessary to deal with the issue of definitions. It would be helpful, therefore, if we could match classification systems for sports development and sports coaching. In doing so, the focus is on 'direct intervention/participation' forms of sports development, rather than sports policy or other socio-cultural descriptors of provision.

There is a great deal of debate about the definition of a coach but this need not detain us. Lyle (2002) examines the concept in great detail, whereas a report (MORI, 2004) allowed individuals to classify themselves as coaches. There would appear to be a continuum between 'any form of leadership that is designed to improve performance' and a narrower conceptualisation of coaching in which there are boundary markers around competition, intensity of preparation and the completeness of the coaching process. The United Kingdom Coaching Certificate (UKCC) is a national endorsement process for certification in coach education (www.ukcoachingcertificate.org). The UKCC endorsement criteria (sports coach UK, 2004) conceive of the coaching role in five levels:

- Assist more qualified coaches, delivering aspects of coaching sessions, normally under direct supervision.
- Prepare for, deliver and review coaching session(s).
- Plan, implement, analyse and revise annual coaching programmes.
- Design, implement and evaluate the process and outcome of long-term/specialist coaching programmes.

- Generate, direct and manage the implementation of cutting-edge coaching solutions and programmes.

It immediately becomes obvious that the functionaries within these levels are likely to be occupying different spaces and roles within the objectives of sports development. It assumes that there is a continuum of 'coaching' from the first level to the fifth. An alternative is that 'coaching' is delivered by individuals who have different levels of expertise but operate within distinctive domains. Thus the sports facilitator, the sports teacher, the multi-skills coach, the sports club coach and the high-performance coach may be a more useful role descriptor and framework than a 'level' of coach certification. This conceptualisation has the potential to enhance the compatibility between developed coaching expertise and specific sports development domains. However, this is not a current conceptualisation within the sports coaching policy community. The issue is one of professional boundaries and occupational growth. An all-embracing leadership definition provides a significant scale of occupational presence but does not establish professional boundaries based on extensive and exclusive expertise.

A COMMON PURPOSE?

Sports development is a term that embraces a broad range of initiatives and activities. Table 10.1 illustrates how the goals that are common to participation-led sports development are complementary to those of sports coaching. Sports coaching can perhaps be best conceptualised in three different forms: participation, development and performance (Lyle, 2002). These 'forms' are differentiated by their levels of preparation intensity, performance standards, competition involvement, development objectives and the scope of the coaching process. The notion that coaching and coach education must be considered within its domain-specificity is supported by Trudel and Gilbert (2006). Their categorisation of domains into recreational, developmental and elite has a self-evident match between coaching practice and the exigencies of the sporting context.

The *UK Action Plan for Coaching* (Sports coach UK, 2006: 4) avers that coaches play a 'vital role in developing and increasing participation in sport, as well as in the attainment of international success'. The document goes on to identify what it terms the key principles and benefits underlying quality coaching:

- Welcoming children and adults into sport.
- Making sport fun.
- Building fundamental skills in participants.
- Improving sport-specific skills.
- Developing fair play, ethical practice, discipline and respect.
- Enhancing physical fitness and a positive lifestyle.
- Guiding children, players and athletes through the steps to improved performance.

Table 10.1 Common goals between sports development and sports coaching

Sports development as:	Common goals	Sports coaching as:

▨ Improvement in sport participation
  – Developing and pursuing excellence
  – Developing and maintaining multi-level competition sport
  – Developing feeder avenues towards competition sport
▨ Initiative-led intervention activity (targeted at non-participants, social disadvantage)
▨ School-based intervention to increase participation
▨ Facility-led provision (casual, recreational, educational and entry level)
	Increase the scale and reach of participation
	Prepare athletes/teams to take part in competitions
	Identify and develop talented sports people
	Provide opportunities for participation through multi-level, multi-sport and multi-site provision
	Improve standards of performance (and competition achievement)
		▨ Participation coaching
		  – Initiation into sport
		  – Basic skills teaching
		▨ Development coaching
		  – Developing sports-specific skills
		  – Talent identification
		  – Transition into performance sport
		▨ Performance coaching
		  – Preparation for competition
		  – Co-ordination and management of athletes' specific goals
		  – Manage variables/lifestyles influencing performance

▨ Placing a high value on the development of the whole person.
▨ Keeping children, players and athletes safe in sport.

(Adapted from Sports coach UK, 2006: 10)

It would be difficult not to see this as a sports development agenda!

It is tempting to revert to the simplistic 'sports participation almost always involves a form of leadership to give it direction, purpose, structure, cohesion and quality'. Such leadership may range from the less technically demanding animateur to the high-intensity coach of professional sportspersons. *Sport participation on which development depends is therefore inextricably linked with sports coaching*. However, the term development also implies a process of change within a progressive structure. The implication from juxtaposing sports development and coaching is that there are some forms of coaching that are more or less appropriate for different sports development domains.

EMERGING ISSUES

The most significant development in recent years has been the emergence of the multi-sport, multi-skills coach. In so far as such coaches have tended to operate within initiative-led sports development and school-based interventions, their specificity (and, in some ways, non-specificity) of expertise provides an interesting exemplar of the need to match context, expertise and function. The demand for multi-skills/multi-sport coaches has emerged from an insinuation of the Long Term Athlete Development model (Balyi, 2001; Balyi and Hamilton, 2003), with its emphasis on the initial stages of development, in which sports practice is less sport-specific. This context emphasises variety (Sallis et al., 2000), and it should not be forgotten that these coaches increase deployment flexibility across different sites and groups. The inception of multi-skill academies and clubs is part of the government's all-embracing strategy for young people in sport, the national PE, School Sport and Club Links (PESSCL) strategy (www.teachernet.gov.uk). The establishment of opportunities such as these has provided the catalyst for the further employment of coaches and teachers.

The clearest expression of an impact on development provision is the Community Sports Coach Scheme (www.sportengland.org). The intention is that there will be the incremental establishment of '3,000 paid qualified Community Sports Coaches working at local level to increase the number and range of coaching opportunities'. The coaches operate across school, club and local authority contexts, with a focus on FUNdamental/Learning to Train stages of the LTAD model. The Sport England web site above provides a catalogue of the diverse ways in which the coaches have become part of sports development, principally at the initiation stage.

The term 'development coach' may seem to imply that it has more in common with sports development. The term applies to a sports domain that is characterised by being in the transition phase between becoming more fully committed to a sport and being prepared and ready to engage in performance sport. It is often considered to be synonymous with age-group sport but may be broader in its coverage than that. Development coaching provides an interesting example of the interplay of development objectives and coaching practice. The range of objectives within the domain may extend from pursuing excellence to retention of participants, and from growing the sport to the personal development of young people. These sports development objectives are influenced greatly by sports coaches' practice. This phase is one in which there is considerable emphasis on talent identification and development. A report has demonstrated that the quality of coaching is a key factor (**sport**scotland, 2004). For example, talent identification and development are dependent on opportunity, provision structures and coaches' selection policies. Coaches who emphasise early specialisation and the short-term gains necessary to achieve success at this stage may not be fostering the conditions likely to prepare athletes for subsequent optimal performance and lifelong participation.

Another way of demonstrating the relation between sports coaching and sports development is to examine the issues considered to be significant in large-scale interventions. For example, School Sports Partnerships (SSPs) have been established by the Department for Education and Skills and the Department for Culture, Media and Sport to achieve a number of policy objectives related to increased participation in sport and high-quality physical education by school-age children. The partnerships provide a network of personnel and programmes designed to achieve these objectives (www.teachernet.gov.uk). One of the key policy outcomes is the 'number of qualified and active coaches, leaders and officials'. Perhaps more significantly, coaching figured high in the identification of barriers to expanding SSP activity (Loughborough Partnership, 2005). Another large-scale initiative is Active Schools (www.sportscotland.org.uk) in Scotland, with a similar aim of increasing participation and improving performance. This initiative provides a network of co-ordinators across all schools in Scotland whose role is to facilitate and develop increased opportunities for young people. The year 1 monitoring report for Active Schools (**sport**scotland, 2006) identified the recruitment of volunteers as a potential weakness, but reinforced their role in achieving sustainability of the initiative and integration between participation sectors. The Monitoring Survey data[3] for 2005/06 record the constraints identified by Active Schools co-ordinators. The co-ordinators in primary schools identified 'lack of deliverers' as their No. 1 constraint on development (and it was ranked No. 2 with secondary co-ordinators).

The consequence of a close connection between coaching domains and sports development is that coach education should emphasise particular competences. Sports coaching education/certification has traditionally neglected the pedagogical delivery skills, and this may render such coaches less suitable for the initiation-level demands in school-based interventions. However, it may be argued that the more episodic, short-horizon participation coaching requires 'direct intervention' or delivery skills, whereas the meta-strategic co-ordination and planning of the high-level performance coach (Jones and Wallace, 2005; Bowes and Jones, 2006) are redolent of the intensive programmes characteristic of that domain. As a picture gradually emerges of coaching roles with specialised functions and expertise being associated with specific domains, there is also potential for the 'wrong' forms of coaching to be adopted. This is generally thought to describe the deployment of (usually) higher level sports-specific coaches whose emphasis on technical development and preparation for competition is assumed to be less suitable for the less committed beginner, for whom sport is often a means to achieving other benefits.

PERFORMANCE PATHWAYS AND COACHING

In an earlier study (Lyle, 1997) I pointed to the work of Hardman and Fielden (1994), who dismissed the mass participation–elite sport pyramid and spoke instead of a notional performance ladder. This notion of a performance ladder is now commonplace in sports development, particularly within discrete sports. The focus in provision of sporting opportunities has moved to the comprehensiveness and appropriateness of the 'ladder of sporting opportunities'. At the level of the individual, the use of the term 'opportunity' implies both a redressing of entry-level exclusion barriers and a richness of provision that addresses variable abilities and motives. At a structural or system level, 'opportunity' implies ensuring that provision and delivery structures are in place to (1) ensure sufficient progression in terms of quantity, (2) provide transition mechanisms that ensure quality, and (3) provide an element of 'inclusivity' or 'care' in tracking individuals.

The clearest example of the link between sports development and sports coaching has been the diffusion of the LTAD model (Balyi, 2001; Balyi and Hamilton, 2004) throughout sports provision in the UK, and the extent to which this model has been adopted by, or rather incorporated into, the emerging United Kingdom Coaching Certificate (www. ukcoachingcertificate.org). The LTAD model is a form of long-term periodisation of an athlete's performance development in sport. It appears to owe much to the East European systematic model for the development of high-level sport performance. The model describes the athlete's development as going through six stages: FUNdamentals, Learning to Train, Training to Train, Training to Compete, Training to Win and Active for Life (Balyi and Hamilton, 2004).

The model is not without its criticisms (see www.sportdevelopment.org.uk), which are centred on the absence of research support or impact evaluation data, lack of clarity in the rationale for development (confusion between elite, retention, inclusion or under-standing) and perhaps overestimating the potential for an integrated system across sports that eschews early recruitment or specialisation. Perhaps surprisingly the LTAD model has been adopted almost uncritically by policy makers in the UK. The model was an underpinning assumption of the *Game Plan* document (DCMS, 2002) and the National Framework for Sport in England (2004). Funding agencies now require governing bodies of sport to have diffused the model throughout their planning documentation. Perhaps more interestingly, the early stages of the model have been the catalyst for multi-sport provision and the justification for many initiatives variously termed Fundamentals, Basic Movement, and so on.

However, the most relevant issue here is that sports coaching levels or forms have become aligned with LTAD stages, perhaps most evidently in the UK Action Plan for Coaching (sports coach UK, 2006). The proposals create an alignment between LTAD stages and levels of coaching, and this is achieved through the coach's role function rather than coaching domain. The coach's development through the certification levels enables her/him to be most prepared for LTAD progressions. It is worth noting that the LTAD model assumes progression through performance levels, whereas this is not a principle of the UKCC (see documentation available at www.ukcoachingcertificate.org). The language of Balyi's work has come to dominate the discourse about development, and coaching development is now termed Long Term Coaching Development (see also Stafford and Balyi, 2005).

This is best illustrated in Way and O'Leary (2006), where LTAD stages are matched to stages in the career development of coaches. In a comprehensive model, coaches are said to go through stages of volunteer coach, part-time coach, career coach and coach for life. At the same time, their roles progress from instructor, through assistant coach to club coach and finally head coach. The model recognises a number of sports development domains: community coaching, competition introduction, competition development and high-performance competition. Although such development planning is at an early stage in terms of national diffusion, it illustrates a welcome attempt to bring together diverse elements of the sports 'system'. Two further examples illustrate this. First, the integration of LTAD and coaching has been adopted by individual sports. *FUNdamental Movement Ideas* (British Gymnastics, 2005) provides an illustration of performance progression with levels of certification. Second, *Building Pathways in Irish Sport* (www.nctc.ul.ie) is an exemplar of the fusion of sports development and coaching at a national level.

The chapter goes on now to illustrate the relationship between sports development and the coaching environment by examining a case study of the development of Scottish volleyball.

SCOTTISH VOLLEYBALL: SPORTS DEVELOPMENT AND SPORTS COACHING

One of the key factors in establishing the success of the coach's endeavours in high-performance sport is the extent to which the coach is able to develop an environment that is supportive. This is a very direct example of the relationship between coaching and sports development. Such an environment is characterised by a pervasive climate of support for excellence in sport, an integrated and co-ordinated effort by national federations to focus on excellence, a provision and delivery structure designed to identify and develop talented performers, a specific programme for pursuing excellence within the national team framework, and the political and resource support of relevant government agencies.

This part of the chapter outlines the development of the programme put in place to enhance performance and excellence in a relatively small national governing body, and in the context of what were, at least initially, apparently unsupportive conditions. There is an attempt to identify the principles underpinning the programme. The content is based on the reflections of the national team coach, who was instrumental in driving through the required changes.[4] It examines the characteristics of the programme put in place to develop the senior men's national team and the adjustments made by the national governing body of the sport to support this. It identifies a catalogue of key issues in support structures and coaching philosophy that will be of value in demonstrating the links between coaching at this level and 'sports development'.

IMPLEMENTING THE NATIONAL TEAM PROGRAMME IN SCOTTISH VOLLEYBALL

Background

In comparative terms, Scottish volleyball has played a modest role in Europe. Traditionally the national team has occupied a place in the C division of European volleyball. Competition is divided into three divisions, with the A division featuring several of the world's top ten national teams. Although the national team had been established for many years and there is both a national league structure in place and also a significant presence in schools' curricula, it had become clear that progress was limited.

Despite the very considerable efforts of successive national team coaches, and a number of very committed performers, the volunteer status of the programme and the absence of a planned, resourced and concerted approach to developing performance and excellence had severely constrained progress. The introduction of ring-fenced funding from the Sports Lottery Fund, and the resulting initiatives, which enabled support programmes for targeted sports to be developed, provided an opportunity for a rethink in Scottish volleyball.

The challenge

In December 2000 a full-time professional high-performance coach for Scottish volleyball was appointed. At the same time, a performance target was established specifying that the national team should reach the top eight of European B international competition within four years. At that time the Scottish team was one of the top two sides in the C division and there were approximately sixteen to twenty different countries that could be placed in the B division. It was acknowledged that the target was ambitious and demanding, and would require a paradigm shift in attitude and practice not only from the players and staff in the programme but from all those more widely involved in Scottish volleyball.

Strategy

The first step was to identify the strategic objectives that would lead to improved performance. Three very simple targets were established for the players and the programme, and three targets for the organisation of Scottish volleyball, necessary to support the national team players. The targets set for the National Team Programme were: the players to become physically stronger, an increase in the volume of practice time, and an increase in the number of competitive matches at the correct performance level. The Scottish volleyball contextual targets were: to establish stronger links between the NTP and the Division I national league clubs, the adoption of national team performance standards by the Division I clubs for national league play and the establishment of a 'Team Scotland' concept.

This establishment of organisational/contextual or developmental targets was viewed as an essential element for the progress required. The strongly held belief was that there was little relevance in using the full-time coaching position to develop the NTP as a pocket of excellence in isolation from the rest of the Scottish game. If it was possible to achieve the desired change in the performance capacity of the team, it would only be with the active help and support of the Scottish Volleyball Association (SVA) and in particular the active participation of the Division I national league clubs. All the countries that featured in the B and A bands of European play had substantially stronger domestic leagues than the one in Scotland; in fact most countries had professional leagues. This is significant because it provides consistent access to a higher and more intensive level of play, which in turn creates the demand for a higher quality of coaching input, strength and conditioning programmes, and so on.

This part of the chapter considers the steps taken to build this supportive framework.

Communication issues

The key to achieving the contextual targets was creating a climate of positive communication between the national team programme (NTP) and Scottish volleyball in general. The NTP was perceived to be elitist and isolated from the Scottish game by the majority of the coaches, players, members of the Executive Committee, etc. who were not immediately involved with it. This lack of communication and consequent understanding could be attributed to the amateur status of the programme and the lack of time available to the national team coaching staff. Members of the national team staff were in full-time employment, mostly in the education sector, and they were also extensively committed to club-level play. Therefore there was a limited amount of time and energy available for the national team work. This time was inevitably used to develop the players and the competition framework within the NTP. The resources required for an element of 'outreach' to involve the rest of Scottish volleyball in national team activities were simply beyond the capacity of the individuals concerned. The appointment of a full-time coach immediately changed that situation. The increased time resource was immediately deployed to improve all aspects of communication.

A series of papers, reports and newsletters were written and circulated to as wide an audience as possible. The object was to raise awareness of all aspects of the NTP, to help identify the range of people who were involved, and to elicit support for the programme targets. This awareness raising was then supported by a series of one-to-one meetings with every coach of a national league Division I team. There were several purposes attached to the meetings, but in the first instance they were designed to establish a database of information about the personal details of the coaches and the training circumstances of their teams. The meetings were also used to identify areas where the national team coach and the NTP could help the club teams.

It was evident that the SVA web site could prove to be an invaluable resource for transmitting positive images and information about the NTP. A part of the site was devoted to the activities of the national team, and a series of articles entitled 'iNTouch' were established. The iNTouch articles were used to explain and report on national team events, competitions and training camps, and were updated regularly. It was also felt that there was an overwhelming need to have a series of action photographs featuring Scottish players to add to the match reports. This was crucial to overcome the general perception that the Scottish game lagged behind the European version, and that Scottish players were physically disadvantaged. A programme to establish a library of such photographs was undertaken. Each of these initiatives was designed to create a positive image of the NTP, and of Scottish volleyball.

Changing practice

A number of changes were required in the way that the players and clubs engaged in the game. Targets centred on increasing the volume of practice, increasing the number of matches played at an appropriate level, and the Scottish clubs adopting national team performance standards were viewed as complementary. Without doubt, the key to implementing these changes was enlisting the active support of the Division I club coaches. The dilemma arose from establishing a situation in which there were common standards of performance and a climate of mutual support between clubs and the NTP, yet at the same time acknowledging the uniqueness of each of the participating clubs, and their need to compete against and attempt to beat each other.

There were two clear schools of thought in evidence during National League play. One was orientated towards winning matches in any fashion, without regard to the performance criteria. The other recognised that being able to win matches consistently was dependent on operating to planned and measurable performance standards. This is simply a version of the process/product debate; that is, focus on the outcome (product) or focus on the method with which the outcome has been achieved (process). In reality, of course, both are required. Sustainable and consistent success cannot be achieved if the process is flawed, and therefore the process is crucial. At the same time there must be a product that is deemed worthwhile and is measurable, if the quality of the process is to be established. If the NTP was to benefit from the assistance of the clubs then the contribution of both approaches had to be established and worked towards.

Action

This position was achieved by the establishment of an initiative entitled the First Division Alliance (FDA). A number of projects were undertaken under the banner of the FDA, all of which received the unanimous support of the Division I coaches. The most significant was a series of performance clinics on specific aspects of the game. These were presented by Division I coaches and members of the national team staff recognised as having expertise in that aspect of the game. Topics for the clinics were selected by the national team staff conducting a statistical analysis of Division I club play and comparing the results with the national team performance and the performance of European competitors in the B division. For many of the coaches involved this was the first set of objective performance criteria to which they had been exposed, and the statistical analyses and subsequent clinics met with enthusiastic support.

The FDA initiative was also fundamental in increasing the volume of practice time to which national team players had access. A regime of daily practice sessions had been established, for which local authority support was provided in the form of free access to specific facilities during the mid-day period when there was less demand for the facilities. However, access was limited in that it was available only to players from a limited geographical catchment who had time available mid-day. The FDA coaches agreed that players who were members of the national team squad could attend several different clubs during the week in order to increase the total volume of their practice time. This was a significant step, as none of the clubs involved practised more than three times per week and most were limited to two nights for financial reasons. The potential problems associated with players moving from one club practice session to another were tackled in several ways: ensuring the highest standards of personal discipline from the players concerned; the national team coach attending club practices to assist the club coach; the sessions being focused on the needs of the club team as a priority; and the alignment of club playing standards with those of the national team over a period of time.

Support from the Scottish Volleyball Association

There were also a number of changes that required the sanction of the SVA itself. One change that was essential for the successful development of the national team performance targets was the active support of the SVA in adapting the national competition structures. One of the principal functions of any national governing body is to develop and support the established national competition structures. All the other functions of the NGB – youth development, officiating, coach education, etc. – flow from this basic requirement. In Scotland the national league structures had been in place for a number of years and were well established. However, the standard of performance was significantly lower than the top levels of European play.

Action

Three major changes were introduced as a result of liaison between the NTP and the Scottish Volleyball Association. The first was to introduce a new competition, which was entitled the Power League. This event was scheduled for dates in the volleyball calendar that had been set aside for development purposes. The format of the competition was a series of single day tournaments, leading to a final event. The normal rules of the game were applied to all matches. However, points in the Power League championship were awarded both for winning matches and also for achieving certain game point tallies. This encouraged both process and product thinking on the part of the match coaches. The Power League featured all the Division I clubs, but also included a team made up of players from the NTP who were seconded from their clubs for the duration of the event. This had the immediate effect of ensuring the event was perceived as an essential part of the NTP, but also increased the level of competition by adding another strong team. Each of the NT staff was involved in coaching at the tournaments, and statistical analyses of game play were provided in all matches.

The second major development was to alter the structure of the national league to accommodate a series of play-offs at the end of the season. Traditionally, regular league play on a home and away basis had decided the outcome of the championship. This was changed to require the top four teams at the end of the round-robin phase to play each other in a 'best of three' match series for first semi-finals, and then the championship final. The best of three series had the added pressure of making the teams play matches on consecutive days. The reason for this was to highlight the need for improved match preparation and coaching. This was aided by good coaching practices such as video analysis, statistical analysis and rotational match-ups.

The third development was the introduction of a 'Player of the Year' award. This was essential to encourage more active interest on the part of the players and the media in celebrating the success of the Scottish game and the players who participated in the national league.

In addition to the changes in the structure of the competitions, the SVA Referees' Commission provided considerable support to the development of playing standards. It became obvious that increasing the volume and intensity of the competitions for the top players also placed a much higher level of pressure on the match officials, and the standards of officiating. The Referees' Commission established a programme of structured support and development for a core group of officials who were encouraged to participate in the key events and matches. Attention to enhanced officiating made a considerable contribution to the overall effort.

SUMMARY

It is possible to identify a number of principles in the developments that took place. (1) It is necessary to derive strategic performance objectives from the externally imposed performance targets. (2) Changes in performance have to be accompanied by changes in supporting structures. (3) A sense of ownership of the NTP was essential. (4) Complementarity between process standards and product outcomes was established. There were also a number of specific changes in competition and practice, designed to increase the volume and intensity of engagement by the players. Creating a coalition of all Division 1 coaches smoothed the way for many of the changes.

There is no doubt that a measurable shift in attitudes took place. The success of the overall change in attitude to performance and excellence in the Scottish game is attributable to two main factors: a realignment of the perception of the primary aim of the Scottish Volleyball Association, and the acknowledgement by all the top coaches in the game of the reality of the performance continuum concept. The primary aim of the Association has to be the development of the playing structures, and the standards of performance. The significance of recognising this is that it provides all those who are involved with a common purpose for their participation. It acknowledges and allows for contributions in many different forms, and encourages opportunities for the different inputs to be fused into a coherent effort.

For the purposes of this chapter, the notable message was that the achievement of the coach's objectives was viewed as an issue of sports development. Performance improvements were perceived to be symbiotic with competition structures, common performance models, and the recognition of a playing continuum to which all agencies were contributors.

CONCLUSION

Coaches can be thought of as 'service agents'; that is, they are capable (if fully trained and educated) of delivering services in response to specific sports development demands, whether school-based, club, high-performance, local authority programmes, and so on. Coaching is not context-free. It may well be argued that it takes on meaning only in its social (and sporting) context, and indeed such a conceptualisation would be helpful in delineating roles, expertise and education. We have seen that a broad and inclusive definition of terms could describe sports development as entirely dependent on sports coaches. While this may have a headline value, it is more useful to apply the analysis described in this chapter in order to gain a much fuller appreciation of the links between them.

There seems little doubt that much of the sports development that is initiative-led focused on the early stages of performance development, intended to address outcomes beyond participation itself; is not primarily competition-focused; and is delivered by coaches who operate in circumstances in which the fullest expression of the coaching process is neither possible nor desirable. In the longer term it may not be helpful in terms of recruitment, education and professional development to conceive of a coherent, integrated continuum of coaching roles. For example, there is evidence that coaches are recruited from within the playing/performing base of a sport and that coaches operating in higher level sport differ in their previous performance experience, motives, recruitment and aspirations from those whose role does not extend beyond participation coaching or 'teaching'.[5] This, however, may not be the case for multi-sport coaches, with consequent implications for recruitment.

A number of questions were posed in the introduction, and the analysis within the chapter has provided us with a set of thought-provoking responses. It does seem likely that the social agenda of many sports development initiatives requires a coaching approach that reinforces practices leading to retention, enjoyment and a form of sporting literacy that is transferable between sports. There is little doubt that this coaching requires a particular set of coaching skills (Lyle, 2002). However, it also brings with it potential for flexibility and multiple applications that are beneficial in sports development practice. Such a capacity may also present the coach with an increased range of employment possibilities.

Attention to the nature of the experience for the participant raises the issue of the 'quality' of the coaching episode or programme. Useful criteria here may be enjoyment, activity levels, sociability, success, achieving competence, and so on. However, there has been little research work in this area. Enjoyment leads to 'coming back' (adherence) for the participation coach and this may be a simple but useful measure of perceived quality. However, it is also worth pointing out that there remains some doubt about the extent to which this form of engagement promotes sufficiently the competence, meaningfulness and commitment necessary for sustained participation. There may be another measure of quality that is related to the adequacy of the content in its sports-specific developmental context. The quality of the experience for the participant is strongly influenced by the quality of the coach. Although this cannot be associated solely with certification, the evidence from the MORI report (2004) and from questionnaire surveys of coaches[6] in Scotland confirms that there is a significant proportion of unqualified coaches operating at all levels of provision.

There is strong support for a significant level of domain-specificity in coaching practice. A further question therefore is centred on the adequacy of coach education for providing levels of expertise that are commensurate with the demands of the context. The analysis suggests that there are quite specific coaching domains and that these describe different roles and functions. Coaching education is currently focused on levels of certification that are insufficiently orientated to these domains. This assertion is related to the final question, that of professionalisation. To service fully the complete range of sports development contexts sports coaching requires a broad inclusive definition and a classification framework that embraces the barely trained volunteer, the part-timer and more highly trained, full-time professional coaches. This conceptualisation is too broad and is not conducive to the professionalisation of coaching. The academic development of sports coaching studies has made substantial progress in recent years. However, one of the gaps is the awareness of development stages in expertise, and the relation of these to different roles both horizontally (responsibility within the same level of sport) and vertically (with increasing standards of performance). The breadth and scope of sports development tends to separate the coaching roles. This may be useful for sports development but not necessarily for the professionalisation of coaching and the establishment of a threshold status for entry to the profession.

As the chapter has shown, sports development and sports coaching have a symbiotic relationship. The distinctive forms of sports development and the sporting domains within which they occur create 'service leadership demands' from coaches and these in turn lead to distinctive roles, functions, levels of expertise and education. It would be a mistake to treat sports coaching as an unproblematic element of sports development. In many ways the success of sports development is dependent on the capacity of the 'coach' and the coaching environment created.

NOTES

1   It is illuminating that the Sport England/UK Sport Value of Sport Monitor (www.sportengland.org/vsm) seeks evidence that sport has an impact on other measures of social cohesion/behaviour. There has been less work on how to develop sport successfully in order to achieve these outcomes.
2   This is intended to imply similar agencies in other 'home nations'. The principle applies throughout the chapter.

3 These are unpublished **sport**scotland data derived from an annual survey of participation and provision across all schools in Scotland. The survey contains quantitative accounts of provision, but also qualitative responses from Active Schools co-ordinators.
4 The appointment of the national team coach was supported by an initiative of **sport**scotland, through Sports Lottery funding. The author was involved in an impact evaluation of this scheme for **sport**scotland, and the insights gained at that time, including multiple discussions with the coach himself, are reflected in this part of the chapter. The author acknowledges the contribution of **sport**scotland and the coach, Thomas Dowens, to the text.
5 This is available in data collated by the author to inform workforce development plans for two governing bodies of sport in Scotland.
6 Data obtained from research conducted in Scotland to support the evaluation of Active Schools and governing body workforce development plans.

REFERENCES

Balyi, I. (2001) *Sport System Building and LTAD in British Columbia*, Vancouver: SportMedBC.

Balyi, I. and Hamilton, A. (2003) Long term athlete development update: trainability in childhood and adolescence, *Faster, Higher, Stronger*, 20, 6–8.

Balyi, I. and Hamilton, A. (2004) *Long-term Athlete Development: Trainability in Childhood and Adolescence, Windows of Opportunity, Optimal Trainability*, Victoria BC: National Coaching Institute and Advanced Training & Performance.

Bowes, I. and Jones, R.J. (2006). Working at the edge of chaos: understanding coaching as a complex, interpersonal system, *Sport Psychologist*, 20, 235–45.

British Gymnastics (2005) *FUNdamental Movement Ideas*, Newport: Gymnastics Enterprises.

Cassidy, T., Jones, R. and Potrac, P. (2004) *Understanding Sports Coaching*, London: Routledge.

Coghlan, J. (with I.M. Webb) (1990) *Sport and British Politics since 1960*, London: Falmer Press.

Cushion, C., Armour, K.M. and Jones R.L. (2003) Coach education and continuing professional development: experience and learning to coach, *Quest*, 55, 215–30.

Department for Culture Media and Sport (DCMS) (2002) *The Coaching Task Force: Final Report*, London: DCMS, http://www.culture.gov.uk/global/publications/archive_2002/sport_coach_task.htm.

Department for Culture Media and Sport (DCMS) and Strategy Unit (2002) *Game Plan; a Strategy for delivering Government's Sport and Physical Activity Objectives*, London: DCMS/Strategy Unit.

Gilbert, W.D., Côté, J. and Mallett, C. (2006) Developmental paths and activities of successful sports coaches, *International Journal of Sport Sciences and Coaching*, 1, 69–76.

Hardman, K. and Fielden, C. (1994) The development of sporting excellence: lessons from the past, in P. Duffy and L. Dugdale (eds) *HPER: Moving towards the Twenty-first century*, Champaign IL: Human Kinetics.

Henry, I.P. (1993) *The Politics of Leisure Policy*, Basingstoke: Macmillan.

Houlihan, B. and White, A. (2002) *The Politics of Sports Development*, London: Routledge.

Hylton, K., Bramham, P., Jackson, D. and Nesti, M. (eds) (2001) *Sports Development: Policy, Process and Practice*, 1st edn, London: Routledge.

Jones, R.L. and Wallace, M. (2005) Another bad day at the training ground: coping with ambiguity in the coaching context, *Sport, Education and Society*, 10, 119–34.

Jones, R.L. and Wallace, M. (2006) The coach as 'orchestrator', in R. L. Jones (ed.) *The Sports Coach as Educator: Reconceptualising Sports Coaching*, London: Routledge.

Loughborough Partnership (2005) *Schools Sport Partnerships: Annual Monitoring and Evaluation Report*, Loughborough: Institute of Youth Sport, Loughborough University.

Lyle, J. (1997) Managing excellence in sports performance, *Career Development International*, 2, 314–23.

Lyle, J. (2002) *Sports Coaching Concepts: A Framework for Coaches' Behaviour*, London: Routledge.

Lyle, J. (2004) *Ships that pass in the Night: An Examination of the Assumed Symbiosis between Sport for All and Elite Sport. Innovation in Cooperation: Proceedings of the Twelfth EASM European Sport Management Congress*, Ghent: Publicatiefond voor Lichamelijke Opvoeding.

Martindale, R.J.J., Collins, D. and Daubney, J. (2005) Talent development: a guide for practice and research within sport, *Quest*, 57, 353–75.

MORI (2004) *Sports Coaching in the UK*, Leeds: Sports Coach UK.

Pickup, D. (1996) *Not another Messiah: An Account of the Sports Council, 1988–1993*, Edinburgh: Pentland Press.

Sallis, J.F., Prochaska, J.J. and Taylor, W.C. (2000) A review of correlates of physical activity of children and adolescents, *Medical Science of Sports and Exercise*, 32, 963–75.

Sport England (2004) *The Framework for Sport in England*, London: Sport England.

sports coach UK (2004) *UKCC Endorsement Criteria (Levels 1–3)*, Paper 18, Leeds: NCF.

sports coach UK (2006) *UK Action Plan for Coaching: Consultation Draft, June 2006*, Leeds: sports coach UK.

sportscotland (2006) *Active Schools Networks: Year one Progress Report and Next Steps*, Edinburgh: **sport**scotland.

Stafford, I. and Balyi, I. (2005) *Coaching for Long-term Athlete Development: Improving Participation and Performance in Sport*, Leeds: Coachwise.

Trudel, P. and Gilbert, W. (2006) Coaching and coach education, in D. Kirk, M. O'Sullivan and D. McDonald (eds) *Handbook of Research in Physical Education*, London: Sage.

Way, R. and O'Leary, D. (2006) Long-term coach development concept, *Perspective* (magazine of the British Columbia Coaches Association), 24–31; www.coaches.bc.ca/resources.

Web references

www.teachernet.gov.uk
www.sportscotland.org.uk
www.ukcoachingcertificate.org
www.sportengland.org/vsm
www.sportdevelopment.org.uk
www.nctc.ul.ie
www.positivefuturesresearch.org.uk

CHAPTER 11

RESEARCHING AND EVALUATING SPORTS DEVELOPMENT

Jonathan Long

One of the problems with sport is that everyone thinks they are an expert (of course in many ways they are) and experts know what is right. But get a few of these experts together and you are likely to find that they disagree about what it is, that there are gaps in their knowledge and that some of the things taken for granted as true are based on belief rather than evidence. What is needed to try to ensure that our policy and professional practice are well informed is good-quality research, but we are operating in an under-researched field.

Quite often we lack even data on basic patterns of participation and information on who those participants are, never mind the non-participants. There are certainly gaps in knowledge about the reasoning that underpins that (non)participation and even bigger gaps in appreciating the broader social, economic and political processes at work. Just as Hylton and Totten in Chapter 4 raise issues around the evidence base for understanding inequality, policy makers criticise sport and leisure professionals for basing arguments on inadequate research evidence.

When the government (in the UK) addressed the contribution that sport makes to achieving a range of social goals they have been unconvinced by the research base. Like several writers in the field (e.g. Glyptis, 1989; Allison and Coalter, 1996; Long and Sanderson, 2001), the report of Policy Action Team 10 (1999: 37) to the Social Exclusion Unit, while positive, concluded that there is little 'hard' evidence of the social costs and benefits involved. The subsequent *Game Plan* strategy for sport and physical activity observed:

> The greatest challenge in assessing the state of sport and physical activity has been the lack of reliable data . . . although this does not invalidate the case for action, it weakens our ability to develop evidence-based policy interventions.
> (Department for Culture, Media and Sport/Strategy Unit, 2002: 21)

It is therefore not surprising that the Sport England research strategy notes the need to 'strengthen the evidence base for decision-making in sport at all levels and . . . put in place a coherent framework for sports research that is responsive to the wider social policy agenda' (Sport England, 2005: ii). In support of this, Sport England and UK Sport have set up the Value of Sport Monitor which identifies research demonstrating the benefits of sport (www.sportengland.org/vsm/vsm_intro.asp).

Many sports development professionals seem to mistrust research, perhaps because it is seen to be conducted by 'outsiders'. The intention here is to give 'insiders' some guidelines for conducting good-quality research. It should be fairly evident that researchers think about the research enterprise differently depending upon the challenge being addressed. Those who want to improve the performance skills of athletes tend to go about their research in a rather different way from those who are picking up the concerns of developing Sport for All (Hylton and Totten, Chapter 4) about the need to understand inequality. These various research communities may use the same techniques, they may use different techniques or they may use the same research techniques in different ways. Clearly it is impossible to provide recipes for what to do in all possible circumstances, so this chapter is about ways of thinking and exploring, and it will also provide leads for finding out more detailed information from elsewhere.

In line with that approach the next section emphasises the need to be clear about the problem to be addressed and the information needed to do that. Without this clear specification vagueness will threaten the validity of the research, so researchers are constantly exhorted to be critical thinkers. This does not mean criticising anyone and anything, but carefully analysing arguments and propositions to see whether they stand up under scrutiny (see Bowell and Kemp (2005) for some guidance). The chapter then emphasises the value of assessing what previous research has to offer and considers some of the issues associated with different styles of research (questionnaires, interviews, observation and evaluation are featured here) . That leads to a case study of a small-scale project using multiple research techniques that was conducted at the Carnegie Research Institute (see Hylton and Totten, Chapter 5). The chapter concludes with an encouragement to question the research being conducted and to consider how the findings can best be put to use.

IDENTIFYING WHAT YOU NEED

Irrespective of the particular techniques used, research in this area may come in different forms, for example:

- Audits of people's needs or current provision.
- Market research to establish people's attitudes and behaviour.
- Feasibility studies to test the viability of some proposed provisions.
- Project evaluation to assess the success of an initiative.
- Forecasting future demands or behaviours.

The crucial thing is to plan these carefully, dissecting the research challenge in order to identify what needs to be done. There are some people who take this advice too far and use 'planning' as a way of procrastinating to avoid doing the research, but it is important not to jump in and start gathering data without proper preparation. The two watchwords typically associated with good research are *systematic* and *rigorous*, but this should not underplay the contribution of creativity, intuition and empathy.

Ouseley's report (2001) into the ethnic divisions in Bradford suggested that community cohesion might be helped by good sports provision. Research might be needed to support projects by informing what they do, but the more challenging task is to assess whether the sports projects have achieved what was expected. So where would you start if you had to do the research that would assess the benefits?

Some important principles:

- *Define key terms*. It is important to be precise about what you are investigating. Can sport be taken to encompass leisure and recreation? Sports facilities or projects? What is meant by social cohesion and how can it be assessed?
- *Narrow the focus*. Break big problems like this down into more manageable chunks. You might decide to examine whether those involved in a sports project have more social contact with people from other ethnic groups than people who are not.
- *Decide what evidence you will need*. How would you measure social contacts? Do you need a quantitative measure or is this an occasion when qualitative data would tell you more?
- *Question the (potential) findings*. If there does prove to be a relationship it may be because of some other factor: e.g. those involved in the project are younger than those who are not and they may have more extensive social networks as a result.

At the same time as working out what you need you also need to be sensitive to who it is for. Who are you trying to inform/convince? Sometimes it may be research purely for yourself in that you feel you need to know something to let you do your job better. Alternatively your line manager may require the information for shaping departmental practice, or it may be to support sporting arguments in the face of challenges or doubts from potential partners in health, education or regeneration, or it may be for the council or board to decide on policy and priorities, or it may be for course tutors. This is more than just a question of presenting results in different formats, though that may indeed be crucial, but a recognition that different kinds of research are likely to be more appropriate for different audiences. I am certainly not suggesting here that you 'fix' your findings in order to satisfy these different audiences, but you need to be alert to what kind of evidence they are likely to believe.

To make your research effective it is important to understand the policy context and work out which are the main 'drivers', what is the local context and who are the key stakeholders. For example, as the sporting imperative shifts from medals to participation to regeneration to health to inclusion to a new policy issue the research questions will need to change too.

However you resolve these issues you should consider the ethical implications of your research to make sure that people do not suffer harm or distress that they would not be subjected to if it were not for the research project. This, of course, is not a hard-and-fast rule as there may be some greater good that outweighs any apparent unfairness to these individuals. The institution you work in or for may require you to get formal ethical approval for the research before you start. Whether or not that is the case, you should be your own conscience and consider carefully the consequences of conducting the research in the way you intend.[1]

USING EXISTING KNOWLEDGE

Despite the concerns about gaps in our research knowledge there is a lot of information already in existence that might go some way to satisfying many research needs. These may contain data collected to represent the national picture or have been conducted in another part of the country or even overseas. So evaluate carefully whether you need to collect your own data or whether those sources will suffice. Some research may be done entirely as a desk study; alternatively this might be one element in a larger whole. Table 11.1 gives examples of data sets that are available in the UK.

But you need to ask yourself several questions before accepting the findings into your report/assessment:

- Were their categories for age, etc. the same as you are interested in?
- How useful were the questions they actually asked?
- Is it reasonable to expect the patterns revealed by a national survey or one done in some other part of the country to be the same as the area you are involved with?
- Have things changed since that research was conducted?

QUESTIONNAIRE SURVEYS

For many people it is the questionnaire survey that is synonymous with social research. Undoubtedly a useful tool if well constructed and administered, unfortunately it is commonly misused. I have often heard it said that any fool can design a questionnaire. Unfortunately many do, but the basic skills can be easily acquired (see, for example, Oppenheim, 2000; de Vaus, 2002; Long 2007).

A few years ago the Carnegie Research Institute was approached by a local authority undertaking its Best Value review of the Parks Service. What the council needed was information on people's patterns of use and assessment of the different elements of provision, not just as a 'one-off', but to provide a baseline for future assessments. This is typical territory for questionnaire surveys, but different styles were used for different constituencies of interest (e.g. some were looser, with more open questions than others, and were administered in different ways). We did all these 'in house' apart from a home interview survey of residents aged sixteen and over, which was conducted for us by a

Taking Part

A home interview survey of (non)participation in culture and sport in England. First conducted for the Department for Culture Media and Sport in 2005/06 with a sample of some 29,000 a year.

www.culture.gov.uk/global/research/taking_part_survey

Active People

A telephone survey conducted on behalf of Sport England to record participation in sport and recreational physical activity. Nationally (England) it has a very large sample of some 350,000 to give 1,000 in each local authority.

www.sportengland.org/active_people

General Household Survey

A survey of some 20,000 people aged sixteen and over in Great Britain. Questions on sport have been included in 1973, 1977, 1980, 1983, 1987, 1990 and 2002. Those questions have been accompanied by others on leisure/arts/social activity/holidays, though the mix has varied.

http://www.statistics.gov.uk/ssd/surveys/general_household_survey.asp

Expenditure and Food Survey (previously separate as the Family Expenditure survey and National Food Survey)

Around 7,000 households a year provide data on all aspects of household expenditure and income, including 'recreation and culture', which is subdivided into twenty-one categories.

www.statistics.gov.uk/ssd/surveys/expenditure_food_survey.asp

Mintel Leisure Intelligence

Reports compile existing data and generate their own to provide an analysis of consumer trends. They operate in several countries. In the UK, for example, there have been reports on computer and video games, multi-leisure parks, snow sports, days out, family leisure trends, cricket and rugby, corporate hospitality, fitness classes, dog and horse racing, student leisure, etc. It is a subscription service.

http://reports.mintel.com/sinatra/reports/view&name=reports_subs/&levels=67267#1

market research company. Our team administered a site survey of the users of three parks; distributed postal questionnaires to sports clubs, allotment holders and councillors; conducted a telephone survey of the secretaries of tenants and residents' associations; and distributed questionnaires in eighteen schools. Interestingly, the lowest level of response came from the councillors, who have other arenas to voice their views. Let us consider now some of the issues we had to address then.

At the outset consider the key issues in designing a questionnaire survey:

■ Who is meant to answer the questionnaire? How will they be identified and selected? Who might get left out or refuse?

- Will there be enough of them to give confidence in the findings?
- What questions should be asked?
- How should they be worded?
- And the big one at the end: do the data justify the conclusions?

The first two relate to sampling; the second two to questionnaire design. It would be unfortunate to say the least if your research report were to be dismissed because it was found to be based on twenty people you happened to bump into at the weekend. Whether you consider it an art or a science, at its most basic sampling here is about selecting a sub-set that can be accepted as being representative of the entire set of people or facilities or schemes that is of interest in the research. In most circumstances more is better in terms of the confidence the findings will command. Ignore the siren calls of those who try to suggest the sample has to be some constant percentage of the population; it is the absolute size of the sample that is more important (de Vaus, 2002).

Questionnaire surveys may take many forms:

- *Site surveys* conducted at the stadium or sports centre by definition cover participants only, so the majority of the population who are non-participants are ignored. But not all non-participants are potential participants anyway.
- *Street surveys* are a quick and easy way of gathering data, but it is unclear who the respondents represent, as some sections of 'the public' are very unlikely to be included.
- *Home interview surveys* are more expensive, but can be more representative of the whole population. Of course those involved in sport and recreation activities may be out pursuing those activities, so the interviewer has to call back, taking even more time.
- *Telephone surveys* can reach large numbers quickly and make direct data entry to the computer easy. Although market research companies are refining ways of sample selection, for most people reading this it will probably be difficult unless there is something like a membership list available. People are also getting increasingly suspicious of 'cold calls' and it can be hard to establish rapport.
- *Postal questionnaires* can be very useful to accommodate a wide geographical spread but often have *very* low response rates which can call into question the findings. The response can be improved by: an accompanying letter explaining the importance of the study; offering a reward; sending reminders; providing a reply-paid envelope.
- *Electronic questionnaires*, if delivered by e-mail, are similar to postal questionnaires. Alternatively, if they are web-based they are dependent on the 'right people' finding them. However, they can be linked directly to a database/spreadsheet, thereby avoiding the errors that might occur as someone in the research office enters data from the questionnaire into the computer.

It should be fairly obvious that with these different styles of survey not only does the cost vary but so too do likely sample sizes, the number of questions that can be asked and the detail sought.

When it comes to designing the questionnaire itself the key is to understand what you want to know. Without that kind of critical reflection there is a danger that questions will not get at the issues at stake, there will be completely unnecessary questions wasting the time of the respondents, or, just as bad, too few questions to allow a proper examination of the issues at stake. The advice to avoid questions that are ambiguous (e.g. Do you *train* and *play* sport at school?) or leading (suggesting a particular response) or hypothetical (the 'what if?' questions) is good for the most part, but not that easy to follow. It can be difficult for the questionnaire designer to spot questions they have written that are leading people to answer in a particular way, so it is useful to have fresh eyes to review the questions. The general principle has to be to give people the chance to report as accurately and honestly as possible what they do and think.

It is worth examining the questions used by other people doing related research. This can give useful ideas, and if the questions are replicated it may be possible to compare findings.[2] Doing this should introduce you to careful wording and useful classifications, and give you an appreciation of how to balance different types of question to help both the researchers and the respondents.

Using closed questions (people select from a predetermined set of responses) makes it much easier to handle the resultant data, with matched numerical codes simply entered into a spreadsheet or database. However, this does mean that the researcher's view of the world is being imposed on the research; open questions that invite a free response give respondents more chance of self-expression.

Rather than asking people what they might do in the future it is better to ask them what they have actually done, but then it is necessary to consider how accurately people can recall what happened at different times in the past. Consider the implications of imperfect memory for the following challenges that might be of interest to researchers: asking them as they leave the sports centre what they have done on that visit; asking them what they have done in the past four weeks or twelve months; asking adults what they did while they were at school. It is generally assumed that the more recent the memory the more detailed the recall, but this is not always the case.

In studies of participation one of the key variables is the frequency of that participation. Researchers have to tread carefully here. For a start much sports participation is seasonal, so when the question is asked can be crucial. Terms like 'rarely', 'occasionally' and 'frequently' are not very helpful, as they can mean different things to different people (and to the same person in the context of different activities). It is important once again to consider what needs to be known. It might be the number of people who participate, the number of participant occasions (tickets sold) or the percentage of the population who (don't) participate. The following forms are frequently used:

> Have you taken part in [gymnastics] in the past day/month/year?
> How many times have you taken part in the past day/month/year?
> Do you take part in [gymnastics]

Daily?
At least once a week?
At least once a month?
At least once a year?
Less than once a year?
Never?

When asking for the details of participation, rather than asking about normally/usually it is better to ask about a specific occasion – 'normally' the most recent or favourite/best.

Sport psychologists in particular are keen to explore people's attitudes and beliefs, typically using some kind of scaling technique. Collectively known as psychometric scaling, this basically means trying to put numbers on what is going on in people's heads (typically 1–5 or 1–7, but there is considerable variation). The two most commonly used approaches involve:

- Rating (say) a youth programme on a set of bi-polar scales – e.g. flexible/rigid; friendly/unfriendly – the *semantic differential*.
- Asking people to assess the extent to which they agree or disagree with a series of statements – *Likert scaling*.[3]

The key consideration here is whether individual items and composite scales measure what they are supposed to. To do that they have to be unambiguous so that everyone understands them in the same way.

Read a book about questionnaire design and it will stress the need for a pilot exercise. There are good reasons for this. For a trial run there is no need to involve large numbers of people, but it is useful to check that others understand the questions in the way that was intended when they were written. At the same time the categories given for answers to closed questions can be checked, as can the flow and sequencing of the questionnaire as a whole. It also makes sense to check the link to the spreadsheet/database that will store the coded responses.

You need to consider whether your survey instruments will be administered by an interviewer or self-administered. Although it is not always possible, or even sensible, my normal preference is to use interviewers to ask the questions, but of course they have to be good at their craft; a bad interviewer can severely damage the research. Interview staff should be able to encourage participation by people who would otherwise not bother to respond, encourage people to take the exercise seriously and clarify any confusion about the meaning of the questions. Apart from cost and convenience, one of the main arguments in favour of self-administered questionnaires is that people may feel more able to give honest answers in more anonymous circumstances.

There is no point in having a carefully designed questionnaire if the interviewers are casual in the way they administer it – not being rigorous in the selection of respondents or off-hand in the way the questions are asked and recorded.

IN-DEPTH INTERVIEWS

Questionnaires are good at gathering data to reveal basic patterns in a standard format. On the other hand, questionnaires can seem regimented and restricted in the way they seek to compartmentalise people and knowledge. They may also recreate knowledge in the image of researchers' preconceptions, with standard questions packaged in standard configurations leading to constrained outputs via fixed categories. Some interviews may be similarly very structured but be based around more open (less easily quantified) questions. In this section I am concerned with more flexible forms of interviewing designed to gather qualitative data to advance our knowledge of how people understand what happens in and around their lives. The central idea is that people should be given the chance to explain what is important to them.

That was why, although we did use questionnaires among club officials and spectators, when we were investigating the nature and extent of racism in sport we used one-to-one interviews with players and group interviews with match officials (Long et al., 1995, 1997, 2000). Our assessment was that we would be able to find out much more about people's experience of racism and their own attitudes by talking to them rather than asking them to respond to a standard questionnaire. Racism is such a sensitive subject that asking brusque, direct questions may mean people (white or black) will not give a natural response. Some people think that African Caribbean and Asian players are too ready to blame racism for all their problems. Far from it in our research; it was only because we were talking to them for some time that they became sufficiently confident to discuss such experiences. To my mind this vindicated the decision to use this way of gathering data because we found out things we would not otherwise have done.

Some people like a fairly structured approach, while others want it to be as free-flowing as possible (Bell, 2005; May, 2001). Of course, having no structure at all can be very disconcerting for respondents. You need some idea of what your research is trying to achieve, especially if research is being conducted to a tight time scale. Consequently most people use an interview schedule to provide a framework. The basis for the questions may come from 'brainstorming', a literature review or preliminary discussions with 'experts' and other contacts. Instead of standard wording the interviewer frames questions that slot naturally into the flow of the conversation, and typically tries to use the language of her/his respondent. In large part the reason this research approach is referred to as 'in-depth' lies with the follow-up questions used to get beyond the initial response. These do not have to be complicated or clever, just something that gives the message that more information would be helpful. Some of the principles that apply in questionnaire design are equally appropriate here – group questions together in blocks and work out logical sequences, learn your 'script' but be prepared to be flexible.

Trial runs are as important to pilot this kind of interview as they are with questionnaires and other research approaches. You need to know how to introduce the various topics in such a way that you will get a full, honest and informative response from the person you are interviewing. The 'trick' is to get people to talk freely about what they think are the most important aspects of what you are examining without going off at a tangent; the interviewer then acts as a guide. Unlike the questionnaire survey, the analysis is not a separate stage that follows the data gathering; a lot of analysis has to be done during the interview so that you know how to direct it most profitably.

Interview technique

Some researchers think that questionnaires are a bit inquisitorial. It has been suggested that we should try to escape the authoritarian approach of questionnaire surveys, where all the power rests with the researchers, and establish a more equal relationship so that the experience is less like an inquisition. Some researchers believe that the relationship between researcher and respondent is so crucial to the success of the research that they should be carefully matched, according to sex, ethnicity and age. In part this is because of the importance of empathy (the ability to put oneself in the shoes of another) in this style of research.

This process of empathy also helps in designing the interview by imagining what would make you most forthcoming in your responses were you being interviewed. My proposition is that you need to feel comfortable and able to relate to the person you are talking to, who in turn probably needs to be non-judgemental. Good interviewers give the impression of being 'good listeners' but also carefully guide and draw out. They manage not to hurry respondents, giving them plenty of time to develop their answers, and also probe beyond the initial responses to get at underlying reasons.

These interviews will normally, but not necessarily, be longer than questionnaires – an hour is not unusual, and sometimes longer. So it is important to select the venue carefully so that the respondent feels comfortable and can give their full attention to the interview.

Given the significance typically given to the way in which people 'construct' the world, it is important to have an accurate record of what they said. While some may be cautious, most people do not object to the interview being recorded as long as it has been explained to them how their comments will be used. Removing the need to scribble notes all the time offers the interviewer the major advantage of being able to concentrate on what is being said and guiding the interview. Through the course of the project this may result in hours of recordings. What then? I like to have full transcripts, but not all researchers have the energy (or staff) for that.

There may be occasions when you feel it would be inappropriate to record the interview in any way at the time (perhaps you are talking to a young person on the project about their encounter with the police last night). As full an account as possible then has to be written soon afterwards, which is a surprisingly difficult thing to do.

For those who are phobic about numbers this kind of interviewing may seem an easy alternative. It may be a rewarding alternative, but it is not an easy one. Understanding statistical procedures may be difficult, but they at least provide a formal procedure to follow: take the right steps and an answer is delivered. Processing and analysing the qualitative data from in-depth interviews is less straightforward. So it is good to ask at the outset how all the information that is going to be so diligently collected from respondents will be examined in the context of existing/emerging theories and analysed. Whatever happens you will almost certainly have to be selective and reduce the amount of data that you have while classifying it in some way.

OBSERVATION

Observation can be used to gather quantitative data (e.g. the number of times a player receives abuse or encouragement), but is probably more commonly associated with qualitative data (e.g. about the way people react to stress or how they generate team spirit even on a losing run). Although this can be a particularly revealing way of doing research (after all, 'seeing is believing'), its findings are often dismissed by decision makers as inferior knowledge. Researchers who use observation as their preferred approach tackle this in one of two ways. The first is to try and devise a robust framework intended to convince people that the process is objective. The second is to insist that their aim is to use observation to understand the subjective experience. While some want to draw on concepts and categories from established theory to guide their analysis and reporting, others insist on the blank slate – going into 'the field' with a completely open mind.

McCall and Simmons (1969: 3) suggest rather grandly that participant observation involves 'repeated genuine social interaction on the scene with the subjects themselves as part of the data gathering process'. The extent to which the researcher becomes immersed in the activity can vary considerably. (*Note.* it has been argued that it is not possible to be a non-participant observer, as any observation will have some impact on the observed.) Gans (1962) identified three different stances that can be adopted. (Others identify more – the point is to recognise that there is no single way to 'do' observation.)

- Observer: present, but apart.
- Participate, but as a researcher.
- Participant, temporarily abdicates study role.

The methodology was originally devised by social anthropologists going into unfamiliar surroundings (e.g. among tribes they considered to be 'primitive') and trying to explain how that society/culture operated. More recently people have used it in their own life worlds on the basis that it is there that they have the best chance of working out how the world works (e.g. Blackshaw, 2003). So the observation may be conducted in the immediate setting of the project/team the researcher works with anyway (Holt and Sparkes, 2001), with other similar projects/teams or a less familiar environment like the committee structure. Participant observation is also used where people might be motivated to distort what they do when questioned (e.g. using drugs to improve performance, drinking behaviour or sexual encounters). Moreover, it allows the researcher to examine structures not recognised by those taking part, and hence not accessible through questionnaires or interviews.

You may be well advised not to follow my example in this case. I had a moment of brilliant insight that led me to try to do some participant observation to find out why the kind of spectator violence frequently experienced at football matches rarely occurred at rugby league games even though both are essentially masculine, working-class sports. Trying to observe why something is not happening is not the easiest challenge to set yourself. Equally, while observing children playing may be the best way of getting a window into their world, spending a lot of time watching the play area in the local park may mean that others start watching you.

Those who have not come across participant observation may be forgiven for wondering how hard it can be to go and watch what is happening. Well, it is much harder than it initially sounds, as it involves trying to make sense of everything around you, picking out the key aspects and turning all that into a set of generalisations. But it can be very fruitful. As a research methodology, participant observation conventionally tends to be considered very much a qualitative approach, but it can in fact use a suite of techniques (Gans, 1962) such as:

- Using and observing at local facilities.
- Attending meetings, gatherings, etc.
- Informal visits to friends and neighbours.
- Formal and informal interviewing.
- Special informants.
- Day-by-day observation.

In addition to deciding whether they are there to observe or participate, those doing participant observation have a decision to make about whether to declare their position as a researcher. Not to do so may be seen as deceitful and unethical, whereas broadcasting the role may mean that people alter the way they would normally behave. Either way, the researcher has to find a role to play so that they have something to do rather than just look conspicuous. When the researcher is not operating in their usual environment, they have to find a way 'in' and then win trust and establish relationships so that people feel comfortable with this newcomer around. This is especially important if the research is into something like the use of drugs to improve performance. The best data are likely to come if rapport is established. Irritatingly for those who have been successful in doing this, they have sometimes been criticised for over-rapport and 'going native' to such an extent that they no longer think like a 'proper' researcher. Some are so concerned at jeopardising their relationships in the field or changing the direction of behaviour that they consider it wrong to ask questions. Writers in this field do nearly all agree, though, that the researcher should adopt a low profile and not pass moral judgements on those around them.

One of the things that worries some who use participant observation is that the people with whom they have worked intensively may not be typical of wider populations, thus preventing generalisations. If your interest is purely with your team, project or committee structure this hardly matters. However, even if that is so, you cannot be there all day every day, so some sampling is inevitable, as it is with any style of research.

Participant observation does seem to highlight ethical issues, most obviously over whether it is legitimate to do covert research by not telling people they are being observed for research purposes. Then when 'in the field' the researcher has to decide to what extent s/he can intervene in what is happening when the study is intended to study the people encountered, not the consequences of the researcher's own actions. Even if people have been informed, when it comes to reporting it may prove difficult to write without betraying confidences.

Critics suggest that participant observation produces neither reliable nor valid data, as it may simply recycle hearsay and is subject to observer bias, being dependent on the personal observation and interpretation of someone who may have 'gone native' and suspended their critical faculties. Moreover, it can be difficult to draw inferences that warrant generalisation and provide proof of a causal link (two highly prized functions of research) and there is no shortage of ethical dilemmas to address. Do not despair, there are advantages in using participant observation. Its proponents argue that in practice it is less likely to be biased, unreliable or invalid because it provides more internal checks. Being in the field for a long time allows information to be checked, emerging explanations to be tested and unsatisfactory explanations discarded. The research can be very flexible (not the hypothesis–data–test tramway) which makes it more responsive to the data than imposed systems of 'scientific' research. It allows researchers to get really close to the realities of social life. Which ever set of techniques you think is the best, take time out to question again whether this is the right approach (Table 11.2).

Table 11.2 Asking questions of yourself

You cannot afford to be mechanical in your research. Always ask yourself questions to make sure you are not taking things for granted.

So you want to do a questionnaire survey . . .

Why?

> How are you going to phrase the questions?
> Open/closed/scales?
> Has someone already worked out how to do that?
> How many questions do you need?
> Why are you including each question?
> Will your respondents be able to understand them?
>
> Who is going to answer the questionnaire?
> How many?
> How are you going to select/identify/get to them?   } What are the
> Who do they *really* represent?   consequences?
>
> Have you arranged necessary access? Why should they take part?

Table 11.2 continued

Can you do anything to improve response rates?
Do you need special approval to question children?

Are you sure you don't need to ask the questions directly, face to face?
If it is a postal survey do you think many people will reply?

Who will your pilot be administered to?

How will you code the responses?
How are you going to analyse the data?
Are pie charts really enough?

So you want to do in-depth interviews . . .

Why?

What questions will you use?
What makes them 'in-depth'?
What kinds of follow-up questions could you use?
Have you got the language right?
How structured will it be?
Is this different from a questionnaire?

Who are your respondents going to be?
Why will they agree to take part?
Who do they represent/speak for? Really?

Can you interview children on this topic?
Do you need police clearance?

How can you practise interviewing?

Are you going to transcribe your interviews?

How will you process the data?
How will you analyse it rather than just write it down?

How will you demonstrate the data are real and really did come from your respondents?

How will you present the data?

So you want to do some observation . . .

Why?

Will you declare your purpose? To everyone?
How will you find your subjects, get 'in' and be accepted?
What will you do while observing in order to fit in?

Are you entitled to 'spy on them'?

What behaviour do you expect to observe?
What will you actually record?
How will you know what is important and what isn't?
How will you record it?

How much time will you have to spend there to be sure you *know* what is going on?

Table 11.2 continued

How will you analyse and make sense of your observations?

How will you present this to others so that they are persuaded by what you say?

So you want to use multiple approaches . . .

Often a good idea, but do you need to?
What will one approach get you that the others won't?
Can you combine the data you get from different approaches?

EVALUATION

Evaluation is not a technique or even an approach in its own right but a challenge that may draw on a range of different kinds of research. Particularly strongly associated with policy research, it typically tries to assess the impact or effect of some intervention. As such it has been of considerable interest to the Sports Councils in recent years (e.g. Coalter, 2002; Sport England, 2001). Some evaluations have enormous financial resources available (though probably never enough in the eyes of the researchers), but many more are small-scale projects (Robson, 2000). At this more modest level, Nichols (2005) makes use of the 'realistic evaluation' principles proposed by Pawson and Tilley (1997) when examining the contribution of sports-based projects to reducing crime.

The most common kind of question that an evaluation is expected to address is, 'Has a change occurred?' If it can be demonstrated that change has occurred it is then important to assess whether it can be attributed to the intervention or is the result of other factors. Both policy makers and practitioners will also be interested in what made it work (or stopped it) and whether it represents value for money.

Ideally, to assess change there should be some measure of how things were before the project started and then clear measures of performance used to see what has changed by how much by the end of the project. Assessments at various stages during the project would also be useful to track progress and allow feedback. And assessments some time after the project to find out how long the benefits last. It may be possible to avoid the need for all these sets of data by asking people involved with the project to assess retrospectively what change there was (e.g. whether they are physically more or less active now as a result of their involvement).

It is difficult to find appropriate quantitative measures of many of the things that currently interest people responsible for sport projects: skills, confidence, esteem, deviance, team work, community cohesion, etc. Unfortunately many have therefore thrown their hands in the air in despair and given up the evaluation exercise, relying instead on anecdotal evidence. If valid and reliable quantitative measures are available, all well and good, otherwise the challenge is to work out what does constitute 'evidence'.

Few people doubt that sport *can* produce social benefits, so pointing out that someone has grown from being a youngster 'at risk' to an Olympic medallist does not get us much further forward. What we need to know is to what extent such benefits occur and whether there is a direct causal link. So what is needed is a more rigorous analysis of all the people involved and careful consideration of any counter-examples. That might allow us to work out why there should be the different outcomes.

Coalter (2002) encourages a distinction between three different types of outcomes (and a fourth might be added). *Sporting* outcomes are things like improved performance or increased participation; *intermediate* outcomes are the impact on the individuals taking part like improved health and well-being; *strategic* outcomes are the wider impacts like lower levels of crime in the community; and *process* outcomes relate to how the goals were achieved like the success of partnership working. The other key considerations for policy makers are the efficiency of the project (e.g. the number of people involved per £), whether it is effective (e.g. whether it really does deter people from antisocial behaviour) and, sometimes, who benefits (equity).

Coalter (2002) is also quite insistent that any evaluation exercise should be conducted against the aims of the project. (Of course, different people may see different aims for the project.) However, the task may be not just to assess change within a single project but to compare one with another. While that suggests using identical methods of evaluation in each project, doing that might be inappropriate if they have rather different aims.

Probably the two biggest problems facing evaluation exercises are identifying suitable indicators and establishing cause (see Case Study 11.1). In an example I have used elsewhere (Long, 2007), if we want to know whether health has improved as a result of an Active Lifestyles project, would it be best to measure the number of visits to local doctors, the number of prescriptions dispensed, individual blood pressure or cholesterol levels, or self-reported health? Which of those offers the best indicator depends on the underlying assumptions about what constitutes the link between activity and health. Making those explicit also helps to deal with the second problem. Just because the health of someone involved in the project improves, it may not have been their increased activity (always assuming the project was successful in increasing activity levels) that caused it. For example, their health may have improved because they changed job and experience less stress, or they got a job as the economic climate improved so they earned the income to allow a better diet, or they gave up smoking because their best friend died of cancer. The change may also have more to do with positive social interaction with the person running the project and the other participants than with physical activity itself. If it was part of a major national evaluation these personal experiences might not be enough to distort the overall picture, but in small-scale evaluations they can be crucial. Setting out clearly at the start what the presumed links are between physical activity and health not only clarifies what the expected outcome should be but also helps identify the most appropriate kind of evidence.

Of course, project evaluation is an intensely political exercise. Whatever nice words surround the exercise, people and processes are being judged and project funding may be dependent on the outcome. It is often seen to be a major advantage to engage external evaluators, as they will be seen by others as relatively dispassionate, with no particular axe to grind. The down side is that they lack the accumulated knowledge of existing staff that can play such an important part in interpreting data about outcomes and processes. Ideally, both project workers and participants should be integrally involved in a collaborative enterprise. In such politically charged environments evaluators need to be able to recognise arguments driven by vested interest and then to have the confidence in the quality of their research to defend their findings. Appreciating the difficulty of providing research evidence to demonstrate positive outcomes, one of the project teams in our study for the Department for Media, Culture and Sport (Long *et al.*, 2002) decided that the best way to ensure future funding was to let decision makers 'see it with their own eyes' by inviting them to an open evening each year.

RESEARCH PROJECT: AN EVALUATION OF SPORTSWEB

Background

As discussed in Chapter 5, Sportsweb was a community sport and recreation initiative based in the Manningham and Girlington areas of Bradford. The aim of the project was to bring about an integrated and sustainable sporting regeneration of the area by co-ordinating the various local initiatives.

Coming towards the end of its funding, the project team and the city council were keen to assess how successful the project had been. What they needed was not a particularly large project, but it was beyond the staff resources of the team. More significantly, though, they were well aware that an evaluation conducted by outside interests would carry more weight in the eyes of others than one they did themselves. So Kevin Hylton and colleagues from Leeds Metropolitan University were commissioned to do the work (Hylton, 2003).

The research

The research had to be sensitive to the nature of the project. Remember, this was an area with a young population and over two-thirds of the people living there were from minority ethnic groups. Prior to any data gathering the researchers clarified Sportsweb's guiding principles: to consult on community needs; promote healthy lifestyle messages; encourage educational and training opportunities in sport and recreation; ensure equality of opportunity by focusing on young people from excluded groups; reduce crime and antisocial behaviour; and break down cultural and religious barriers. To do this Sportsweb operated through its development centres for cricket, football and rugby league, through schools (and their associated out-of-school clubs) and a programme of summer events. There was a strong emphasis on opportunities for girls and women and on training coaches.

It was seen to be important that all the constituencies of interest should be heard in the evaluation, but different kinds of research were conducted with each.

- *Stakeholders*. Focus groups were conducted with the sports steering group and the community coaches.
- *Coaches*. Individual interviews to construct case studies.
- *Key partners*. Individual interviews with key partners (schools, those making holiday provision, development centres and existing clubs), and a survey of their clients.

Although quantitative techniques dominate in evaluation studies generally it was only the last element of the study that could be subjected to conventional quantitative analysis.

The focus group interview with the coaches was based around nineteen open-ended questions. This is more than would typically be used – once several people start talking there is a limited number of questions that can be addressed – but here the questions were grouped/themed around:

- The nature of the coaching experience in the Manningham/Girlington area.
- Relationships between the project and the community.
- The running of the project through the management and advisory group.
- The training of coaches.
- Effectiveness in the use of resources.
- Reactions to the project's guiding principles.
- The future.

The questionnaire, completed by 105 young people participating in Sportsweb activities, was more structured and comprised mainly closed questions about:

- Getting involved in Sportsweb.
- The sessions.
- Possible improvements.
- The characteristics of the participants.

One of the questions asked what they would be doing if they were not at the session. Almost half said they would just be hanging around with friends, but a third would still have been playing sport.

This allowed the data to be assessed against the three considerations identified by **sport**scotland (Coalter, 2002) for community sports development projects – planning, delivery and participants – and to make recommendations for each of those (Hylton, 2003). Generally the research confirmed that Sportsweb is a 'respected and identifiable symbol of sports development' in the area (p. 33).

MAKING USE OF THE FINDINGS

So the brilliant research project has been completed: what next? If it was to inform your own practice you need to show that you can learn the lessons of your research. If it was done for almost any other purpose the findings have to be communicated to others. I was about to suggest that you have to find the best way to present the research, but just as you had to be aware during the research that people react differently to what they encounter in everyday life, so they will respond in different ways to what you produce. The implication is that it may be necessary to use more than one format, depending upon your audience. Those who share your new-found enthusiasm for research may be prepared to read a lengthy report, but board members or the council may want no more than two or three sides of A4, and the media probably less. Within some professional cultures a slide presentation has become the norm, whereas in others people will be bored by 'yet another' PowerPoint presentation.

Within the reporting there are alternative ways of presenting data too, e.g.:

- Extended arguments for your peers who crave the detail and want to be reassured that you are alert to the subtleties of the problems they have to grapple with.
- Tables of figures for the data-hungry.
- Diagrams for those who respond better to visual representations.
- Direct quotes for those who like the original voices to show through.
- Short, topical thought pieces for the media (and politicians).

Once again, people respond in different ways and they may not even be consistent in this. In my own case:

- I feel quite comfortable dealing with large tables of figures, but sometimes feel that researchers let the numbers take over from the reality.
- I respond to diagrams and figures, but feel frustrated by the lack of precision and detail in the commonly produced pie charts and question graphics in newspapers and magazines that hide the true nature of the data behind the impact message.

- I like to read what reflective respondents have had to say, but sometimes wonder why certain quotes have been selected in preference to all the others.

The tone of your research report needs to suit your audience and this is often a tough challenge (see Fairbairn and Winch (1996) for advice).

FINDING OUT MORE

Useful sources of further information about doing research are Long (2007) and Gratton and Jones (2004) but there are several other useful guides and introductions. The main point to bear in mind is that which ever books you use you should not try to follow them slavishly, but use them to give you ideas and help you to think through the various issues associated with your research.

There are also several good web-based sources, like the one set up by the Higher Education Academy Network for hospitality, leisure, sport and tourism to provide a gateway to useful research resources: http://www.hlst.ltsn.ac.uk/gateway/gateway.html.

NOTES

1 I am lucky – where I work I can always get advice on these tricky issues. If you lack that immediate support you may have guidelines issued by a professional association, or you can find information on the web site. I try to adhere to the principles of the Social Research Association: http://www.the-sra.org.uk/ethical.htm.
2 In the UK the Question Bank contains the questions used in publicly funded surveys: http://qb.soc.surrey.ac.uk/.
3 Although the term tends to be applied to any such exercise, it more properly refers to a set of statements (items) reflecting a concept like competitiveness or orientation to fair play, and it is the composite (reflected in the summed values for all items) that is the Likert scale.

REFERENCES

Allison, M. and Coalter, F. (1996) *Sport and Community Development*, Edinburgh: Scottish Sports Council.

Bell, J. (2005) *Doing your Research Project*, 4th edn, Maidenhead: Open University Press.

Blackshaw, T. (2003) *Leisure Life: myth, masculinity and modernity*, London: Routledge.

Bowell T. and Kemp, G. (2005) *Critical Thinking: a concise guide*, 2nd edn, London: Routledge.

Coalter, F. (2002) *Sport and Community Development: a manual*, Edinburgh: **sport**scotland.

de Vaus, D. (2002) *Surveys in Social Research*, 5th edn, London: Routledge.

Department for Culture Media and Sport/Strategy Unit (2002) *Game Plan: a strategy for delivering the government's sport and physical activity objectives*. London: Cabinet Office.

Fairbairn, G. and Winch, C. (1996) *Reading, Writing and Reasoning: a guide for students*, 2nd edn, Buckingham: Open University Press.

Gans, H. (1962) *The Urban Villagers*, New York: Free Press.

Glyptis, S. (1989) Public sector sport and recreation initiatives for the unemployed in Britain's inner cities, in P. Bramham, I. Henry, H. Mommaas and H. van der Poel (eds) *Leisure and Urban Processes: critical studies of leisure policy in Western European cities*, London: Routledge.

Gratton, C. and Jones, I. (2004) *Research Methods for Sports Studies*, London: Routledge.

Holt, N. and Sparkes, A. (2001) An ethnographic study of cohesiveness in a college soccer team over a season, *Sport Psychologist*, 15 (3): 237–59.

Hylton, K. (2003) *Sportsweb: an evaluation of the Sportsweb project*, Leeds: Leeds Metropolitan University.

Long, J. (2007) *Researching Leisure, Sport and Tourism: the essential guide*, London: Sage.

Long, J. and Sanderson, I. (2001) The social benefits of sport: where's the proof? in C. Gratton and I. Henry (eds) *Sport in the City*, London: Routledge.

Long, J., Hylton, K., Welch, M. and Dart, J (2000) *Part of the Game: an examination of racism in grass-roots football*, London: Kick it out, http://www.leedsmet.ac.uk/ces/lss/kioreport.htm.

Long, J., Nesti, M., Carrington, B. and Gilson, N. (1997) *Crossing the Boundary: a study of the nature and extent of racism in local league cricket*, Leeds: Leeds Metropolitan University.

Long, J., Tongue, N., Spracklen, K. and Carrington, B. (1995) What's the Difference? A study of the nature and extent of racism in rugby league, Leeds: RFL/CRE/LCC/LMU.

Long, J., Welch, M., Bramham, P., Hylton, K., Butterfield, J. and Lloyd, E. (2002) *Count me in: the dimensions of social inclusion through culture and sport*, report to the Department for Culture Media and Sport, http://www.leedsmet.ac.uk/ces/lss/research/countmein.pdf.

May, T. (2001) *Social Research*, Buckingham: Open University Press.

McCall, G.J. and Simmons, J.L. (eds) (1969) *Issues in Participant Observation*, Reading MA: Addison-Wesley.

Nichols, G. (2005) Reflections on researching the ability of sports interventions to reduce youth crime: the hope of scientific realism, in K. Hylton, J. Long and A. Flintoff (eds) *Evaluating Sport and Active Leisure for Young People*, Eastbourne: Leisure Studies Association.

Oppenheim, A.N. (2000) *Questionnaire Design and Attitude Measurement*, 3rd edn, London: Continuum.

Ouseley, Lord H. (2001) *Community Pride, Not Prejudice*, Bradford: Bradford Vision.

Pawson, R. and Tilley, N. (1997) *Realistic Evaluation*, London: Sage.

Policy Action Team 10 (1999) *Arts and Sport: a report to the Social Exclusion Unit*, London: DCMS.

Robson, C. (2000) *Small Scale Evaluations*, London: Sage.

Sport England (2001) *Performance Measurement for the Development of Sport: a good practice guide for local authorities*, London: Sport England.

Sport England (2005) *A Strategy for Sports Research, 2005 to 2008: towards evidence-based decision-making in sport*, London: Sport England.

INDEX